*Behavioral Problem Children
in the Schools*

Behavioral Problem Children in the Schools

RECOGNITION, DIAGNOSIS, AND BEHAVIORAL MODIFICATION

Robert H. Woody
University of Maryland

New York

Appleton-Century-Crofts

Division of Meredith Corporation

Dedicated to My Wife

Jane Divita Woody

Preface

It scarcely needs saying, especially to an experienced educator, that behavioral problem children constitute a major concern in the field of education. Not only are the children who manifest the problem behaviors affected, but their classmates and teachers suffer the effects of the unacceptable behaviors.

As opposed to certain other types of exceptional children, such as the physically handicapped, the behavioral problem child is not to be placed permanently in a category of exceptionality. Rather it seems that virtually every child has, or could conceivably have, behavior problems at some point in his life and could, therefore, be considered a "behavioral problem child." There are, of course, some children who, because of social-emotional or neurological factors, may display chronic unacceptable behaviors.

Since behavior problems have such a critical influence on the effectiveness of the total educational program and may possibly affect such a great percentage of the children, it is a bit surprising that more professional efforts have not been directed at combating these difficulties. Granted, there are numerous approaches to meeting the needs of these children, but they seem to represent rather segmented positions, and there is often little cohesion between them.

It would be pretentious to claim that this book offers a panacea. But the position set forth is based on three assumptions: first, behavioral problem children merit immediate attention for their own welfare as well as for that of their classmates, teachers, families, and society; second, because of the potentially great expense involved in establishing a new, comprehensive program, services must and should be provided by existing educational sources and personnel; and third, since educators differ in their personal and professional capabilities, the approach to serving behavioral problem children must be broad in scope, yet allow for specific direct action from each type of educator.

Part one of the book deals with the recognition and diagnosis of behavioral problem children. The educator must be capable of recognizing problem behaviors with some degree of objectivity, and this necessitates understanding the psychology of behavioral problem children. Psycho-educational diagnosis is essential, since it is only from an appraisal of the probable causes or etiology of the problem, a description of the past and present behavioral characteristics, a collection of psychological and educational data, and the positing of a prognosis that the psychoeducational staff can propose a realistic treatment program for the behavioral problem child.

Part two deals with the theory and techniques of behavioral modification. Since no one specific theory and its set of techniques are suitable for all children or for all problem behaviors, an eclectic position labeled *psychobehavioral* or *integrative therapy* is set forth. This approach does not represent a new theory for behavioral modification, but simply maintains that learning theory or conditioning techniques, as used in behavior therapy, can be combined or integrated with the insight-oriented techniques of counseling and psychotherapy for the benefit of the behavioral problem child. Analysis of experimental and clinical evidence shows that these seemingly diverse theoretical positions actually have elements in common; and when used conjointly, they probably constitute the most effective means for meeting the needs of most behavioral problem children.

Since some of these procedures are relatively new and have had only limited application in educational settings, considerable attention is devoted to the task of implementing behavioral modification services in the schools. Guidelines are offered that will, it is hoped, allow each reader to ascertain his own personal and professional competencies in regard to the use of behavioral modification.

This book is designed to provide a basic introduction to the psychology of behavioral problem children and to the means of coping with the behavioral difficulties. The contents are directed primarily at three major types of educational personnel: classroom teachers, both in regular and special education classrooms; school counselors on both the elementary and secondary levels; and school psychologists serving all age and educational levels. Although attention is focused on these professionals, it is recognized that school administrators, speech and hearing therapists, school social workers, itinerant teacher-consultants, and others within and outside of the school also have a responsibility to behavioral problem children; and their roles are also discussed.

The materials in this book are presented on the assumption that the reader has a basic knowledge of educational psychology—that is, that he has the qualifications at least of a teacher trainee. Many of the principles and techniques are appropriate for use only by persons of graduate-level training, probably in special education, guidance and counseling, and educational, counseling, school, and clinical psychology. These advanced materials are not included in order to teach the reader how to use them, but it behooves every educator to have at least a basic orientation to the functions of all professionals who service behavioral problem children. It is possible, however, that many professionals will find that the text offers an adequate understanding to allow immediate implementation of some of the procedures.

Writing this book has achieved two things for me: I have acquired from the task of synthesizing the materials increased academic knowledge about the psychology of behavioral problem children, and I have found in the process that my own motivation to serve the needs of these children is even greater than I originally thought. I only hope that the reader can benefit as much.

Numerous people have contributed directly and indirectly to the production of this manuscript. Its completion was facilitated by a post-doctoral fellowship from the United States Vocational Rehabilitation Administration; this allowed me to spend one year at the Institute of Psychiatry (the Maudsley Hospital), University of London, and afforded me the time to conduct research, write, and study with some of the prominent psychologists in the field of behavioral modification. Many of my ideas were fostered by the professors with whom I have studied at Western Michigan University, Michigan State University, and the University of London. My public school and university colleagues, past and present, have contributed to my professional development. Similarly, I can recall a number of students whose impact on me is reflected in the pages of this book. Professor Donald C. Smith, of Ohio State University, has given incomparable assistance by providing a detailed critique of the original manuscript. His comments and suggestions greatly aided my revisions, but he is in no way responsible for any shortcomings in the contents. I wish to express my appreciation to each of these persons.

Special acknowledgment must be given to my wife, Jane Divita Woody. Not only did she keep the domestic scene undisruptive, but she fostered my efforts with more unconditional positive regard than any counselor could give, and she worked diligently on the manuscript. Her skills as a professor of English literature proved to be invaluable, and she carefully criticized, sometimes to my chagrin, each principle that I set forth.

R. H. W.

Contents

List of Tables

Part one

RECOGNITION
AND DIAGNOSIS

1

The School and the
Behavioral Problem Child

All educators, even those in positions that are only peripherally connected with the classroom, have encountered behavioral problem children in the course of their professional duties. Behavioral problem children are found in every educational program and influence it to some degree; and obviously when there are children with problems, there will be potential problems for the others with whom they come in contact. Children who are typically well-behaved may be influenced toward unacceptable behavior by their behavioral problem peers. Special educational resources, such as personnel and facilities, have to be allocated to meet these problems. And, in fact, there is evidence that behavioral problem children present such unpleasant situations to their teachers that their presence—or rather their behavior, with which the teachers cannot adequately cope—is one of the primary reasons why teachers leave the teaching field.

The behavioral problem child, whether his problems are aggressively acted out or are manifested in quiet withdrawal, eventually has an effect on those with whom he comes in contact, and unless the adult, such as the teacher, is able to manage the child's behaviors, there will be interference with the learning processes. This, in turn, leads to a series of potentially critical confrontations: the teacher and the students may have to function in an unhealthy learning environment; educators may be faced with new sources of interpersonal contention; school personnel and the community may discover conflicting objectives; and the individual teacher may experience dissatisfaction that will modify both professional and personal aspects of his life.

Behavioral problem children constitute, therefore, a major concern to all educators. Failure to meet the challenge set forth by these children can lead only to a steady sapping of human and institutional resources.

EVOLUTION OF RESPONSIBILITY

Even the most superficial look at the history and evolution of American education reveals that public education has assumed an increasing number of different responsibilities for the development of the student. At one time, particularly during the nineteenth century (before the impact of John Dewey's writings and the sociological and technological advances of our society), the educator had essentially one responsibility to the student: to educate him in the basic academic skills. But this one-sided approach to education had many limitations. During this early period, the teacher did not have to assume the obligation for preparing the student for a specific vocation, or for helping him select a vocation, or for helping him plan his further education. Now, however, with the great emphasis on pupil personnel services, and with the services of specialists such as school counselors and school psychologists, and through within-the-classroom guidance practices, these tasks are very much part of education. Moreover, at one time the psychological development of the student could be virtually disregarded by teachers. Social relationships generally involved a limited number of peers, most of whom lived within walking distance of the student and the little red schoolhouse, and these few other children were often the only persons of his age that he knew to pattern his own behavior after. But disregard for psychological development is no longer acceptable.

It should be noted that this change in importance given to the student's psychological status is not due solely to philosophical and cultural trends, nor should it be interpreted as suggesting that educators were previously negligent of student needs. Rather, it is evident that much of the emphasis on a psychological frame of reference is due to research advances made in the field of psychology during the past few decades. These newly derived psychological data have gradually received increased application in many areas. The influence on education has been to provide the educator with a fairly comprehensive scientific basis for dealing with the psychological as well as the academic factors of teaching and learning.

The modern public educational system is much more diverse and comprehensive in its responsibilities to students than it was a generation or two ago. These responsibilities have evolved from informal public opinions and social mores to formal designation of responsibilities through legal statutes and policies officially acted upon by boards of education. And these responsibilities have been indirectly extended and perpetuated by numerous fiscal procedures, as exemplified by school aid reimbursement policies on the state level and federal funds for educational research, program development, and personnel training.

Despite the diverse and numerous responsibilities held by contemporary educators, most of them, if asked their primary function, would probably reply that it was to help the student learn the academics necessary for him to lead a productive life. While this statement indicates that educators define their role in a rather narrow sense, in actual practice they are necessarily involved in many facets of the student's life. The aims of contemporary education definitely go beyond the "academic" function. The goal of helping the student lead a productive life is actually multifaceted. It is necessary that the educator—whether classroom teacher, school counselor, school psychologist, or administrator—assume some degree of responsibility for the student's sociological, psychological, and often physiological functioning in meeting the challenges presented by social, educational, and vocational situations. Academic knowledge, then, is but part of the *total education* of the student; and "helping the student learn the academics necessary for him to lead a productive life" cannot really be fulfilled unless these new additional responsibilities are met. Without this help the student may not be adequately prepared.

To exemplify this position, as previously mentioned, the student of several decades ago had only a limited number of opportunities for social relationships with peers, and usually these were limited to neighbors and family members within a relatively short distance of the student's home. And the teacher supposedly did not need to be concerned with the student's social skills, at least not to the same degree as is the case today. Today the American student is certainly not confined to his immediate geographical area for finding social models for his behavior. One cannot help thinking of how British entertainers have influenced the current hair styles and dress of students (and adults) all over the world, and how behaviors, such as slang expressions and behavioral standards and ideas, are quickly transmitted from teen-agers in one country to teen-agers in another. The student, partly because of changes in the vocational demands with which he must cope, is painfully aware of the importance of effective social relations. Such additional complexities of modern life and the changes in standards for students' behavior, imposed by adults and students alike, have quite naturally resulted in new responsibilities for professional educators.

Within this frame of reference, it is apparent that the educator should not only be trained in the teaching of academic subject matter, but must also be prepared personally and professionally to help the student with numerous concrete and abstract situations that may possibly affect his quest for a fulfilling and productive life. This requirement, needless to say, places a heavy professional burden upon the shoulders of the educator.

THE EDUCATOR'S ROLE

The educator must be aware of the factors that influence his carrying out of these numerous responsibilities. Some of these factors are endogenous to or developed within the educator, while some are exogenous or developed outside of the educator—for example, social or institutional guidelines and influences.

Perhaps the endogenous sources can be dichotomized into personal characteristics and professional capabilities. Personality factors or personal characteristics of the educator can obviously influence the way in which he perceives behavior problems, reacts to them, and deals with them. These characteristics will receive repeated attention throughout this book; however, at this point it should be acknowledged that just as the efficacy of personal-social counseling depends greatly upon the counselor's *knowing himself,* so will the efficacy of the educator's dealing with behavior problems depend upon *self-knowledge.* For example, some teachers might consider it a blessing to have a quiet, withdrawn child in the classroom. This introverted behavior may really be reflecting psychological problems, yet the needs of this type of teacher lead to neglect of the problem. Thus, the thing to strive for is self-understanding—an understanding of one's own inner dynamics. Only through self-understanding can the educator achieve any degree of objectivity in dealing with behavioral problem children. The second endogenous area, professional capabilities, might best be understood as the necessity of receiving academic training in the psychosocial development of children. Unfortunately, although most teacher-education programs require training in child development and educational psychology, relatively little attention is given to the theories and techniques of guidance and counseling that should be a part of every teacher's professional armament. It is only on the graduate level that a teacher typically receives this training, and then only if it is personally elected.

Exogenous characteristics are usually defined as the regulations and expectations imposed by the society and institution within which the educator lives and works. Each of the educator's responsibilities must be practiced and upheld within the walls of an institution: the public school. From this institution, the educator is provided with both positive and negative stereotypes or regulations or expectations to which he must adhere. He is given a somewhat structured role for helping the student, and is also restricted by lay opinions as to what are acceptable techniques, theories, and subject matter to be used in the educational processes. The teacher's "laboratory" or "office," his classroom, is placed under many more societal restrictions than are other professionals' "offices," such as those of the medical physician or of the scientist. In other words, the reality of the situation is that the role of the educator when dealing with behavioral problem children cannot be determined solely by theoretical formulations based on research; consideration must be given to the limitations imposed by exogenous sources. The educator's goal should be a judicious blend of sound theory and realistic practice.

These limitations should not be discounted or considered to be all bad. Many are both needed and justified. For example, some childhood emotional problems are essentially direct reflections of a disturbed home environment. To expect the school to assume full responsibility for helping a severely disturbed child in this situation would be illogical. If the child's difficulties stem from the home or perhaps disrupting neighborhood influences, efforts from the school alone would be rather impotent. A more appropriate approach would involve intensive intrafamily therapeutic effort, such as might be achieved only through the guidance of a multidiscipline mental health center, and maybe even residential treatment services—that is, placing the child in an institution for the emotionally disturbed. Thus the school is not, and should not be, impervious to limitations imposed exogenously.

MEETING THE NEEDS
OF BEHAVIORAL PROBLEM CHILDREN

One of the major obstacles to creating an effective classroom learning environment is the behavioral problem child: *the child who cannot or will not adjust to the socially acceptable norms for behavior and consequently disrupts his own academic progress, the learning efforts of his classmates, and interpersonal relations.* This working definition is given at this point to allow discussion of general considerations.

Reference to "behavioral problem" children in this book does not indicate a type of child who will always be exceptional or atypical. The physically handicapped child may carry his physical impairment throughout his life, and the severely brain-injured mentally deficient child may always have essentially the same level of functioning; but the behavioral problem child may be a child who is experiencing a temporary or transitory problem and who, in areas unrelated to the unacceptable behaviors, may be quite normal and possibly even superior to other children. Behavioral problem children are not a select, permanently classed group. Indeed, nearly every child has behavior problems at some point in his life, and could thus be called a "behavioral problem" child during that time. Therefore, the term is used in this book to denote children with unacceptable behavioral patterns. With some the problems may be longlasting; with others they may be short-lived.

The behavioral problem child may present a wide variety of symptoms; this area will receive elaboration and clarification in Chapter 2. The symptoms or problem behaviors may stem from either psychological sources (which would include social and emotional disturbances), or neurological impairments, or a combination of the two. Social and emotional disturbances may develop from a number of possible situations; these include traumatic incidents, feelings of insecurity or inadequacy fostered within the family, cultural deprivation, unresolved conflicts, uncontrolled anxiety, and detrimental social learning experiences or lack of beneficial social learning experiences. In regard to neurological impairments, since more and more persons are surviving the potential hazards of prenatal life, infancy, and childhood, it may be assumed that there is an increase in the number of children who have at least some minimal degree of brain injury. And research has revealed that any injury to the brain, regardless of how mild or minimal it may appear, is capable of producing behavioral changes, and that this damage may alter the child's behaviors in learning and social situations (Bakwin & Bakwin, 1960; Bradley, 1957). There are, however, many behavioral problems that have no neurological basis. It should be emphasized that the child who has a behavioral problem need not be neurologically impaired. Similarly, the child who is neurologically impaired, although in general the impairment makes the person potentially susceptible to behavior disturbances for organic reasons, does not necessarily have a behavior problem.

Behavioral problem children are receiving far more attention at the present time than at any other point in the history of the behavioral sciences. No longer is the study of the physiological-psychological-sociological behavioral relationships limited to the medical specialties of neurology, pediatrics, and psychiatry; increased research and interest are being contributed by the disciplines of education, psychology, sociology, and anthropology. Diagnostic and treatment programs are developing rapidly on the national, state, and local levels. Colleges and universities are enlarging their curriculums to provide the professional training necessary for the personnel needed in these programs. The educator's increased responsibility for the behavioral problem child has placed new emphasis on the importance of the classroom teacher, the school counselor, the school psychologist, and other school personnel being involved in the identification, diagnosis, and treatment phases. Consequently, it is crucial that educational personnel, particularly the classroom teachers and members of the psychoeducational services staff, such as school counselors and school psychologists, be prepared to contribute effectively their share in meeting the needs and problems presented by the behavioral problem child.

The initial question confronting educators, particularly classroom teachers, is: How do I identify the behavioral problem child? Then, after the child has been identified: What should I do? How do I deal with the child? To whom can I turn for help? In many cases the classroom teacher may feel that his academic training does not qualify him to identify *real* behavior problems, at least not in the same manner as a skilled psychological or medical clinician. But, as will become evident at a later point, *teachers can identify real behavior problems,* and although they may use criteria that are different from those used by psychologists or psychiatrists, they can still determine which children need help. In any case, the teacher is left with the responsibility of coping with the child's daily behavior and, in most instances, of making the initial efforts to obtain the parents' cooperation in locating professional services to help attain behavioral modification.

Thus the classroom teacher is faced with two difficulties: identifying the behavioral problem child and obtaining, through referral, professional services for him. Naturally the first place to turn would be to other members of the school faculty, such as the school counselor or the school psychologist. There are, of course, many school systems in which these professional allies are not available to the teacher, and the only recourse then is to seek help from outside the faculty. Even when there are auxiliary or ancillary pupil personnel staff members, it may be that they too are not equipped to provide all of the psychological services necessary. There is the further problem, then, of determining referral sources.

The possibility of another complicating situation exists. There are instances where pupil personnel or psychoeducational personnel, such as school counselors or school psychologists, may take one of two erroneous positions: they believe that they are incapable of performing a specific service that they are actually qualified to offer; or they believe that they are capable of performing a specific service that they are in fact personally or professionally incapable of ethically providing. Although the latter, seemingly delusions of grandeur, may possibly be the more dangerous of the two, both contribute to an ineffective attitude.

What all of this points to is that one of the primary objectives of all school personnel should be to recognize realistically what professional skills they are and are not able to exercise. Their title alone does not indicate what they can and should do. Just as not all school psychologists can do an acceptable personality evaluation, not all school counselors are capable of handling a counseling relationship that can lead to modification of personal and social problems. Similarly, there are classroom teachers who cannot recognize behavior problems and who, moreover, are incapable of dealing effectively with them.

If educational personnel are to be involved in the processes of recognition and identification, diagnosis, and treatment or modification of the behavioral problem child, guidelines or criteria must be established for each aspect. The teacher must know what types of behavior are suggestive of specific disorders. The objective instruments used in the diagnosis must be valid and reliable in delineating the disorder; perhaps more important, the subjective judgments of the diagnosticians, such as might be formulated during a social case history, must be stabilized and accepted as subjective but professionally derived evidence. And, finally, educational, psychological, and medical services must be provided to all children, regardless of socioeconomic, racial, or geographical factors. In regard to the latter services, when treatment is necessary, it must be professionally and ethically given by the most suitable person.

There is reason to believe that the legal mandate of compulsory education necessitates that *each school system must have the professional resources to meet the needs of all behavioral problem children,* such as the emotionally disturbed and brain-injured (Bower, 1959a). Experts who have surveyed the problem of implementing these services conclude that adequately serving the behavioral problem child is one of the most critical and desperate problems that most schools face (Bower, 1959b). And there is a distinct, pressing need for improved preparation of professional workers to meet the educational programing requirements of behavioral problem children (Knoblock, 1963). It is on these grounds, in part, that much of the content of this book will be based: the premise is that many educators currently employed in schools, as well as those in teacher training programs, can prepare themselves to cope more effectively with the behavioral problem child. Many of the techniques set forth in this book will be directed toward implementing that goal.

A prerequisite for *total education* is that the modern classroom must provide a flexible curriculum that can be modified for each child. This is especially important for the behavioral problem child. The over-all curriculum can benefit from provisions for special staff personnel and referral sources for diagnosis and treatment, psychological and medical consultants, and the inauguration of various types of educational-therapeutic activities—for example, adjustment classes, child study programs, group and individual counseling, parent counseling, and human relations classes. Many of these provisions will obviously cost a great deal of money, something that most school systems certainly do not have an abundance of. Thus the most prudent and perhaps equally effective way would be to capitalize upon available resources. In other words, many extra expenses could perhaps be avoided if classroom teachers, school counselors, and school psychologists, aided of course by appropriate administrative policies, were able to provide more direct service, such as attempts at behavioral modification, to the behavioral problem children. It is necessary for the educator to be aware of new personal and professional responsibilities, and to strive continually to develop the abilities necessary to cope with the problems (Bower, 1960; Juul, 1959). The chapters in this book on behavioral modification will present approaches that are applicable to educators within their existing positions.

The foregoing statement should not be interpreted as meaning that all behavioral problem children can be "treated" by the educational staff. But it is believed that there is far more potential for behavioral modification within existing school personnel than is actually realized. There will, however, be behavioral problem children who will have to be referred to other sources, such as the local child guidance clinic.

The classroom teacher will find that criteria for referrals for professional services are ambiguous. Although some distinct guidelines for referrals are presented in chapter 3, it will become clear that one cannot easily make definitive statements about behavior. For example, while some studies have shown that the lower the academic achievement the higher the tendency toward problems (Olson, 1930), the experienced teacher will recognize immediately that poor achievement alone does not necessarily reflect behavior problems. Therefore, there is a distinct need for incorporating the classroom teacher's perception of behavior problems with those of the school counselor and the school psychologist, which may be more clinical in nature. This combination of percepts may lead to criteria that can be generalized to behavior problems exhibited in the classroom. These criteria, we may hope, would make identification of the children possible and also help clarify the relationship between teachers' opinions and the data obtained from counseling interviews, diagnostic instruments, and clinical judgments.

The diagnosis of a behavioral problem is a complex process. The goal is not solely to arrive at a diagnostic category or label; labeling is essentially meaningless. Rather, the diagnostician attempts to determine the characteristics of the problem, such as the possible causes and related emotions, and to derive a recommended approach to treatment or modification to eliminate or at least alleviate the problem. Diagnostic instruments can provide a number of indications of possible etiological factors and current characteristics, but the real task is attempting to synthesize the data into a valid and reliable diagnostic opinion and then trying to determine the best treatment procedure to recommend. As if this were not difficult enough in itself, there are many pitfalls in the processes of diagnosis; these will be presented in detail in chapter 4.

The comprehensive diagnosis of behavioral problem children, such as those who are emotionally disturbed and/or brain-injured, could include a physical examination, a social case history, psychological testing with the psychologist's impressions, an electroencephalographic examination, and a neurological and/or psychiatric examination. This would be the comprehensive approach, but there are many cases—and it might even be safe to say that these are the majority of cases—that do not receive and possibly do not require each of these diagnostic approaches. Unfortunately, not all of the techniques are considered to be of equal validity and reliability, since the final judgment is frequently based on the *opinions* of a clinician. Opinions are subjective and are subject to error, but some would state that that is one of the "prices you pay" in clinical services. The key thing to remember is that clinical judgments are subjective and may be erroneous. The judgment of a single clinician, regardless of professional training or degree, should not be considered absolute. Attempts to establish statistical interrelationships between the various sources of clinical diagnostic data have been rather minimal because of the uncertainty of an empirical basis for comparison. Consequently, there is a need for intertest and intratest reliability and validity studies.

Because of the complexity involved in the identification, diagnosis, and treatment or modification of behavioral problems, there seems little doubt that a multidisciplinary approach is usually the most advantageous. Thus far, the functions of the classroom teacher, the school counselor, and the school psychologist have been emphasized. Frequently, however, it is necessary to go beyond these persons and to involve other professionals, such as social workers, speech therapists, general medical practitioners, pediatricians, and psychiatrists. As Gildea says:

The school mental health program cannot stand alone but must be closely integrated into the matrix of social institutions in the community. For optimum functioning a child guidance clinic should be available where psychiatric treatment for individual children and parents can be found, if necessary. And for the sickest children, an in-patient service should be at hand. The school mental health program should function as one branch of the comprehensive community mental health services.[1]

In other words, although the educator is indispensable in the professional services designed to meet the needs of the behavioral problem child and has a responsibility to initiate and assure continuation of treatment programs, other social agencies, such as the public mental health department or child guidance clinic or family service center, must also be included within the constellation of referral sources.

Attempts to change or modify the unacceptable behavior patterns of these problem children will undoubtedly meet with various limiting factors. As mentioned previously, the comprehensive mental health program necessitates the involvement of several professions, and there are many

[1] From Margaret C.-L. Gildea, "School Mental Health: Orientation, Methods, and Screening," in M. Krugman (Ed.), ORTHOPSYCHIATRY AND THE SCHOOL (New York: American Orthopsychiatric Association, 1958), p. 133. Copyright, the American Orthopsychiatric Association, Inc. Reproduced by permission.

school systems that will not have access to needed professional personnel. Not only may it be difficult to find the services of a psychiatrist (and even more difficult to find a *child* psychiatrist), neurologist, and electroencephalographer; but many school systems may not have access to either a clinical or a school psychologist—or even a school counselor. Thus, one of the basic challenges involved in adequately meeting the needs of the behavioral problem child is the obtaining of multidiscipline services. Moreover, even if the school system is fortunate enough to have a school counselor and/or a school psychologist, these persons are restricted in the types of services that they can provide. No one person, regardless of discipline, can adequately fulfill all of the requirements for providing diagnostic and therapeutic services to behavioral problem children. Another limiting factor is that the school setting may influence the services that are offered. For example, there are still some school systems that refuse to let school psychologists, regardless of their level of training, provide services that are labeled "therapeutic" or to do certain types of testing. It should be realized, therefore, that any attempts to work with behavioral problem children will require that the educator be willing to exercise initiative in pioneering in a new area which justly needs his attention and that he be prepared to face the critical attacks which may be leveled at him for his courage. It should be added that it takes an equal amount of courage for the educator to draw the line on what services he can provide. Just as there are school systems that restrict professional services, there are also those that expect more services than can ethically be justified. This will be particularly relevant when some degree of acceptance has been accorded to behavioral modification techniques within the school program; unless care is exercised, the educator may find himself pressured toward attempting behavioral modification with children who are too severely disturbed for his capabilities, and problems may be referred to him that are philosophically incompatible with the psychological objectives of behavioral modification.

SCOPE OF THIS BOOK

This book covers two broad areas. In the first part, emphasis is placed on the recognition and diagnosis of behavior problems in school settings. Definitions of types of behavior problems, epidemiological data on types of problems, and the roles of classroom teachers, school counselors, and school psychologists in the detection of behavior problems will be presented to clarify the factors involved in recognizing and initially dealing with behavioral problem children. The diagnostic processes emphasized will be those procedures that are typically used by school psychologists or by clinicians who service schools, and a review of research will exemplify the extent to which the reliability and validity of the diagnostic techniques must be considered.

The second part will present means of accomplishing behavioral modification in an educational setting. The theoretical position that will be presented is an eclectic one: a combination of aspects from various theories of counseling, psychotherapy, and behavior therapy. Emphasis is placed, however, on principles of client-centered counseling and on a conditioning or behavioristic approach based on principles of learning theory. Although these two approaches, client-centered and conditioning, may seem incompatible, evidence will be cited which indicates that there are indeed areas of theoretical agreement and that this is probably the most efficacious for dealing with behavioral problem children in the schools. This eclectic method is suitable for the three main types of educational personnel: classroom teachers, school counselors, and school psychologists. And although certain aspects of it may be controversial, particularly those that are behavioristic, they may be readily adapted to the educational setting and used for the alleviation of most behavior problems. Further, its efficacy, in terms of relieving the problems for the student and the amount of time, effort, and training required of the educator, seems to more than justify its priority over other, more conventional approaches. Specific techniques and procedures for application in the classroom, in school counseling, and in school psychology will be discussed and will be supported and illustrated by related research and case studies. Following the methodology, consideration will be given to how these procedures can be introduced into the public school setting and how certain practical problems, such as combating misconceptions and erroneous stereotypes, can be confronted. Although there is only a limited amount of directly relevant research, recommendations regarding the training of educators to provide this type of behavioral modification will be made.

This book is not intended to totally train the reader to cope with behavioral problem children; it is not a "do-it-yourself" text. It is expected that the reader will already possess some degree of training in educational psychology, and that to be fully trained, he will undoubtedly need to receive further training in psychology, education, and sociology, and will require some degree of individual supervision, such as in a practicum experience. However, this material will serve as an introduction to the theoretical rationale for recognition, diagnosis, and modification of behavior problems and will relate existing research to the theoretical constructs. And the examples regarding the use of the behavioral modification principles in classroom teaching, school counseling, and school psychology will serve as models from which unique approaches for use in practical situations may be developed. Although, in general, further training is necessary, the contents of this book should give the reader some definite practical techniques that can be immediately applied with behavioral problem children in the schools.

REFERENCES

Bakwin, H., and Bakwin, Ruth M. *Clinical management of behavior disorders in children* (2nd ed.). Philadelphia: W. B. Saunders, 1960.

Bower, E. M. The emotionally handicapped child and the school. *Exceptional Children,* 1959, 26:6-11. (a)

Bower, E. M. The emotionally handicapped child and the school: an analysis of programs and trends. *Exceptional Children,* 1959, 26:182-188. (b)

Bower, E. M. *Early identification of emotionally handicapped children in school.* Springfield, Ill.: C. C Thomas, 1960.

Bradley, C. Characteristics and management of children with behavior problems associated with organic brain damage. *Pediatric Clinics of North America,* 1957, 4:1049-1060.

Gildea, Margaret C.-L. School mental health: orientation, methods, and screening. In M. Krugman (Ed.), *Orthopsychiatry and the school.* New York: American Orthopsychiatric Association, 1958, 131-134.

Juul, K. D. Education for the mentally ill. *Michigan Education Association Journal,* 1959, 37:286, 314.

Knoblock, P. Critical factors influencing educational programming for disturbed children. *Exceptional Children,* 1963, 30:124-129.

Olson, W. C. *Problem tendencies in children: a method for their measurement and description.* Minneapolis: University of Minnesota Press, 1930.

2

Causes and Characteristics
of Behavior Problems in Children

In attempting to delineate causes and to describe characteristics of behavioral problem children, we run the risk of having to resort to generalizations or, worse yet, overgeneralizations. Yet to claim exactness is presumptuous, since precise knowledge is not available thus far. When considering causes and characteristics, it is necessary to settle for categorical positions that are general but that possess the value of not going beyond what is validly known.

Thus, to achieve some sort of common frame of reference for the ensuing chapters, the most appropriate approach would be to accept guidelines that are admittedly general, yet reasonably definitive. Three stages are involved: defining the term "behavioral problem children," reviewing studies that cite the behavioral characteristics of these children, and considering the possible etiological, or causative, sources of the problem behaviors. This sequence conforms to the components of *epidemiology*—that is, the study of causes, characteristics, and control of a given condition (in our case the behavioral problem child). Following this sequence, research evidence on behavioral characteristics that reflect specific conditions will be presented.

DEFINING THE TERM
"BEHAVIORAL PROBLEM CHILD"

As is the case with many technical words used in the behavioral sciences, the definition of "behavioral problem child" is complicated by numerous factors. There appear to be four primary complicating factors.

First, what is a behavior problem in one situation may not be in a different situation. In other words, the acceptance of a particular behavioral act will depend upon the norms for the specific group and setting in which the act is performed. For example, a certain behavioral act may be acceptable when it is performed in relation to a sibling; that is, at home during a rough-and-tumble play session, a boy may "clobber" his brother and receive no rebuke from anyone (granted, however, that the brother may "clobber" him in return). But if the same boy hits his brother or another student during a spelling lesson at school, it is a safe bet that he will be admonished by the teacher for his behavior. Thus, the definition of a behavior problem must involve the setting in which the behavior occurs.

Second, the personal opinions of the observer or judge, such as the classroom teacher, will influence the definition. For example, it was mentioned in Chapter 1 that a silent, withdrawn child in the classroom may not be perceived by the teacher as having a behavior problem, possibly because that particular teacher feels insecure or extremely threatened (challenged) by the acting-out, aggressive child and therefore perceives any quiet, nondisruptive behavior as acceptable. Another teacher might perceive this behavior in an entirely different manner. This teacher may feel no more threatened by acting-out, aggressive behavior than by passive, withdrawn behavior, and may be capable of dealing with all kinds of behavior with equal effectiveness; thus this teacher's definition of behavior problems quite likely includes the withdrawn child who is unable to participate as well as his peers in social or learning activities. Or to return to the previous example of the boy who hits his brother, the brother who has been struck during a play session might view the act as a playful gesture or an act done for the purpose of getting him to react in a like manner, whereas such an act in the classroom might be viewed by the teacher as a show of hostility and aggression, or as a challenge to his effectiveness as a teacher, and would definitely be deemed unacceptable behavior. The person assessing the act, such as the brother or the teacher, holds his or her own set of opinions as to what response or behavioral act is appropriate in view of the situational events. Indeed, the "eye of the beholder" is significant in the definition of behavior problems. It should be clear at this point that teachers, because of—or at least in part—their own personal characteristics, will define behavior problems in their own individual ways; and any attempt to determine an exact definition will have to be based on a consensus.

Third, the theoretical orientation of the professional observer or judge will influence the definition. A school psychologist who accepts certain principles derived from developmental psychology or various theories of personality might view certain behaviors, such as childhood masturbation, as expected because of developmental factors, whereas another school psychologist who bases his theoretical approach on different grounds, such as a position that relies on specific moralistic ideas (which may or may not be scientific), would react to such behavior as being a sure sign of a behavior problem. Because of the potential differences in theoretical positions, each person who is going to judge or evaluate behavior professionally must be familiar with the different theories of behavior and be able, through evolving a comparative analysis, to derive at least loose theoretical parameters to use in their work. It is totally unethical for a person to pose as a "professional judge" of behavior without having the academic knowledge to justify this status.

Fourth and finally, the professional orientation or discipline of the observer or judge will influence the definition. Although this factor will receive further elaboration at a subsequent point in the book, it should be mentioned now that the criteria which classroom teachers use to define behavior problems are naturally rooted in what they observe in their setting, the classroom, and are influenced by the goals for their role. In contrast, the school counselor or school psychologist who is engaged in helping the child achieve personal adjustment or personality modification may well overlook certain behaviors because they do not contradict the goals of his role. For example, the teacher may base the definition on educational achievement factors—that is, on how easily the child learns or whether the specific behavior being judged influences the learning process—whereas counselors or psychologists may give little or no consideration to learning factors and may instead place emphasis on behaviors in relation to others—that is, social interaction or interpersonal behaviors.

There is little doubt that any definition of "behavioral problem child" put forward by anyone is bound to be relative. This same type of relativity is found with other terms, such as "abnormal" and "deviant." Thus it is acknowledged that definitions may vary, and the consensus may vary among groups or types of professionals; a definition that represents the consensus for classroom teachers might easily differ from the definition that represents the consensus for school psychologists.

Several decades ago, an impressive array of American educators, psychologists, and medical physicians came together to form the White House Conference on Child Health and Protection (1931), and in their publication on special education they emphasized the importance of meeting the needs of behavioral problem children in the schools. Their definition of behavior problems seems a bit broad, but perhaps it is a good starting point. They divide behavioral difficulties into three general classes: the nervous, the emotionally unstable, and the delinquent. As will be seen from a perusal of other sources, these categories are certainly limited in how well they delineate problem behaviors, but they do broadly separate behavioral characteristics. This example was purposely selected to illustrate the fact that definitions offered, sometimes from even the most esteemed sources, are not necessarily going to establish clearly a working definition.

Many definitions are based on classifications of behaviors. It is believed that by classifying the behaviors, a meaningful definition can be developed. As one example, Gilbert (1957) placed referrals of children to child guidance centers in the following categories: academic difficulties; mental retardation; aggressive and antisocial behavior; passive, withdrawn, asocial behavior; hyperactivity and motor symptoms; sexual behavior problems; toilet training; speech defects; and miscellaneous. While these categories exemplify the problem areas and thereby, in a sense, possibly provide a classification of the children who would be serviced in that particular setting, there is admittedly only limited value because the actual definition was determined in the first place by the individual who initiated the referral for the child with "deviant behavior." Thus a definition by characterization may be of value, at best, for developing a *generic* definition; further attention will be given to characteristics shortly.

In general, the definitions of behavior problems in the school context emphasize the judgments of teachers; for example, one group of writers defines "problem behavior" as

. . . all types of misbehavior in school, including violations of rules and work requirements and violations of moral standards. Admittedly, there are some obvious limitations to using the term problem behavior in this way. Teachers differ in the way they look at pupil behavior and in what they consider to be problem behavior. However, this is the way such behavior is usually identified, so for the purposes of this study the teacher's judgment was considered sufficient. (Eaton, Weathers, and Phillips, 1957, p. 130)

In other words, this position would allow each teacher to make an individualistic definition, as long as the behavior evaluated was within the school setting.

In Chapter 1, the following definition of the behavioral problem child was set forth: *the child who cannot or will not adjust to the socially acceptable norms for behavior and consequently disrupts his own academic progress, the learning efforts of his classmates, and interpersonal relations.* This definition is about as specific as can be logically justified. It is somewhat restricted to behaviors that are manifested within the school; it recognizes that there are socially determined norms to which the child must conform if the behavior is not to be deemed inappropriate or a "problem"; and it places importance on learning or academic activities. Admittedly, this definition does not include behaviors that could be readily classified as problems outside of the school. For example, it is possible, at least theoretically, that a severely disturbed child could behave in an acceptable manner within the school and go unnoticed as needing help, especially if the educators involved were impervious to certain cues to the underlying problems. But the final phrase, "disrupts his . . . interpersonal relations," broadens the definition from emphasis on just behaviors in learning situations and should adequately encompass essentially the same social and behavioral cues that could feasibly be observed outside of the school. The final point about this definition is that it allows for the inevitable necessity of permitting each teacher to use his own criteria for what are acceptable and unacceptable behaviors. But in regard to this factor, Chapter 3 will include other materials that should facilitate agreement between teachers' ratings or appraisals of behavior.

CLASSIFICATIONS OF BEHAVIOR PROBLEMS

Before elaborating on the characteristics and causes of behavior problems, one should consider how behaviors might be classified. Such groupings could have implications for defining and diagnosing the problem areas.

Probably the classification system most often used today is the one published by the American Psychiatric Association (1952). In summary, mental disorders are divided into the following categories: I. Organic brain disorders (acute and chronic); II. Functional disorders, including psychotic, psychophysiologic autonomic and visceral, psychoneurotic, personality (character), and transient situational personality disorders; III. Mental deficiency. Rosen and Gregory (1965) provide a more comprehensive discussion of this system. Beller (1962) has developed a similar classification system specifically for childhood personality disorders; his system subdivides these into functional behavioral disorders, mental subnormality, and behavior disorders with an organic basis (each of these three categories has numerous subcategories). Such attempts to group behaviors seem to emphasize the dichotomy of problems caused by organic (neurological or physiological) factors and those caused by functional (nonorganic) factors. Kessler (1966) notes that the classification systems also emphasize whether the disturbance results from inner conflict or external conflict (between the child and reality), whether the disturbance causes only the child to suffer or other people as well, and whether the child's general functioning is disturbed.

It should be noted that frequently more than one term is applied to the same type of behavior. This difficulty will receive additional attention when consideration is given to characteristics *per se* of behavioral problem children. Suffice it to say that comparisons between studies are often tenuous because of inconsistent use of terms—for example, different criteria for a given term or different terms for identical criteria. And, as will be brought out in Chapter 3, the degree of pathology or intensity and the chronicity of the symptoms may also be necessary parts of the classification process.

CHARACTERISTICS OF CHILDHOOD PROBLEM BEHAVIORS

Systematic investigations of the problem areas of children reveal that specific characteristics cited generally vary with each investigator. This seems to be due primarily to the lack of precision of the classification systems. For example, one investigator might measure "timidity" and "withdrawal" as separate behaviors, whereas another investigator might group them together. Moreover, a comparison of categories from different studies is of little value, because it is virtually impossible, or at least impractical, to ascertain whether the definition for a given characteristic, such as for "introverted," is exactly the same as used in each of the different studies.

As might be expected from the lack of precision in recognizing and classifying behaviors, estimates of frequency of occurrence are diverse. Despite the ambiguous meaning and value of such estimates, a brief review should aid in developing a perspective of the complexity of deriving specifics about behavioral problem children.

Martens (1944) estimated that 2 to 3 percent of school-age children presented behavior and/or emotional problems that were severe enough to incapacitate them for regular school. Rogers (1942), in a study of elementary schools, concluded that 7 percent of the girls and 18 percent of the boys were seriously maladjusted. Ullmann (1952) found that junior high school teachers judged 8 percent of the students to be severely maladjusted. These figures are obviously estimates of the children with rather severe problems, and certainly are much lower than would be figures that included children who experienced transitory and situational behavioral problems. Although the discussion on incidence will be carried further, it should be emphasized at this time that the majority of disturbed children are to be found in the regular classroom (Morse, 1958) and that the critical involvement of the school personnel hardly necessitates mention.

The diversity in investigations of the characteristics of behavioral problem children is exemplified in Table 2–1, which presents the categories and percentages found in two studies. The data from Cummings (1944) are based on an analysis of 239 British children between the ages of two and seven years, and each percentage represents the frequency with which that particular category was found in the behaviors of school

children, as observed by classroom teachers. The data from Rogers, Lilienfeld, and Pasamanick (1954) are from a comprehensive analysis of the
developmental psychology of American behavioral problem children;
the percentages represent the frequency with which specific unacceptable
behaviors were found in teachers' referrals for 363 white behavioral
problem children. These two studies are based on two different cultural

TABLE 2-1.   Frequency of Unacceptable Behaviors in Childhood

Cummings (1944)—British Study		Rogers, Lilienfeld, and Pasamanick (1954)—American Study	
	Percent		*Percent*
Excitability and Restlessness	28.9	Nonconforming Attitudes	51.0
Daydreaming, Lack of Concentration, and Laziness	28.9	Nonconforming Physical Behavior	46.3
Generalized Anxiety, Timidity, and Shyness	23.0	Inadequate School Work	37.5
Specific Fears	22.2	Hyperactivity	37.5
Bladder Control, Frequency of Micturition Difficulties	21.3	Nonconforming Verbalizations	32.2
Nervous Habits	18.9	Assaultive	30.9
Cruelty, Aggression	15.1	Delinquent	30.6
Speech Difficulties	14.2	Confused-Disorganized	22.9
Lack of Appetite, Food Faddiness	11.3	Withdrawn	14.9
Babyish Behavior and Frequent Crying	11.3	Physical Complaints	11.0
Lying and Stealing	10.1	Fear	10.2
Tendency to Constipation, Headache, Stomachache	9.2	Bodily Manipulation	5.5
Obstinacy, Disobedience	8.8	Sexual Activity	4.1
Bedtime Problems	7.1	Hypoactivity	0.0
Undesirable Sex Habits	6.3	Other (not classified)	14.6
Easily and Frequently Tired	4.6		
Obsession	4.2		
Hysterical Outbursts	4.2		

samples: one is British and one is American. Some of the differences,
therefore, may represent cultural factors.

The significance of cultural differences has been borne out by an
international comparative study by Wall (1955). In this investigation,
Wall summarized eight studies, encompassing samples ranging from five
to sixteen years of age. He concluded that the estimates of children showing some symptoms of maladjustment ranged from 22 percent to 42 per-

cent of the population; the estimates of children appearing to be seriously maladjusted ranged from 4 percent to 12 percent of the population; the estimates of total percentages of children showing evidence of maladjustment, including all degrees of severity, ranged from 7.6 percent in New Zealand to 49 percent in the United States. It is interesting to note that the studies in the United States, as compared to the United Kingdom, New Zealand, and France, consistently reported higher incidences of maladjustment.

As part of a larger study (Woody, 1964), an investigation of the manifested characteristics of behavioral problem children was conducted by a county department of health.[1] In this project, an analysis was made of teachers' descriptions of behavioral problem children referred to a special psychological and neurological program. The referrals were made by classroom teachers within a given geographical area, a county school system, and included all first-time referrals seen during the initial two and one-half years of the program. Since this county had never had any sort of comprehensive mental health program, the referrals were from a virtually untapped population of children and it is believed that the sampling essentially represented the entire body of behavioral problem children in the county. Although there were some written guidelines for referrals, the teachers were generally free to establish their own criteria and definitions for behavior problems. It should be noted that this program was not intended for those students thought to be mentally retarded, since the special education program serviced this type of referral. This study of problem areas included 133 boys and 39 girls. The boys ranged in age from 4 years and 3 months to 18 years and 6 months; their mean chronological age was 10 years and 2.5 months. The girls ranged in age from 5 years and 0 months to 17 years and 1 month; their mean chronological age was 12 years and 1 month. Table 2–2 presents the percentage of the children that displayed any one of twenty-one different behavioral characteristics. It is interesting to note that the number of behavioral problem areas per child, as described by his classroom teacher and categorized by the program's clinical staff, ranged from one to nine, and the mean number of descriptive characteristics was 4.23 for the boys, 5.18 for the girls, and 4.45 for the combined sexes. It seems that the classroom teachers referred most of the behavioral problem children, approximately 50 percent of them, because of poor social relations, presumably due to numerous overt behavioral acts displayed toward members of their peer group in the school setting. The second and third rankings, poor reading skills and poor concentration or attention, are obviously related to academic requirements in the classroom; and this

[1] This project was supported in part by a Neurological and Sensory Disease Project grant from the U. S. Public Health Service. Grant No. N2405 A62 was under the administration of W. R. Storer, M.D.

TABLE 2–2. Reasons for Referring Behavioral Problem Children

Characteristic	Males N = 133			Females N = 39			Males and Females N = 172		
	No.	Percent	Rank	No.	Percent	Rank	No.	Percent	Rank
Poor Social Relations	63	47.36	1	18	46.15	1.5	81	47.09	1
Poor Reading Skills	51	38.34	2	17	43.49	3	68	39.53	2
Poor Concentration or Attention	47	35.33	3	16	41.02	4	63	36.63	3
Hyperactivity	44	33.08	4.5	13	33.33	7	57	33.14	4
Emotional Problems, Undifferentiated	44	33.08	4.5	11	28.20	10	55	31.97	5
Resents Authority	38	28.57	6.5	15	38.46	5	53	30.81	6
Nervous	38	28.57	6.5	14	35.89	6	52	30.23	7
Poor Motivation	35	26.31	8	12	30.76	8.5	47	27.33	8
Immature Behavior	24	18.04	10	18	46.15	1.5	42	24.41	9
Aggressive	33	24.81	9	8	20.51	12.5	41	23.83	10
Lies and Exaggerates	23	17.21	11	12	30.76	8.5	35	20.34	11
Poor Motor Coordination	19	14.28	12.5	9	23.07	11	28	16.28	12
Speech Problem	17	12.78	14	7	17.94	14.5	24	13.95	13.5
Withdrawn	19	14.28	12.5	5	12.82	16.5	24	13.95	13.5
Lacks Confidence	14	10.52	16	7	17.94	14.5	21	12.20	15
Poor Comprehension	15	11.27	15	5	12.82	16.5	20	11.62	16
Cries	10	7.51	19	8	20.51	12.5	18	10.46	17
Poor Bowel and Bladder Control	12	9.02	17	4	10.25	18	16	9.30	18
Uses Profanity	11	8.27	18	2	5.12	19	13	7.51	19
Sucks Finger	4	3.00	20	1	2.56	20	5	2.90	20
Uncontrolled Salivation	2	1.50	21	0	0.00	21	2	1.16	21

adds support to a statement made earlier that teachers are likely to define behavior problems on the basis of interference with learning activities.

A comparison of the data in Table 2–2 with the study by Cummings (Table 2–1) reveals similarities, particularly in regard to the most frequently noted characteristics, but there are differences between the two in some of the symptoms or characteristics of lesser frequencies. Likewise, it seems that these data compare closely with the study by Rogers, Lilienfeld, and Pasamanick (Table 2–1), especially in the area of hyperactivity; but again there are also differences.

As mentioned earlier, comparisons of this kind are of questionable value. Each study is based on a unique sampling selection procedure; and the fact that the results are usually categorized according to an original set of descriptive characteristics makes the assumption of sameness for categories, even though they are labeled with the same term, of dubious validity. It seems lamentable that there is not a common set of manifested characteristics with distinct, clear-cut definitions available for describing behavioral problem children. This type of classification system has proved to be of great value in other areas of exceptionality. For example, professionals in the field of mental retardation have developed and adopted an approach to terminology and classification, which should provide the bases for standardization of procedures and allow comparisons of the results of research studies regarding mental retardation (Heber, 1958). Unfortunately, such a unifying approach to terminology and classification is still lacking in the area of behavior problems.

After considering all of the aforementioned frequencies, differences in approaches to classification, and the possibility of divergent definitions, one might feel that even a consensus would be a rough estimate of definitions and characteristics. And indeed that is true. But to proceed any further, it is necessary to accept the fact that precision is limited.

These sources of variance might also lead to doubts about the reliability of teachers' selections of behavioral problem children. In other words, one might question whether the entire scope of behavior disorders is represented in referrals from classroom teachers. It has been found, however, that teachers are able to select approximately equal numbers of children who are aggressive or defiant and who are withdrawn or timid (Bower, 1960). This finding serves to contradict the belief held by many that teachers do not recognize the shy, passive child who may possess a behavior problem, but tend to refer only the acting-out child for special diagnostic services. As may be recalled, just such an example was used earlier; this occurrence is possible with certain teachers, but should not be considered to be generally the case. Characteristics of teacher identification will receive specific consideration in chapter 3.

Thus far in this chapter, a working definition of "behavioral problem children" has been arrived at. And several studies have exemplified the characteristics attributed to behavioral problem children and the frequencies with which they are found.

CAUSES OF BEHAVIOR PROBLEMS

In examining causes of behavior probléms, one should stress that any etiology or cause is only assumed to be true, and that there is always the possibility that a diagnosis will have to be changed. After further observations or additional diagnostic data, it may become evident to the diagnostician that his initial beliefs about cause were possibly wrong, or were only partially correct, and his thinking about etiology should be modified; on the other hand, it is, of course, possible that his initial impressions will be strengthened by the supplementary evidence. Thus whenever the *cause* or the *etiology* is discussed the reader should bear in mind that the terms should always be mentally qualified with the word *possible* and that it is entirely appropriate that a diagnosis regarding causes be changed with the advent of further knowledge about the conditions.

Any attempt to delineate a specific cause, even with the most obvious and seemingly clear-cut evidence, is always contaminated with the effects of interactions between the possible causative factors. For example, a behavioral problem child may seem to be manifesting behaviors caused by brain injury, but underlying the undeniable neurological impairment there may also be the effects of another causative source, such as environmental pressures. In other words, when any statement about etiology is made, what is really being dealt with is what seems to be the primary or most likely cause. There may well be other secondary causes or factors of lesser effects. In fact, there are multiple causations underlying most problem behaviors (Stroh, 1960).

When a diagnostician sets forth a hypothesis about the causes or etiology of a condition, he is influenced by two factors. First, the etiological concept will be influenced by the level of explanation that is necessary for the particular situation. And second, the theoretical orientation of the diagnostician will influence the way he views the possible causative sources (Kessler, 1966).

There are different levels of etiological explanation; all diagnoses of causes will not be—and, moreover, need not be—on the same level; that is, some may seemingly be more highly refined than others. For example, if a classroom teacher is presented with a boy who acts out during the social studies lesson, the teacher may wish to delve into the cause for the behavior. In a situation like this, the cause may simply be designated in terms of two possibilities: the boy could not fulfill the academic requirements of the lesson and had to resort to acting out as a defensive measure against failure, or the boy was lacking in social-behavioral controls. In the first of these possibilities, the boy's problem behavior would appear to be caused by his poor academic achievement, and thus special reading services, developmental or remedial in nature, might be provided, rather than, as in the second possibility, pursuing some sort of guidance approach that would help the boy realize that his behavior was inappropriate for that setting and that, in order to make his behavior acceptable, he needed to develop better social-behavioral controls. In other words, determining such causes as these might appear rather superficial, yet this level of explanation would be adequate and appropriate for this type of situation.

Now a contrasting level of diagnosis may be considered. Let us assume, for example, that the same boy (who acted out in the social studies class) was in the school psychologist's office for testing (perhaps he had been referred by the teacher to find out whether he was below average in reading skills), and that while the boy seemed to be cooperating and accepting the examiner, he suddenly stood up or began fidgeting in his chair. In this situation and in view of the differences in role objectives between the school psychologist and the classroom teacher, observations and other evidence would probably be aligned with a deeper or more refined level of diagnostic explanation. In this case, the school psychologist might look for supportive or contradictory evidence in the test data, such as from a mental abilities test profile, to see whether the boy has difficulty in maintaining concentration, or whether the type of task (verbal comprehension versus manipulation of materials, for example) influences his behavior, or whether the information in the boy's cumulative folder suggests extreme anxiety when in the presence of adults. And there would be numerous other possibilities that could be considered. From this approach, the school psychologist might try to infer whether the hyperactive behavior that disrupted the testing was due to a neurological impairment or emotional problem (such as being anxious when with adults perceived to be authority figures) or to some other type of etiological explanation. Thus, the same boy and quite similar behaviors might be attributed to different causes by different observers, and the diagnostic explanation of probable cause would depend upon the observer's personal and professional attributes, and his role objectives, and the level of explanation necessary for the given situation.

The theoretical orientation of the diagnostician will influence the manner in which causative sources are determined. This factor will probably have greater influence as deeper explanatory levels or more refined diagnoses are used; that is, theoretical orientation might exert greater influence for school counselors and psychologists than for classroom teachers. The reason for this belief is that school counselors and psychologists typically approach their roles from one of several possible theoretical positions, whereas the classroom teacher is not typically aligned with a specific theoretical approach but more probably employs his or her own unique approach to teaching. The word "theory" in this case is used primarily in conjunction with theories of personality. Underlying most counseling or psychological approaches is a theory (or a combination of theories) of personality development, and from this theoretical framework the diagnostician derives the bases for establishing possible causes for behaviors. The scope of this book does not allow for a detailed review of theories of personality. Suffice it to say that personality theories may be grouped into psychoanalytic, client-centered, learning or conditioning, and numerous others; the theories vary in regard to defining the development of normal and abnormal behavior; and consequently views regarding the possible etiologies of behavior problems are also different. Even within each of the groups there are differences: for example, within the psychoanalytically oriented group there are differences between Freudian and Adlerian diagnosticians; and in the learning-theory group there are differences between the diagnosticians that are aligned with the work of Eysenck and those aligned with the work of Mowrer.[2]

In regard to these factors in the setting forth of possible causes for behavior problems, the most appropriate level of explanation or degree of refinement of diagnosis for the educators to whom this book is directed would be an analysis expressed in terms of groups of factors that influence behavior but that may or may not be the actual causative sources of the behavior in question. This type of approach does not necessitate a comprehensive formal knowledge of theories of personality and development (although this knowledge would obviously strengthen the reader's ability to grasp and derive relevant ramifications), but some theory of personality, although informal, is necessary for whoever makes an assessment of behavior.

Rogers (1939), in his early book on problem children, grouped factors that influence behavior into six categories: the hereditary factor, the organic influences, the family influences, the cultural and social influ-

---

[2] These examples, especially the names of theoreticians, may mean little to some readers. While many educators pursuing a graduate-level training program will at some time be exposed to material on comparative theories of personality, it is recommended that the reader plan to assure himself of some familiarity with these theories. For those interested in doing some special reading in this area, overviews of a number of theories can be found in books by Hall and Lindzey (1957), Lindzey and Hall (1965), Sahakian (1965), and Wepman and Heine (1963). In the area of psychoanalysis there are materials relevant to behavioral problem children in books by Freud (1966) and Kessler (1966). There are a number of other fine books available on theories of personality; the aforementioned ones are cited primarily because they have proved personally useful.

ences, the needs of the organism, and the interaction of factors. Although some would say that this is a rather arbitrary division of factors, this categorization should serve sufficiently to illustrate the important etiological sources for problem behaviors.

The importance of *heredity* as a source of behavior problems is still subject to dispute among behavioral scientists. In fact, it is very difficult, if not impossible, to establish exactly what the current thinking on the subject is, because the minute an impressive position paper is issued by one person, a contradictory one emerges from another. Essentially, it seems that hereditary factors do set the boundaries for the person's capacities, development, and some actions. With intelligence, for example, it is known that heredity endows the person with a certain innate capacity; but it is also known that environmental influences can modify, to some extent, what seems to be the capacity. In other words, if an estimate of intellectual capacity is made at the age of five and again at the age of ten, there may be differences in the estimates. These differences could, of course, be the result of the crudeness of the instruments; that is, the differences may be due to errors in measurement. Body developments serve as another example of the role that heredity plays in behavior. The boy who is physically small and weak, as compared to his peers, may well tend to be passive or uninvolved in behavioral activities that require robustness or physical size and strength. And there seems to be evidence that certain mental problems or conditions may be inherited (Myerson, 1925), but there is other evidence that heredity is not the primary cause of all behavior problems in children (Rutter, 1966). It seems, therefore, that inheritance may contribute to a child's physical and mental (both intellectual and emotional) conditions, and these may in turn influence his behavior.

Organic factors are closely related to hereditary factors and include such conditions as glandular imbalances and other aspects of body chemistry that could easily influence personality and behavioral development. Similarly, illnesses and injuries may contribute to behavior problems. During recent years there has been an increasing amount of professional interest in the neurological components of behavior. A wide variety of studies indicates that certain neurological conditions, due to impairment or damage, produce specific behavioral disorders. As in so many other areas of the behavioral sciences, the research literature is often contradictory; and perusal of the studies sometimes produces the idea that at this stage it is impossible to sort out, order, and summarize the evidence related to neurological causes of behavior problems. There seems reason to believe that neurological impairments constitute one of the most crucial areas for professionals interested in behavioral problem children. Consequently, later in this chapter detailed evidence will be presented regarding neurologically based behavior problems; and in chapter 4 several diagnostic techniques that can be used for determining this condition will be set forth.

The significance of *the family* hardly needs emphasis. Most persons are well aware of how children's behaviors reflect the attitudes, ideas, standards, and conditions presented to them within the family. Such factors as parental conflicts, sibling rivalry, affectional deprivation or affectional smothering, immature behavioral standards or pressures for too-mature behaviors, and countless other situations within the home can definitely be the causes of behavior problems. Needless to say, the importance of the intrafamily situation makes it essential that the educator be willing and able to become involved with the family members if the behavior of the child points to family factors. On this basis, later chapters will include several techniques for behavioral modification in the schools that will involve the parents and possibly even the siblings. At this point, it is enough to say that the family or home environment is undoubtedly one of the most important influences on the behavior of children.

Cultural and social influences are of diverse character. There can be conflicting sets of standards for behavior within a given geographical area. That is, one child in the classroom may have one set of culturally determined standards for his behavior, while another child within the same classroom may be influenced by an entirely different set of culturally determined standards for his behavior. A good example may be found in the large urban setting; within a city there will be numerous subcultures, formed by racial, ethnic, and socioeconomic factors, that will have quite different behavioral expectations. Thus a child raised in one culture and suddenly deposited in another culture, perhaps because his family changes residences in search of better employment, may find himself under cultural influences to change his behavior; yet he has been conditioned to accept a set of behavioral norms that are, at least in part, contradictory to the new standards. Similarly, some children have more opportunities for constructive learning from social influences. The socioeconomic conditions of the family largely determine what opportunities will be available for social learning. And the attitudes and actions of a child's peer group will have a significant effect on his over-all behavior. Behavioral problem children, therefore, represent social learning or social experiences in their behaviors, and the educator who attempts to reckon with behavior problems will likewise have to reckon with cultural and social influences. These influences can cause behaviors that are considered to be unacceptable in the school setting.

To pursue in depth the *needs of the organism,* one would have to become immersed in theories of personality, an endeavor previously mentioned as being outside of the realm of this book. However, to summarize briefly, psychological theories hold that there are fundamental desires or needs, and these may be grossly categorized into affectional needs and sexual needs. Certain theories, such as psychoanalysis, are much more specific; and as with other aspects of development, theories often assume contradictory positions. It seems that, regardless of the specific theoretical position, it is safe to generalize that it is believed that people have a set of needs and that these needs influence the person's behavior. The means by which these needs are satisfied change as the person matures, experiences, and develops a style of life. Perhaps one of the most obvious examples within the classroom may be found in the boy who is not accepted by his peers and yet needs attention; he may resort to unacceptable behavior, such as fighting on the playground with his peers, not because it will win acceptance but because it satisfies his need for attention—negative attention being better than no attention.

One final example of possible need-influenced behaviors might be drawn from the variables measured by the Edwards Personal Preference Schedule (Edwards, 1959). This instrument is based on manifest needs, hypothesized by Murray (1938), and includes the following variables: achievement, deference, order, exhibition, autonomy, affiliation, intraception, succorance, dominance, abasement, nurturance, change, endurance, heterosexuality, and aggression. Without going into a detailed description of each need, the name of each variable should adequately illustrate that an exceedingly high score on any one of these variables could be reflected in related behaviors. And therefore behavior problems could develop because of high or low manifest needs.

As stated earlier, there is an *interaction of factors* for the etiology of behavior, and there are typically multifactorial causations underlying most problem behaviors. No diagnostician is correct in assuming that he can determine *the* cause of a behavior problem. What really occurs is that the diagnostician will present a hypothesis or will draw an inference as to what he believes are the primary and secondary causes; and this belief may, with the emergence of additional information or clinical evidence at a subsequent time, need to be modified. Moreover, the level of the diagnostic explanation of etiology will be important; that is, for functional purposes it may be appropriate to set forth simply one causative factor, but that does not mean that another diagnostician, working on a different level of etiological refinement, might not derive a different one, or several other causative factors. There is, therefore, an interaction of effects; and although one factor may be stated, it is not a pure factor, since it may contain the influences of any number of factors.

Thus far an effort has purposely been made to avoid bombarding the reader with a lot of experimental evidence that may or may not be of value. At this point, however, it seems advisable to turn toward experimental results that should serve to clarify what signs of what causative conditions may be evidenced in the school setting. In accord with the foregoing discussion of causes, the distinction made will be a broad one; the evidence will be presented along the lines of detecting problem behaviors that result from neurological factors and those that result from social-emotional or functional factors. Obviously, one should remember that even within this categorization there will be the results of interaction between factors; that is, there may be a behavioral problem child whose behavior seems to be primarily caused by neurological damage, but who also reflects the influences of his family's standards or his cultural and social environment.

NEUROLOGICAL AND SOCIAL-EMOTIONAL PROBLEMS IN THE CLASSROOM

Earlier in this chapter, the discussion indicated that teachers can detect problem behaviors, that there are a number of behavioral characteristics of varying clarity, and that there are several possible sources that can interact to cause behavior problems. This section will present information from different investigators that will synthesize the over-all contents of this chapter and will especially help the reader formulate some guidelines for differentiating possible *neurological* and *social-emotional* causes on the basis of observable behaviors in the classroom. The two categories of causes might also be labeled *organic* and *functional*.

It should be recognized that the contents of this chapter, and indeed of the book, are not designed to provide the basis for an empirical differentiation of behavior problems; rather, the goal is to create a general frame of reference. To develop a thorough knowledge of deviant behaviors, to the extent that learned differentiations can be made, the reader would need an academic knowledge of the psychology of exceptional children. Although there are fine texts in this area, such as the ones by Kessler (1966) and Cruickshank (1963), the reading of books does not take the place of formal training to achieve refined professional skills. The subsequent discussion, therefore, should be viewed as a means of developing a relatively simple, yet very necessary, frame of reference on which to base psychoeducational services, and particularly efforts at behavioral modification, in the schools.

A number of behavior problems can be recognized in the classroom. One writer concludes that there are five criteria that may be visible in the classroom:

. . . an inability to learn which cannot be explained by intellectual, sensory, or health functions, . . . an inability to build or maintain satisfactory interpersonal relationships with peers and teachers, . . . inappropriate types of behavior or feelings under normal conditions, . . . a general, pervasive mood of unhappiness or depression, . . . a tendency to develop illnesses, pains, or fears associated with personal or school problems.[3]

A review of the data presented in Tables 2–1 and 2–2 readily reveals that there is a relationship between these characteristics and these five criteria. The neurologically impaired child is often labeled brain-injured or brain-damaged, perceptually disturbed, hyperkinetic, or possessing organicity. All of these terms, and others, mean essentially the same thing in relation to etiology. A distinct definition may be found in two brief statements by Strauss and Lehtinen (1947):

A brain injured child is a child who before, during, or after birth has received an injury to or suffered an infection of the brain. As a result of such organic impairment, defects of the neuromotor system may be present or absent; however, such a child may show disturbances in perception, thinking, and emotional behavior, either separately or in combination.[4]

The behavioral aspect is given the greatest recognition by some writers; for example, Lewis (1951) states:

Behavior is the main clue to the parent that a disturbance exists. Because of perceptual and conceptual disturbances, the child tends to behave incongruously. Oddities appear in his behavior pattern which becomes uneven and unpredictable from the normal viewpoint. (p. 31)

The behavior of the neurologically impaired or brain-injured child may be different from the behavior exhibited by the emotionally disturbed child. The neurologically impaired child will possibly behave in the classroom, the school psychologist's office, or anywhere in the manner described by the parents; but the emotionally disturbed child may be a "holy terror" elsewhere, and yet be quiet and cooperative when he is being observed, tested, or examined by a professional person; and where lesser degrees of organicity are involved, the child may have a history of good first impressions, followed by a rapid "wearing out" process with exactly the same timing in all kinds of situations (Morris and Dozier, 1961).

In general it is believed that the results of neurological impairment may be observed in motor impairment, recurrent convulsions, intellectual

[3] From Bower, Eli M., EARLY IDENTIFICATION OF EMOTIONALLY HANDICAPPED CHILDREN IN SCHOOL, 1960. Courtesy of Charles C Thomas, Publisher, Springfield, Illinois.

[4] From A. A. Strauss and Laura E. Lehtinen, PSYCHOPATHOLOGY AND EDUCATION OF THE BRAIN-INJURED CHILD (New York: Grune and Stratton, 1947), p. 4. Reprinted by permission.

subnormality, and/or organic behavior disorders (Taft, 1958). It should be pointed out that although these conditions may occur, they need not necessarily be present.

There also seems to be a consensus among professionals that there are specific behaviors or symptoms associated with an *organic* or *hyperkinetic* syndrome; the cause of this syndrome is termed "minimal brain dysfunction." Perceptual disturbances seem especially frequent (Fostig, Lefever, and Whittelseg, 1961). Laufer and Denhoff (1947) believe that the essential symptoms of hyperkinetic behavior disorders are hyperactivity, short attention span, variability, impulsiveness and inability to delay gratification, irritability, explosiveness, and poor school work (also see Denhoff, Laufer, and Holden, 1959). Bradley (1957) provides a list of similar symptoms: unpredictable variation in behavior, hyperactivity, distractibility or short attention span, impulsiveness, irritability, and difficulties in abstract thinking. As can be seen, these two lists are fairly comparable and are similar to those characteristics listed in Tables 2–1 and 2–2, but the previously made comments about uncertainty of comparisons between studies are still applicable. There is one more study that merits mention because it summarizes the relevant research. Beck (1961) reviewed the research literature and found forty-three different so-called symptoms of brain damage. The number of symptoms per author ranged from six to thirty-two. And Beck points out, as has been stressed, that comparisons are virtually impossible. He concludes that the symptoms of brain injury, based on the "majority of the writers," can fit into fifteen categories: perseveration, distractibility, disorganization or lack of integration, perceptual difficulties, conceptual difficulties, language disorders, motor incoordination, disparity in development, hyperactivity, emotional instability, insecurity, irritability, convulsions, mental deficiency, and poor retention. These investigators, and others (e.g., Pond, 1960; Schulman, Kaspar, and Throne, 1963), believe that there are behavorial characteristics associated with neurological damage—in other words, that there is a hyperkinetic behavioral syndrome.

In the past few years there has occurred a noticeable change in the thinking on the possible neurological influences on behavior. In general, there seems to be agreement that there are behavioral characteristics associated with neurological impairments, and that "minimal brain dysfunction" (the preferred term) can result in perceptual handicaps and learning disabilities (Frierson and Barbe, 1967). Stevens and Birch (1957) have suggested the term "Strauss syndrome" to describe the child who has this organic-based behavioral difficulty, but others still prefer "hyperkinetic" or one of the other terms. Although recent research seems to have led to a stronger consensus about the possible effects of minimal brain dysfunction, uncertainty remains as to exactly which behaviors have or could have organic bases; the outcome is that an extensive diagnostic appraisal system is necessary, and even then clinical judgment or opinion remains the final criterion (Clements and Peters, 1962). It should be noted that a child may show behavioral effects of minimal brain injury and still have a relatively adequate level of intellectual functioning; in other words, there can be minimal brain dysfunction without mental retardation. But there can, of course, also be mentally retarded persons whose condition results from brain damage or a cerebral deficit. Even with a so-called organic condition, the behavioral problem child should not be permanently assigned a constricting label; there are instances when, with development, maturation eliminates or alleviates the influences of minimal brain dysfunction; that is, in a sense there is a spontaneous remission (but this occurrence is probably the exception rather than the rule).

Observation of neurologically impaired children readily reveals behaviors that would be considered "problems" in the school; thus behavioral problem children in general might be believed to have a relatively high amount of neurological abnormality. This may be true (as will be evidenced by electroencephalographic studies of behavioral problem children to be cited in Chapter 4), but this position has not been adequately validated. It may be that the effects of neurological impairment are reflected in social relationships, learning ability, intellectual factors, self-concept, and even personality (Goldstein, 1952). But it seems unwise to say on the basis of current evidence that the presence of any of these characteristics is a definite sign of brain damage, because it is likewise known that many of these same characteristics are also found to be characteristics of persons with no neurological impairment. Some persons who are emotionally disturbed exhibit these same characteristics. Thus, although it would be convenient to be able to use such easily observed behaviors as the bases for diagnosis and the determination of etiology, the practice is not justified on the basis of experimental research.[5] To use behavioral signs as the sole basis for diagnosis can only lead to errors (Doll, 1951). Care must be exercised to avoid the formation of ill-conceived, unjustified percepts about behavior, which are often a result of overgeneralizations drawn from research on the subject.

One final point on the subject of brain injury *per se* is that the majority of neurologically impaired children seem to receive their trauma early in life. The damage is usually done during the prenatal period, during the birth process, or during the first two or three years of life (Bakwin and Bakwin, 1960; Bradley, 1957; Taft, 1958).

---

[5] It should be noted that *published opinions of professionals* do not constitute experimental research. Experimental research necessitates control and experimental measures that will accommodate statistical comparisons. Too frequently, it seems, medical *opinions* and not the results of experimentation have been used as diagnostic criteria, and this is an unscientific practice.

In addition to the behavioral manifestations of neurological conditions, consideration must also be given to what might be termed social-emotional, or functional, influences on behavior. It is common knowledge that the child is especially vulnerable to influences from external sources, such as family, siblings, peers, neighborhood, and subculture. Interpersonal relations with significant others—for example, parents and peers—can result in both real and imagined anxiety-producing situations that may eventuate in problem behaviors. A child may be hypersensitive to specific types of cues—for example, adult criticism—at certain maturational phases of his life. Besides external influences, inner conflicts, logically unjustified but neurotically developed, can lead to overt problem behaviors. Kessler (1966) and Verville (1967) have discussed in detail the functionally based or social-emotional behavioral problems.

The material in this section has suggested several differences between behaviors resulting from social-emotional disturbances—that is, functional disorders—and those resulting from neurological impairments —that is, minimal brain dysfunction or organicity. But it is apparent that there are probably more behavioral similarities than behavioral differences between these two groups. In other words, research can attest that certain characteristics are found with neurologically impaired children and also that certain characteristics are found with socially or emotionally disturbed children; and while these factors do actually "characterize" the particular disorder, they may also "characterize" a different disorder. Therefore, observable characteristics alone are an insufficient basis for making differentiations—there are too many overlapping symptoms or characteristics.

The question, then, remains: How does one differentiate between various possible etiologies? And the answer simply is: It is possible, but it requires more of the observer than recording the overt behaviors. But that, the reader may say, is not a simple answer. This problem suggests that consideration must be given to some of the necessary qualifications for the observer. Only a few basic concepts will be given at this point, because continued attention will be focused on this problem in Chapters 3 and 4.

In making even the most basic of behavioral differentiations, one of the primary requirements is that *the observer or educator have an understanding of the theoretical bases for expected behavior.* In other words, some degree of familiarity with educational psychology is certainly a much-needed requirement for educators, regardless of position. Special emphasis should be placed on developmental psychology, and here care must be exercised to assure that the differences between adult psychology and child psychology are understood:

Fundamental to all considerations of diagnosis and etiology of children's disorders is the principle that the child is not just a small edition of an adult. A child is a distinct organism. The psycho-biological principles which govern a child's development and adaptation are unique. They must, therefore, be derived from the unique characteristics of the child's life rather than from observation of the problems of living of the adult person. For these reasons, identical criteria for diagnostic classifications cannot be applied to child and adult alike. The issues of diagnosis in children must be viewed independently and in a separate adaptional context.[6]

There is the very real problem that many writings on exceptionality use terminology that was initially applied to adults, and there is reason to believe that the standard psychiatric nomenclature is most often inapplicable to children (Quay, 1963). It is imperative, therefore, that special training with children be required. This is undoubtedly the reason why some states require that school psychologists and school social workers specialize with children in educational settings; that is, holding a graduate degree in psychology or social work does not alone suffice, since it would be possible for the holder to have earned a respectable degree without special training with children or in educational settings.

A second requirement for the recognition of behavioral problem children is *keen, unbiased observation based on skills in assessing with reasonable objectivity the overt behaviors and to make "clinical assumptions" about the underlying reasons or motives for the behaviors.* This requirement will, logically, involve both academic and personal preparation. That is, a thorough academic knowledge of both normal and abnormal developmental psychology is (again) necessary, and the use of this knowledge is subject to the personal characteristics and personality constructs of the educator. Academic and personal sensitivity are requisite for effectively recognizing and thereby beginning to help the behavioral problem child. Although the development of these two types of sensitivity is a demanding process, it is not an impossible one, and one of the goals of this book is to help the reader-educator begin to develop these necessary qualifications.

A third requirement is that *the observer or educator have a basic understanding of diagnostic processes and techniques.* As has been stated before (but the statement merits repetition), observed behaviors alone should not be considered to be valid indications of the causes of behavior problems. A look at any basic text on abnormal psychology will attest to the fact that such behavioral categories as perseveration, distractibility, disorganization and lack of integration, perceptual difficulties, conceptual difficulties, language disorders, motor incoordination, and a number of

[6] From Nathan W. Ackerman, "Psychiatric Disorders in Children—Diagnosis and Etiology in Our Time," in P. H. Hoch and J. Zubin (Eds.), CURRENT PROBLEMS IN PSYCHIATRIC DIAGNOSIS (New York: Grune and Stratton, 1953), pp. 206-207. Reprinted by permission.

others may be found in persons with various causations for their problems. The problem behavior could be due to either neurological or social-emotional factors or a combination of the two types of factors; additional diagnostic techniques are necessary to make even a provisional assumption regarding etiology.

Thus the educator who wishes to help behavioral problem children needs to understand the basic components of diagnostic procedures. This is especially important, as will be seen in Chapter 4, when clinical judgments and psychological test data are involved. This recommendation is justified because all educators, although not actually making diagnoses that would involve these more complex techniques, should be aware of the limitations, values, rationales, and meanings of diagnostic information. This knowledge will increase their ability to use the material in diagnostic reports in their own particular roles.

At this point the reader has presumably achieved at least a working definition of behavioral problem children, and is familiar with the characteristics that are usually attributed to this type of exceptional child. It is evident that a single set of characteristics for behavioral problem children cannot and should not be proposed and that the consensus is as close to resolution of the problem as can logically be expected. The educator who hopes to help the behavioral problem child has a large task, and it has emerged that one of the most significant problems is the preparation of the educator to recognize problem behaviors. And there have been hints that the diagnosis of behavioral problem children involves numerous crucial factors. Thus the next point of consideration is the recognition of the behavioral problem child, especially as would be appropriate for classroom teachers, school counselors, and school psychologists.

REFERENCES

Ackerman, N. W. Psychiatric disorders in children—diagnosis and etiology in our time. In P. H. Hoch and J. Zubin (Eds.), *Current problems in psychiatric diagnosis.* New York: Grune and Stratton, 1953, 205-230, by permission.

American Psychiatric Association. *Diagnostic and statistical manual for mental disorders.* Washington, D.C.: American Psychiatric Association, 1952.

Bakwin, H., and Bakwin, Ruth M. *Clinical management of behavior disorders in children* (2nd ed.). Philadelphia: W. B. Saunders, 1960.

Beck, H. S. Detecting psychological symptoms of brain injury. *Exceptional Children*, 1961, 28:57-62.

Beller, E. K. *Clinical process: the assessment of data in childhood personality disorders*. New York: Free Press of Glencoe, 1962.

Bower, E. M. *Early identification of emotionally handicapped children in school*. Springfield, Ill.: C. C Thomas, 1960.

Bradley, C. Characteristics and management of children with behavior problems associated with organic brain damage. *Pediatric Clinics of North America*, 1957, 4:1049-1060.

Clements, S. D., and Peters, J. E. Minimal brain dysfunctions in the school-age child. *Archives of General Psychiatry*, 1962, 6:17-29.

Cruickshank, W. M. (Ed.). *Psychology of exceptional children and youth* (2nd ed.). Englewood Cliffs, N.J.: Prentice-Hall, 1963.

Cummings, Jean D. The incidence of emotional symptoms in school children. *British Journal of Educational Psychology*, 1944, 14:151-161.

Denhoff, E., Laufer, M. W., and Holden, R. H. The syndromes of cerebral dysfunction. *Journal of the Oklahoma State Medical Association*, 1959, 52:360-366.

Doll, E. A. Mental evaluation of children with expressive handicaps. *American Journal of Orthopsychiatry*, 1951, 21:148-154.

Eaton, M., Weathers, G., and Phillips, B. N. Some reactions of classroom teachers to problem behavior in school. *Educational Administration and Supervision*, 1957, 43:129-139.

Edwards, A. L. *Manual: Edwards Personal Preference Schedule* (rev. ed.). New York: Psychological Corporation, 1959.

Fostig, W., Lefever, D. W., and Whittelseg, J. B. A developmental test of visual perception for evaluating normal and neurologically handicapped children. *Perceptual and Motor Skills*, 1961, 12:383-394.

Frierson, E. C., and Barbe, W. B. (Eds.). *Educating children with learning disabilities*. New York: Appleton-Century-Crofts, 1967.

Freud, Anna. *Normality and pathology in childhood: assessments of development*. London: Hogarth Press and the Institute of Psycho-Analysis, 1966.

Gilbert, G. M. A survey of "referral problems" in metropolitan child guidance centers. *Journal of Clinical Psychology*, 1957, 13:37-42.

Goldstein, K. The effect of brain damage on the personality. *Psychiatry*, 1952, 15:245-260.

Hall, C. S., and Lindzey, G. *Theories of personality*. New York: John Wiley and Sons, 1957.

Heber, R. (Ed.). A manual of terminology and classification in mental retardation. *Monograph Supplement, American Journal of Mental Deficiency*, 1958, 64, No. 2.

Kessler, Jane W. *Psychopathology of childhood*. Englewood Cliffs, N.J.: Prentice-Hall, 1966.

Laufer, M. W., and Denhoff, E. Hyperkinetic behavior syndrome in children. *Journal of Pediatrics,* 1957, 50:463-473.

Lewis, R. S. *The other child: the brain-injured child.* New York: Grune and Stratton, 1951.

Lindzey, G., and Hall, C. S. (Eds.). *Theories of personality: primary sources and research.* New York: John Wiley and Sons, 1965.

Martens, E. H. *Needs of exceptional children.* U. S. Office of Education, Leaflet No. 74. Washington, D.C.: U. S. Government Printing Office, 1944.

Morris, D. P., and Dozier, Elizabeth. Childhood behavior disorders: subtler organic factors. *Texas State Journal of Medicine,* 1961, 57:314-318.

Morse, W. C. The education of socially maladjusted and emotionally disturbed children. In W. M. Cruickshank and G. O. Johnson (Eds.), *Education of exceptional children and youth.* Englewood Cliffs, N.J.: Prentice-Hall, 1958, 557-608.

Murray, H. A. *et al. Explorations in personality.* New York: Oxford University Press, 1938.

Myerson, A. *The inheritance of mental diseases.* Baltimore: Williams and Wilkins, 1925.

Pond, D. Is there a syndrome of "brain damage" in children? *Cerebral Palsy Bulletin,* 1960, 2:296-297.

Quay, H. C. Some basic considerations in the education of emotionally disturbed children. *Exceptional Children,* 1963, 30:27-31.

Rogers, C. R. *The clinical treatment of the problem child.* Boston: Houghton-Mifflin, 1939.

Rogers, C. R. Mental health findings in three elementary schools. *Educational Research Bulletin,* 1942, 21:67-79.

Rogers, Martha E., Lilienfeld, A. M., and Pasamanick, B. *Prenatal and paranatal factors in the development of childhood behavior disorders.* Baltimore: Johns Hopkins University Press, 1954.

Rosen, E., and Gregory, I. *Abnormal psychology.* Philadelphia: W. B. Saunders, 1965.

Rutter, M. *Children of sick parents: an environmental and psychiatric study.* Institute of Psychiatry, Maudsley Monographs No. 16. London, Eng.: Oxford University Press, 1966.

Sahakian, W. S. (Ed.). *Psychology of personality: readings in theory.* Chicago: Rand McNally, 1965.

Schulman, J. L., Kaspar, J. C., and Throne, Frances M. The brain damage behavior syndrome: a clinical-experimental study. Unpublished manuscript. Chicago: Children's Memorial Hospital, 1963.

Stevens, G. D., and Birch, J. W. A proposal for classification of the terminology used to describe brain-injured children. *Exceptional Children,* 1957, 23:346-349.

Strauss, A. A., and Lehtinen, Laura E. *Psychopathology and education of the brain-injured child.* New York: Grune and Stratton, 1947, 1:4, 31, by permission.

Stroh, G. On the diagnosis of childhood psychosis. *Journal of Child Psychology and Psychiatry,* 1960, 1:238-243.

Taft, L. Brain injury—its definition, diagnosis, causes, and treatment. (Printed résumé of a lecture.) New York: New York Association for Brain Injured Children, 1958.

Ullmann, C. A. *Identification of maladjusted school children.* Public Health Monograph, No. 7, Public Health Service Publication, No. 211. Washington, D.C.: U. S. Government Printing Office, 1952.

Verville, Elinor. *Behavior problems of children.* Philadelphia: W. B. Saunders, 1967.

Wall, W. D. *Education and mental health.* Paris: UNESCO, 1955.

Wepman, J. M., and Heine, R. W. (Eds.). *Concepts of personality.* Chicago: Aldine, 1963.

White House Conference on Child Health and Protection. *Special education: the handicapped and the gifted. Section III. Education and training.* New York: Appleton-Century, 1931.

Woody, R. H. The use of electroencephalography and mental abilities tests in the diagnosis of behavioral problem males. Unpublished doctoral dissertation, Michigan State University, 1964.

3

Detection and Referral
of Behavioral Problem Children

Thus far emphasis has been on the general characteristics of behavioral problem children in the schools and the importance of meeting their needs. In regard to the former, research evidence indicates that causative factors are usually not distinct but rather represent an overlapping or combination of factors, and that observable problem behaviors, regardless of severity, are usually nondifferentiating. In other words, the causes of unacceptable behaviors cannot be determined without special diagnostic procedures, and even the most professional diagnostic practices are not infallible or insulated against the possibility of faulty reliability and validity. Between the tasks of acknowledging that there are behavioral problem children and providing diagnostic services, there is a crucial portion of professional responsibility; this lies in the stage of detecting behavior problems and initiating referrals to diagnosticians.

There are two underlying key premises: someone must be willing to accept the responsibility for stating that a behavior problem seems to exist, and someone must be willing to assume the responsibility for initiating a referral. These premises are not always fulfilled as readily as we might think. There are educators who, perhaps because of cultural influences or the institutional expectations for public school personnel, are hesitant—if not strongly resistant—in assuming initiative or taking an action that requires their personal involvement. Just as newspaper accounts cite people on the street refusing to "see" or come to the aid of a victim of a robbery or beating, there are, unfortunately, educators who refuse to become personally involved in situations that are ethically part of their responsibility.

Fulfilling the detection and referral duties—that is, being willing to say, "Yes, I think that this child has a behavior problem and needs professional help"—requires both personal and professional qualities: the educator must be secure enough within himself to face the responsibility, and he must possess the academic knowledge that will provide the basis for making such a decision. All too often children in need of help are bypassed simply because no adult is willing to take the necessary action to obtain services for them.

Similarly, there is action that must be taken after the behavior problem has been detected; this involves making a referral for diagnostic and treatment services. As will be seen shortly, there are special considerations, such as whom should the child be referred to and who should make the referral. The behavior problems must be detected and steps taken to channel the child and possibly the parents of the child to the right professional worker. Although these procedures will receive subsequent elaboration, it is believed that no one type of educator, be he classroom teacher or school counselor or school psychologist or school administrator, can be totally exempted from the responsibility of recognizing or detecting and of helping the behavioral problem child. Helping the child may mean direct service from the given educator, or it may involve the activating of a referral of the child to another professional who can perhaps offer the child and/or the parents more comprehensive services.

Since differences in roles may influence the specific actions and responsibilities of educators, let us consider the respective roles of the classroom teacher, the school counselor, the school psychologist, the school administrator, and other psychoeducational personnel. It will be evident that these positions have many points in common, but it is extremely important to recognize that each does have a responsibility at this detection and referral stage. It should also be acknowledged that this discussion must be limited to generalities about each position; that is, conditions will vary among school systems, communities, and educators, and there will always be the possibility of a necessary exception to what is generally believed to be true.

THE CLASSROOM TEACHER

In some ways it seems that the classroom teacher's role in the detection of the behavioral problem child is the most crucial. There is little doubt that the classroom teacher spends more clock hours (and perhaps more psychological hours outside of the classroom) with a given group of children than do most of the other types of educators; for example, the school counselor and school psychologist typically see only the students who are self-referred or referred to them by the classroom teachers, and regrettably there are many school administrators who may go through their entire workday without coming in direct contact with a student. (Incidentally, it seems logical that educators, even those employed in universities as teacher and counselor educators, can benefit from direct contact with students.) The classroom teacher has at his disposal much more of a sampling of a child's behavior than would the school counselor or school psychologist who "audited" a classroom to look for behavior problems.

Being involved with the children does not, of course, guarantee that the teacher can "see" behaviors in the sense of appraising them. In fact, there are many critics who dispute the teacher's ability or even potential capability of detecting behavioral problem children. Essentially, the question posed by these critics is: Does the classroom teacher perceive behavior problems in the same manner as the clinician who has supposedly specialized in the skills needed for this detection? But a contradictory question might also be posed: Is it really necessary for teachers to view behaviors in the same manner as clinicians? Let us consider possible answers for these questions.

It is logical that teachers do not, because of the content of their training, judge behavior on the same bases as clinicians, such as psychologists and psychiatrists. Teachers are concerned with the individual child, but they also have responsibilities to the other children in the classroom and to the educational objectives of the school, and they must fulfill these latter responsibilities. The clinician, on the other hand, has a much different framework for his role. When he deals with a behavioral problem child, he is concerned solely with that particular child's needs and problems; the child's classroom activities are but a part of the over-all view that the clinician will take, and educational goals may well be secondary to personal or interpersonal behavioral goals. It is no wonder that clinicians and teachers have difficulties when they try to discuss the relation of learning activities to childhood behaviors (Rivlin, 1958). This breakdown in communication is readily exemplified in the reports of some school psychologists. The school psychologist, because of his training and orientation, may state in his report that one therapeutic action is the most advisable, while the classroom teacher will see that action as completely impractical; or the school psychologist may use in his report technical terms or jargon-filled statements that are meaningful to psychologists but have little meaning to teachers who are not trained in the nuances of psychology. And school counselors frequently see the key to behavioral change resting in the development of a particular type of relationship, a relationship that may be quite appropriate within the counseling setting, but inappropriate in a classroom.

Despite the indications that professionals vary in the way they view behavior, there are also indications that they do, in the long run, perceive the same behavior problems, albeit with different sets of criteria for recognition. Research seems to suggest that teachers can make good judgments about behavior (Bower, 1960). Logically, the efficacy of teachers' detections can be improved with special help, either during the course of their academic training or through in-service training with other educators. Bower (1960) concludes: "Teachers' judgments of emotional disturbance were very much like the judgment of clinicians" (p. 62).

One of the main goals of this book is to develop in the reader an appreciation of the differences between opinions and experimental findings. Thus, rather than make only general statements about what is "believed," let us review briefly some of the studies regarding teachers' attitudes toward, and recognition of, behavior problems.

One of the earliest studies of teachers' attitudes toward children's behavior was made by Wickman (1928). This classic study has served as the basis for numerous subsequent studies. One of the most recent emphasizes that the original Wickman study was an indicator of the role of the teacher of that era, but that the role expectations of teachers have since changed; and replications of the Wickman study reveal a trend to greater congruence between teachers' and clinicians' attitudes (Beilin, 1959). In other words, although there are studies that reveal differences between teachers' and other professionals' ideas about behavioral problem children, such as Goldfarb's (1963), which found that teachers and psychiatrists differ in the way they classify children's behaviors, the differences do not seem to be as great as they were several decades ago. In all likelihood, this is due to changes in training for teachers and in what is expected of them; it may also be partly due to an improvement in interdisciplinary research and communication.

As mentioned earlier, differences between professionals do not necessarily mean that the teachers' ratings are ineffective. For example, in a fifteen-year follow-up of children initially referred by the classroom teacher, Fitzsimons (1958) concluded that teachers were capable of selecting the children who needed psychological or psychiatric services. However, potential delinquents and asthmatics were more successfully designated or detected than children who became mentally ill. Although this study indicates that teachers have difficulty in detecting children who will eventually be treated for emotional disturbances, four points should be remembered: first, emotional or functional disturbances may develop in a relatively short time and thus may be more difficult than other problems to detect at a given point in time; second, emotional problems may be camouflaged or covered up more readily than other types of problems, such as those that result from neurological impairment; third, teachers trained today, according to some sources, are better able to detect problem behaviors than those trained some two decades ago, and thus this inability to detect emotional problems may be declining; and fourth, there is other evidence to support that teachers can, in fact, detect emotional problems.

In regard to the last point, Cooper, Ryan, and Hutcheson (1959) tested the hypothesis that emotional disturbance is manifested in class-room behavior and that it can be identified by behavioral observations. On the basis of ratings on a check list and reliance upon a psychiatric evaluation as the criterion for determining emotional disturbance, a comparison of thirty children revealed the rating instrument to be reliable, and a positive correlation between the ratings and the psychiatric evaluation was obtained. Cooper, Ryan, and Hutcheson conclude that classroom observation is an effective screening device for emotional disturbances.

Rating instruments, such as those used in this study, seem especially valuable in the detection processes, and their application by teachers will be discussed later in this chapter. At this point, however, clarification can be gained by focusing attention on one such rating instrument and noting how the findings from its use show that teachers can detect problem behaviors; thus teachers can, given certain techniques, effectively identify problem behaviors and thereby fulfill their total responsibility to the child.

The California State Department of Education has devised a screening procedure to help classroom teachers identify the pupils who probably have emotional problems and who should be referred for special diagnostic services. The research revealed that seven out of ten children who were probably emotionally handicapped were not noted or observed by principals or school psychologists, but subsequent experimentation on the development of rating techniques revealed that the ratings of teachers and peers and self-ratings are sensitive to various types of behavioral and emotional maladjustments (Lambert and Bower, 1961a). It was also found that professional personnel, including teachers, have more difficulty in recognizing patterns of maladjustment in girls than in boys; this difficulty was believed to be due to the fact that overt behaviors or symptoms of boys allow the teachers to make their decisions about the behaviors with greater confidence than is the case with the girls (Lambert and Bower, 1961b). The California studies (Lambert and Bower, 1961a, 1961b), based on the belief that teachers and others, even the children in the classroom, can recognize indications of behavioral and emotional maladjustments, have resulted in the development of a battery of indices, which is still in the process of being fully standardized, but which does offer educational personnel an approach possessing great potential value.

Bower (1966) has since conducted follow-up studies and has found that there is agreement between clinical evaluations of students and evaluations made by teachers using a behavior rating scale. Similar support for teachers' ability to discern behavior problems in the classroom has been provided by Dayton (1967). In an earlier study, Dayton and

Uhl (1966) found that teachers' ratings of student behavior correlated significantly with student ratings of the teacher.

It appears that teachers are capable of holding, and indeed do hold, the responsibility for becoming involved in the detection and referral stage of helping behavioral problem children. Research indicates that teachers vary in the degree of success that they achieve. It is logical that the different frames of reference and objectives inherent in different institutional settings result in the differences in perceiving behavior between teachers themselves and, moreover, between teachers and clinicians. Nevertheless, there is evidence that the classroom teacher is capable—and especially, perhaps, when using a rating scale or similar observational technique—of recognizing potential behavioral and emotional maladjustments. And research has revealed a reciprocal effect; that is, not only can and does the teacher influence the development and behavior of the child, but the behavioral problem child can and does influence the teacher's development, behaviors, and reactions.[1] If it is assumed that the classroom teacher is capable of recognizing behavior problems as well as he seems to be, and has the responsibility of referring the child for special diagnostic and treatment services, it is necessary that he enter actively into this role. As Sarason, Davidson, and Blatt (1962) indicate, the classroom teacher must be "an astute psychological observer and tactician" (p. 36).

Although the classroom teacher is the first in line to detect the behavioral problem child in the schools, other psychoeducational personnel, such as the school counselor and the school psychologist, have not only their own responsibilities to the behavioral problem child but, by virtue of their roles as consultants, also have the responsibility of helping the classroom teacher develop the capacities and skills to fulfill his part in the chain of events, particularly at the detection and referral stage, of helping the behavioral problem child. Obviously the

[1] In regard to this reciprocal effect and the other points under discussion, one study of the reactions of classroom teachers to behavioral problem children deserves special attention. Eaton, Weathers, and Phillips (1957) asked two hundred classroom teachers enrolled in summer graduate study to react to a questionnaire and check list related to behavior problems in the school. They concluded: (1) The majority of the teachers did not feel that the incidence of behavior problems was significantly increasing. (2) The inability to cope with behavioral problem children influenced many teachers, particularly beginning teachers and teachers on the secondary level, to leave the teaching profession. (3) There was diversity in the way that teachers viewed problem behavior, but, in addition to normal growth and development, the three most frequently perceived causes were large classes, inadequate teacher personality, and poor teaching techniques. (4) Many of the teachers felt a "need and desire" to have administrative assistance in handling behavior problems, and it seemed that adequate help in understanding and coping with the difficulties was not being provided. (5) Many teachers requested more in-service training programs as a means of increasing their effectiveness in dealing with behavioral problem children.

teacher cannot unload her responsibilities on one of the psychoeducational staff members; each must assume responsibility for detection and referral. Implementing such actions does, however, involve some potential pitfalls. Let us consider now several factors that classroom teachers must be prepared to cope with and techniques that will facilitate his efforts.

Two basic recommendations are offered in regard to teachers' involvement in the detection and referral stage: first, the classroom teacher (and actually all educators) should be familiar with referral sources; and second, a systematic approach should be used for detecting problem behaviors. Both of these factors are absolute necessities for effectively dealing with behavioral problem children.

Resource Persons

Before making a referral, the classroom teacher needs to know what resource persons are available. This necessitates not only knowing *who* they are, but also *what* they are, and *how* one gets them to help. For example, the classroom teacher needs to be able to distinguish at the detection and referral stage whether a child should be referred to a remedial reading specialist, the school counselor, the school psychologist, or perhaps to a specialist outside of the school, such as a psychiatrist or clinical psychologist at the local child guidance clinic. Obviously the teacher's choice will be what is believed to be the best referral source, and although it may become evident after the initial referral—to the school counselor, for example—that the child really should have been referred elsewhere, perhaps to the child guidance clinic, this type of situation is not really an error of judgment, but rather indicates that with additional information and the opinion of another professional, the referral process can be more definitive than other approaches.

To attain a knowledge of the sources for referral (which would include the *who, what,* and *how* aspects), the classroom teacher must make a conscious effort to meet these persons, either directly or indirectly, to become familiar with what is encompassed in their particular services, and to know how to obtain their cooperation. There are many service agencies with which the teacher should be familiar. Certainly a visit to the local child guidance clinic would be advantageous for anyone who is eligible potentially to use its service, and such a category includes every citizen or resident of that area. This familiarity is especially important for educators; the child guidance clinic should not be looked upon as some mystical, alien medical organization, but as a professional service center that exists to help children and to cooperate with allied professionals, such as teachers.

Furthermore, this quest for information about referral sources provides an excellent opportunity for the classroom teacher to become familiar with the psychoeducational services available in the school. This familiarity with the roles of special teachers and consultants, counselors, social workers, speech and hearing therapists, and psychologists within the school system will result in a number of benefits that will definitely increase the efficiency for everyone, the psychoeducational personnel as well as the teaching personnel.

Although ideally each teacher should show initiative in these matters, it should be acknowledged that the psychoeducational personnel and the school administrators have a responsibility to help classroom teachers achieve an orientation to the factors relevant to the detection and referral of behavioral problem children and to help them become familiar with the resource persons to whom the behavioral problem child may be referred. Needless to say, the classroom teacher and the psychoeducational and administrative personnel alike have the responsibility of being psychologically and physically available to communicate and consult with each other. It is extremely important that the teacher be willing to accept the fact that these other educators, such as the members of the psychoeducational staff, are both wanting to help him do his job and also seeking help to facilitate their own jobs. In other words, a classroom teacher should not be defensive about asking for or allowing a consulting person, such as the school counselor or school psychologist, to enter into the problem situations that arise in his classroom. The presence of a consultant should not be interpreted as a potential threat to the teacher: the consultant is not there to assess the teacher's teaching skills or to jeopardize his professional status; he is there to assume a share of the responsibility for helping the children with problems, for helping the teacher better understand the needs of behavioral problem children, and for helping improve the over-all learning situation for the children in the class who might be adversely influenced by the behavioral problem children. The classroom teacher should consider the opportunity to receive consulting services from these other professionals as a privilege to benefit from their specialized training and experience. Conversely, these specialized professionals should equally feel that it is a privilege for them to receive the acceptance of the classroom teacher, and it behooves them to support sincerely the position of the teacher and not to assume an attitude of superiority.

With knowledge of the *who, what,* and *how* aspects of referral sources, with the achievement of interprofessional acceptance and communication, and with a cooperative seeking of help among educators, the detection and referral processes will function smoothly. These relationships must, however, be fostered by each of the professionals involved. No one is immune to responsibility; job title, position in the institutional hierarchy, and academic degree do not provide any justification for exemption.

Systematically Recording Observed Behaviors

In addition to the classroom teacher's need to know what resource persons are available, there is a second requisite factor: the classroom teacher should employ a systematic approach for recognizing and ranking or assessing the behavior problems and for recording the observed behaviors.

As mentioned in Chapter 2, it would naturally be helpful if there were a set of descriptive and categorical terms that could be used, or if there were specific behavioral characteristics that could be noted and thereby used as the clear-cut bases for detection and referral; but lamentably these desirable tools are not readily available. The proper use of terms can only come from knowing the psychology of exceptional children and, specifically, behavioral problem children. Acquiring this knowledge is, logically, an individual thing with teachers. The materials in this book, and particularly in Chapter 2, are designed to foster the beginning stages of development of this ability, and supplementary reading and study should also help. Such reading and study in the area of the psychology of the behavioral problem child could be augmented by planned in-service training with the various psychoeducational staff members. In fact, such a cooperative in-service training program might well be the first step in the development of a systematic approach to detecting, rating, and recording behavior problems.

It is believed, however, that (given a basic orientation to the psychology of the behavioral problem child) the most valuable adjunct for these detection tasks is the use of a specialized instrument. Such behavioral rating instruments as those previously cited (Bower, 1966; Dayton, 1967; Lambert and Bower, 1961a, 1961b) have great potential value. But additional research, particularly concerning reliability and validity, is typically needed for instruments of this type. Nevertheless, there seem to be four specific types of techniques that can be immediately employed by classroom teachers: observational methods, anecdotal records, lists of descriptive adjectives, and behavioral rating scales.

Observational methods

Observational methods can be divided into two types. *Direct observation* allows the observer to note behavior simultaneously with its spontaneous occurrence, and is generally independent of the child's ability and willingness to report. Direct observations can be made in natural conditions, such as on the playground or in the classroom, or in controlled conditions, such as a planned (staged) problem-solving situation. *Indirect observation* includes such techniques as structured and unstructured interviewing, self-report tests, questionnaires, available school records, and personal documents; in other words, any source of information, excluding direct observation, could be termed an indirect procedure. Obviously, anecdotal records, adjective check lists, and rating scales of behavior, which will be discussed in detail shortly, could be completed on the basis of either direct or indirect observations.

The use of observational methods requires a fairly refined set of assessment skills. Basically, the assessor must be capable of maintaining a high degree of objectivity and must be able to recognize significant behavioral cues. Technically, a specific recording procedure must be developed; for example, behaviors could be sampled at random intervals and for a limited time, or they could be recorded in total (all acts during the period of observation), or they could include only those acts that fitted a previously determined set of behavioral criteria, such as recording only observed aggressive acts.

There are a number of sources of contamination for observational methods. The most obvious perhaps are: the presence of an observer or the knowledge that one's behavior is being observed and/or evaluated (for example, use of a one-way window) could influence the child's behavior and thereby lead to an atypical sample of behavior; and subjectivity, such as personal biases, could easily lead observations toward unreliable and invalid inferences. Kleinmuntz (1967) provides a comprehensive overview of theory and techniques of observational methods; and Richardson, Dohrenwend, and Klein (1965) present a depth analysis of interviewing procedures.

Suffice it to say that teachers have an excellent opportunity to observe their students' behaviors in a variety of settings. If the teacher can employ a systematic method for recording observed behaviors, this procedure may be the basis for a valuable source of information for detecting behavior problems.

Anecdotal records

Anecdotal records offer perhaps the most frequently used method for systematically recording classroom observations. With this technique, the classroom teacher periodically jots down impressions of a child's behavior, development, or learning attempts. There are, however, some shortcomings to this approach. As one might suspect, it would be easy to neglect making these observations at regular intervals or to bypass observations about some children. For example, a well-behaved child might go unnoted in the anecdotal records, yet comments on his good behavior would be very valuable if at a later date he were to become a behavioral problem child; changes in behavior and the possible influences might be detected from the records. Another possible shortcoming, especially when the teacher is responsible for a large class or for several classes of children, is that the anecdotal records might, by practical necessity or fatigue, become brief and contain essentially meaningless comments. Perhaps the biggest problem with this technique is that it is highly subjective; teachers vary in their definitions of words that are used in the anecdotes. For example, when Miss Jones states that a child is "rowdy," does this mean the same thing as when Miss Smith states that another child is also "rowdy"? In other words, the terms may not mean the same thing to each teacher.

Properly written anecdotal records can be extremely valuable, not only at the detection and referral stage but at the diagnostic stage as well. Before setting forth some general "rules of thumb" for the writing of anecdotal records, let us consider several examples of poor anecdotes and how they could be improved.

Example 1. John hasn't made many friends since he transferred to this school.

With this example, we might wonder just how long John has been in the school, whether this behavior is different from that which he exhibited in his previous school, what he does during the periods that he is alone, and whether he has actually been provided with opportunities to make friends. Therefore, an improved example might read:

Improved Example 1. John has only been at our school for five weeks. He transferred from Johnson Elementary School. It seems to me that he has not made many friends yet. According to his cumulative folder, however, he did not have many friends at Johnson either; his previous third-grade teacher said that he usually confined his play activities to a neighbor boy who lived only a few doors away from him, and she also said that he preferred reading in the library to playing with some of the more active boys. These observations seem compatible with his behavior here. I have pretty much left him on his own to make friends; perhaps I will try to structure him into more social activities during the next term.

A second poor example might be:

Example 2. Charles seems listless in class. He frequently puts his head down on his desk and seems to nap. Yet at other times he is very aggressive.

An improvement of this example should clarify what the teacher thinks might be the possible influences for this behavior, whether the behavior was appropriate or inappropriate, and what the word "aggressive" means. An improved example might read:

Improved Example 2. Charles seems to have trouble maintaining attention in class; he is not a disturbance, but he does seem to be tired and frequently puts his head on the desk as if to rest. This may be due to his overcrowded home. At other times, however, he is very active and aggressive. If some other boy tries to bully him, he will fight back without hesitation, but he seldom starts a fight. He is very competitive on the playground.

With this improved version we see more specifically what "listless" and "aggressive" behaviors mean to this particular teacher. If the anecdote had been more detailed, other ideas about why the behavior occurred might have been added; for example, it might be noted from perusal of the other anecdotal records and social case history notes on file in the cumulative folder from previous years that Charles comes from a lower socioeconomic home, shares a bedroom with several siblings, has parents who neglect such things as putting him to bed at a proper time, and has to compete with his siblings for almost everything (from playthings to food to parental attention). If these things were known, the anecdote would take on much more meaning, and the observed behaviors would be better understood. But the comment, "This may be due to his over-crowded home," gives us at least a clue to look into his home environment.

The two preceding examples are short, but they may shed some light on what might be done to improve an anecdotal record. It is recognized that such improvements take more time and effort on the part of the teacher, but in the long run their improved quality will more than compensate for the additional time and effort.

Several books, such as those by Beller (1962) and Warters (1964), have provided good accounts of the components of comprehensive developmental and social case histories and the writing of anecdotal records. As is the case with so many aspects of the behavioral sciences, anecdotal techniques cannot be restricted to a hard and fast format; anecdotes must remain subjective expressions and opinions of the recorder, the teacher. There are, however, some general considerations or "rules of thumb" that will facilitate the keeping of meaningful records.

1. Record anecdotes at specific times. Adhering to a predetermined schedule should assure that the records will be written and not be put off until later. It seems advisable to make these at least twice a year, if not more often. Some teachers have found it beneficial to make weekly notes; in other words, an anecdotal diary is kept for the students throughout the entire school year. (This

seems especially appropriate for special education classes for exceptional children.) If this is done, it is recommended that a certain day and time be designated, and that this task should always take preference over other things during this period.

2. Make anecdotes for all children. The purpose of anecdotal records is not just to record observations about a few children—for instance, the behavioral problem children—but is a means of furnishing developmental information about every child. The child who is well-behaved today may be a behavioral problem child tomorrow, or vice versa, and a retrospective look at behavioral patterns can be invaluable in understanding the child.

3. Record observations of both good and bad behavior. All too frequently only the bad behaviors are noted; good or acceptable behaviors may be equally valuable to a collection of anecdotes. (This is related to No. 2.)

4. Define descriptive terms. When a term is used to describe a behavior, such as "acting out," it will be meaningless unless it is clarified and exemplified. The same term may mean different things to different teachers.

5. Do not sacrifice quality for brevity; similarly, do not "ramble on" with meaningless, repetitious comments. If proper time is scheduled for record keeping, the length of the anecdotes should not be a problem. Hurrying to get through with the task can only lead to poor records. The true value of a well-written anecdote must be appreciated. Likewise, extremely lengthy descriptions and the repetition of material will be as damaging as extreme brevity. Each anecdote should be written with the idea of communicating information to another educator, one who may be as pressed for time as the teacher doing the writing and who will want concise, clearly worded descriptions of recognizable behaviors.

6. If opinions are expressed, as they well might be, state briefly the rationale for each belief. In other words, any statement that is an opinion of the observer-recorder, the teacher, should be justified by an explanation of the bases from which it was derived. Thus if a child is described as being "a threat to others" or "immoral" or by some other description based on the teacher's opinion, the reasons for this belief should be stated.

7. Follow as similar a format for all children as is practical. (This is related in part to No. 3.) That is, precautions against neglecting certain types of behavior should be exercised. Frequently we are more conscious of bad behavior than of good behavior; and we are prone to overlook certain behaviors with one child simply because of our over-all impression or set concerning him, whereas we would readily see them in another child. Thus it is good to have a general set of types of behavior or observational areas that are applicable to all children. Needless to say, there will be cases where a certain behavior may not need to be mentioned with a given child, but at the time of the recording of the anecdote, the teacher should at least give brief consideration to whether that behavior merits comment. At the same time, care must be exercised to be sure that observations are not constricted by the set of categories; there may be behaviors outside of the standard set of considerations that should be noted.

These seven recommendations, if conscientiously and consistently practiced, should lead to improved anecdotal records.

Lists of descriptive adjectives

A second way of systematically recording behavioral observations is to make a list of adjectives that describe behavior. Obviously this is quite similar to anecdotal records, and this technique has many of the same advantages and disadvantages. It has the additional advantage, however, of being quick and easy to record, but it has a distinct disadvantage because of nebulous or differing meanings attached to the adjectives.

It should be acknowledged that terms used to describe behaviors are not only ambiguous in meaning, but numerous as well. Allport and Odbert (1936) studied the English language for terms used to describe human characteristics and to differentiate people from one another; they found nearly 18,000 relevant words. It almost goes without saying that it is literally impossible to derive an all-encompassing set of descriptive words for an adjective check list. Thus, in approaching this technique, one must accept the fact that it is at best a rough device for the assessment of behavior.

To make such a list of adjectives, the teacher (or the teachers as a group) would prepare a list of words describing specific behaviors; such words might include "hyperactive," "aggressive," "self-centered," "hostile," "withdrawing," "loud," "independent," "dependent," "unaccepting of peers," "shy," and so on. Then a special list of definitions or a code for meanings of the terms should be created. Each definition might include a description of the behavior, some typical examples, antonyms and synonyms of the words, and any other information that will help make the terms meaningful. This type of list would only allow for consistency within a given classroom or, if all teachers were involved in the development of a list of adjectives, within the school or, at best, within a school system. But this is still quite an improvement over inconsistency between teachers within the same school or, moreover, inconsistency between ratings at different times by the same teacher.

The list of adjectives and the necessary code of definitions should be developed by the combined efforts of all those who will use it. In other words, the school psychologist or the principal should not alone create the list and the definitions. Rather, one of them might serve as coordinator of an in-service training program in which each teacher would contribute his or her own ideas about behavior problems, key terms, and their definitions. This group effort would not only improve the quality and understanding of the instrument by resolving the conflicts in opinions (it is known from sociological research that group problem solving is usually more productive than individual problem solving), but it would also achieve increased acceptance of the tech-

nique. That is, teachers would not feel that this was another unnecessary duty being forced upon them, since they were involved in the
planning and development: involvement creates better understanding,
acceptance, and usage.

To use this technique, after the list of adjectives has been prepared
and definitions have been established, the teacher would periodically
check off or list those adjectives that best describe each student in the
classroom. Over a period of time, review of accumulated lists of adjectives would be used to postulate behavioral trends.

There have also been adjective check lists standardized for national
use (Buros, 1965). As an example, Scarr (1966) has adapted Gough's
(1960) Adjective Check List for use with children. She found that this
modified instrument was a valid means for personality assessment and
correlated highly with direct and indirect measures of children's behavior.

Behavior rating scales

A third method for recording behavioral observations is to use a
behavior rating scale. This technique is based on the idea that specific
observable behaviors can be defined and that the severity or the importance of the problem can be rated. A number of these scales are available, but it is also possible, and in some cases wiser, to design an
instrument for a particular school system. Table 3–1 is an example of
a behavior rating scale (Rutter, 1967) that is simple yet adequately developed. Rutter presents evidence that the scale has good retest and
inter-rater reliability and is an efficient screening device for children with
behavioral and emotional disorders. The use of a nationally available
instrument, which may be located simply by consulting almost any reference book on testing (for example, Buros, 1965), is especially valuable for
research. That is, the use of the same rating scale in different school systems might facilitate a comparison of opinions regarding behavior problems; the need for these comparisons has been mentioned repeatedly in
this book.

One of the most industrious and potentially promising efforts to
develop a behavior rating scale is being made at the University of Maryland Research Center of the Interprofessional Research Commission on
Pupil Personnel Services (IRCOPPS). This project has extended the previously cited work of Bower (1966) and Lambert and Bower (1961a,
1961b). On the basis of eight items developed by Bower, sixteen additional items were developed; in combination, the twenty-four items constitute the Pupil Classroom Behavior Scale (Dayton, 1967); the scope of

TABLE 3–1. Rutter's Child Behavior Rating Scale *

Below are a series of descriptions of behavior often shown by children. If the child definitely shows the behavior described by the statement, place a cross in the box in column 3. If the child behaves somewhat according to the statement but to a lesser extent or less often, place a cross in the box in column 2. If, as far as you are aware, the child does not show the behavior, place a cross in the box in column 1. Please show one cross for each statement. Thank you.

Statement	*Doesn't apply*	*Applies somewhat*	*Certainly applies*
1. Very restless. Often running about or jumping up and down. Hardly ever still.			
2. Truants from school.			
3. Squirmy, fidgety child.			
4. Often destroys own or others' belongings.			
5. Frequently fights with other children.			
6. Not much liked by other children.			
7. Often worried, worries about many things.			
8. Tends to do things on his own—rather solitary.			
9. Irritable. Is quick to fly off the handle.			
10. Often appears miserable, unhappy, tearful, or distressed.			
11. Has twitches, mannerisms, or tics of the face or body.			
12. Frequently sucks thumb or finger.			
13. Frequently bites nails or fingers.			
14. Tends to be absent from school for trivial reasons.			
15. Is often disobedient.			
16. Has poor concentration.			
17. Tends to be fearful or afraid of new things or new situations.			
18. Fussy or overparticular child.			
19. Often tells lies.			
20. Has stolen things on one or more occasions.			
21. Has wet or soiled self at school this year.			
22. Often complains of pains or aches.			

	Doesn't	Applies	Certainly
Statement	*apply*	*somewhat*	*applies*

23. Has had tears on arrival at school or has refused to come into the building this year.
24. Has a stutter or stammer.
25. Has other speech difficulty.
26. Bullies other children.

How well do you know this child? Very well. Moderately well. Not very well.

Signature (Mr./Mrs./Miss) . . . . Date . . . .

Other remarks.

---

* Appreciation is expressed to M. Rutter for permission to reprint this scale.

the enlarged scale is thus extended from the function of screening for emotionally handicapped students to detecting behavior problems in the classroom and in other school groups. The Pupil Classroom Behavior Scale is presented in Table 3–2. Each of the twenty-four items is a description of a relatively discrete behavioral event. The teachers rate a particular child on each of the items; a five-point frequency-of-occurrence continuum is used (almost never or never, not very often, sometimes, quite often, and most of the time). It has been found that on the average approximately five minutes are required to complete the scale for a student; this means a total time of 2.5 hours for the behaviors of a group of thirty students. Although the scale is not yet completely validated, the investigators are attempting to derive subscores for specific aspects of behavior as well as an over-all numerical behavioral rating. If the validation studies are successful, eventually this scale may have diagnostic value. At present, however, it might best be described as a subjective screening instrument and thus quite appropriate for helping teachers develop inferences of possible behavior problems.

Novick, Rosenfeld, Bloch, and Dawson (1966) have developed the Deviant Behavior Inventory. This inventory contains 237 items of deviant behavior; each item is checked as being true, false, or not sure for the child being evaluated. Special care went into the construction of the

TABLE 3-2. Pupil Classroom Behavior Scale *

1. Comments on the work of other pupils by bringing out good points or suggesting improvements instead of being critical of their weaknesses and faults.
2. Contributes in ways that make class activities more interesting, varied, and meaningful. (For example: brings in materials; relates personal experiences to activities; suggests ideas, plans, projects, solutions.)
3. Acts upon helpful criticism in such ways as: correcting mistake; looking for other solutions; trying to better understand criticism; trying to make his reasoning clear to others.
4. Shows enthusiasm toward learning activities, being with classmates, and, in general, being in school.
5. Cooperates with teacher requests for quiet, for starting work, and for changing activities.
6. Blows up, becomes excited, and loses self-control when unable to do what he wants to do.
7. Uses available school time inefficiently.
8. Shows little concern for the needs, problems, and feelings of others.
9. Tries out new things; puts ideas or things into new combinations. (Creativity may be seen in any subject-matter area, in social, athletic, manual, and fine arts areas. Examples are: the making up of a poem, art object, melody, story, chart, diagram, model, a solution to a social problem, a new football play.)
10. Leads well toward socially desirable goals when given the chance to do so.
11. Follows well toward socially desirable goals when given the chance to do so.
12. Gives up when faced with a difficulty without trying to find a solution.
13. Hands in inaccurate or inadequate written work because he does not review or check work.
14. Has difficulty following teacher directions or instructions.
15. Is unable to keep attention for the necessary time on work tasks.
16. Disobeys or rebels against reasonable school authority (teachers, rules, regulations).
17. Gets into fights or quarrels with other pupils.
18. Has to be coaxed or forced to work or play with others.
19. Has difficulty in learning school subjects.
20. Makes unusual or inappropriate responses during normal school activities.
21. Works extremely hard in learning school subjects to the exclusion of any other interests or activities.
22. Behaves in ways which are dangerous to self or others.
23. Is unhappy or depressed.
24. Becomes upset or sick when faced with a difficult school problem or situation.

* Appreciation is expressed to C. M. Dayton and R. H. Byrne for permission to reprint this scale. Items 17-24 are adapted from Bower's Behavior Ratings of Pupils; items 1-16 are new items added by IRCOPPS personnel.

inventory to minimize and control over- and under-reporting errors. The inventory can be administered to parents or other adults who know the child; or it may be completed by a trained observer of the child's behavior at home or in school.

As might be inferred from these examples of instruments, behavior ratings are generally based on observation by adults, such as teachers, in a number of situations. In the recall of past events, distortion or faulty perception can easily create error in the ratings. One way to minimize the possibility of error would be to videotape a sequence of behaviors; by replaying the sequence several times, ratings could be improved. Haworth and Menolascino (1967) have used such a videotape technique and devised a behavior check list for use in a standard play interview situation.

But possibilities are not limited to nationally distributed behavior rating scales. Any educator can develop a similar instrument. There are four steps in the development of a behavior rating scale. First, create an item for each behavior that is to be rated; for example (using a frame of reference of the average behavior in the class), "social relations with peers." Second, define the behavior or the criteria for rating (as briefly as is practical); for example, "Social relations with peers refers to the ability to give and take socially, to fit into the group's behavioral norms, and to get along with others." Third, establish a rating continuum of categories (from positive to negative); for example, "1. Extremely good; 2. Above average; 3. Average; 4. Below average; 5. Very poor." In regard to the continuum, any number of categories may be used; the number depends upon how fine a discrimination is desired and how capable the rater is (some raters might be effective only at differentiating behavior on a three-point scale—above average, average, below average—whereas another rater might be able to use effectively seven, nine, or eleven categories). In general, it seems advisable to use an uneven number of scale steps, and for educational purposes five or seven categories seem the preferred number. The fourth point is this: Following each of the three-part phases for each item, leave space for a sentence or two to describe the behavior; for example, "Benny works well and becomes involved in peer-group activities in the classroom, but seems hesitant to enter as readily into the rough-and-tumble playground activities."

The development of a behavior rating scale is fairly complex, but certainly not an impossible task. All of the educators who are to use it should, of course, be involved in the developmental stages; this involvement will assure thorough understanding, acceptance, and usage of the scale. The faculty could, therefore, after having a workshop on the psychology of behavioral problem children, formulate a series of items that was the most appropriate for their needs and qualifications.

The behavior rating scale method is obviously related to both the anecdotal and list-of-adjectives techniques. As compared to the anecdotal records technique, a behavior rating scale assures more areas of agreement among the frames of reference used for the observations and covers a set of specific behaviors (but of course this latter point could also be a limitation). As compared to the list-of-adjectives technique, the behavior rating scale technique allows the observer, such as the classroom teacher, both to note the occurrence of a behavior and to place a quantitative value on the behavioral act; the list-of-adjectives technique is essentially limited to noting only what behaviors are present or observable.

The fact that the behavior rating scale technique provides a quantification of behaviors is one of its strongest assets. For example, assuming that the definitions of the terms were the same or comparable, a teacher checking the adjective "withdrawing" on a list of adjectives would know only that the child fulfilled the definition of that particular term; the teacher using a behavior rating scale would have the opportunity to delineate the degree of withdrawing behavior—whether the child withdrew in all social situations, only in classroom activities, only in activities with peers of the same sex or the opposite sex, only in relationships with adult authority figures, or any number of other possibilities. The number of possibilities or degree of refinement is, in general, limited only by the abilities of the observer and the design of the rating scale. There are, of course, possibilities for error with this technique, but controls against error are also possible to some extent (Kleinmuntz, 1967; Novick, Rosenfeld, Bloch, and Dawson, 1966).

As the reader may have inferred, the behavior rating scale technique, all things considered, probably has the most value of the three techniques presented. But, of course, the efficacy of each technique will depend greatly on the qualities and skills of the observer; in other words, the teacher must, regardless of technique, still possess knowledge and technical skills regarding behavioral problem children. In general, a combination of the behavior rating scale and anecdotal records techniques appears most valuable. This combination, if exercised judiciously and consistently, should provide bases for comparing the observations of all the teachers of any one child through the years (which would be inferred from the behavior rating scale data) and should facilitate subjective impressions of the child's behavior in specific situations and under differing circumstances (which would be derived from reviewing anecdotal records).

Thus far this section has emphasized that the classroom teacher is in a position to initially detect behavioral problem children. Teachers must be willing to consult with other school personnel in an effort not only to facilitate their own work with students, but to facilitate the work of all the psychoeducational specialists as well. The classroom teacher should also be familiar with the referral resources available within the school and the community. With knowledge of behavioral problem children and of the available referral resources, the teacher is in a position to draw upon his behavioral observations in selecting one of these other specialized professions for a referral.

The referral process culminates with the teacher's (or another educator's) willingness to state that the child does need additional professional help. Although the final decision ultimately rests with the judgment of the professional involved, there are some guidelines. In summarizing the considerations, Kessler (1966) lists seven indications that suggest whether or not a referral is needed. On the basis of these seven categories, the following questions may be raised:

1. Age discrepancy: Is there a significant difference between actual chronological age and the behavioral age?
2. Frequency of occurrence of the symptom: How often are the problem behaviors manifested?
3. The number of symptoms: Is it an isolated problem area or does the child have a number of problems?
4. The degree of social disadvantage: How much do the behaviors influence the child's interpersonal relations, and how much influence do they have on the behaviors of others?
5. The child's inner suffering: Does the problem "hurt" the child—that is, cause anguish—or is he quite content in and with himself?
6. Intractability of behaviors: Does the problem persist even after others have tried to bring about change?
7. General personality appraisal: Since the most important thing is general adjustment, does the problem cause a significant disruption in the child's general psychosocial, behavioral functioning?

These are some of the questions that must be answered before a decision to initiate a referral can be reached.

When a referral is to be made, it is obviously desirable, and indeed probably essential in most instances, to involve the parents in the decision. In discussions with them, the educator should explain why their child appears to need help, deal with their resistances and objections, and convey a realistic understanding of what a referral involves and what it is likely to accomplish (Kessler, 1966). The primary objective is not solely to gain the parents' approval for the referral, but to get them active in the process (their participation should facilitate any subsequent treatment recommendations) and to encourage them to think about how they can help their child. Moreover, the child should receive a realistic orientation to what he is being subjected to.

With the advent of a referral, and sometimes even without a referral, other educational personnel become involved. Of specific concern herein are the roles of the school counselor, school psychologist, school administrator, and other specialized psychoeducational personnel. As attention is focused on each of these professionals in turn, one should remember that most, if not all, of the factors deemed significant for the classroom teacher in this section are equally applicable to each of these others. For example, just as a classroom teacher might have difficulty in defining terms or in rating behavior, so might any of the other professionals employed in the school setting. Since all are educators, the generalities are applicable to all; it is only the differences in job responsibilities and differences in personal and professional qualifications that lead to different types of actions or responsibilities in the processes of helping the behavioral problem child.

THE SCHOOL COUNSELOR

It has been previously stated that the classroom teacher is typically the first in line to detect the behavioral problem child in the school; this assertion was based primarily on the fact that the classroom teacher spends more working time in a situation involving general childhood behavior and with a more limited number of children than do other educators, such as the school counselor or the school psychologist. The school counselor is assigned numerous duties, such as test administration, record keeping, provision of educational and/or occupational information, and counseling. These duties are directly related to the behaviors of students, but they do not always allow firsthand observation of behavior. Moreover, even the behaviors observed in personal-social counseling are limited to that particular setting and relationship, and certainly lack the variation that is possible in the general classroom activities involving teachers and peers. Similarly, the school psychologist usually spends a good deal of his working time in diagnostic activities. While these activities are very definitely related to behavior and possibly to behavior problems, they are generally but brief samples, point-in-time observations, and their purpose is an assessment of behavior from which *assumptions* about general behavior, such as would be observable in the classroom setting, can be made. The importance of the behavioral impressions received by school counselors and school psychologists should not be underestimated; the roles of these staff members are very important in the detection and referral stage. It is true that their relationships with the child are centered on different professional objectives and that their observations will necessarily be made in a different context from those of teachers. But these different points of view, both in terms of professional orientations and the actual settings, are just as important as the classroom observations and serve as complementary sources of information.

Despite his functions outside of the classroom, the school counselor is in an excellent position to complement the detection and referral efforts of the classroom teacher. In all likelihood, the school counselor will be the first to whom the classroom teacher will (and should) turn for help with a suspected behavioral problem child. The approach may be formal, such as a scheduled consultation period or a written communication about a child, but from personal experience it seems more probable that the initial joint considerations between the teacher and the counselor will be much more informal. Many a behavioral problem child has been called to the school counselor's attention when the counselor has made a visit to the classroom for some other reason. Such comments are frequently made at the classroom door while the teacher and counselor are discussing something, such as the time for the next teachers' meeting or when the new recess time will be.

Some of the most effective interactions between teachers and counselors are in such informal situations. Unfortunately, some educators (in all types of roles) just do not feel comfortable unless their discussions allow them to be behind their desks. This type of behavior can only be interpreted as a reflection of insecurity and defensiveness, and can scarcely lead to effective work with colleagues. There seems reason to believe that many—and perhaps the best—teacher-counselor consultations are held in the faculty lounge over a cup of coffee (Board of Education members and administrators, please take note of this rationalization for a coffee pot in every faculty lounge and time to use it). It is during these coffee-therapy sessions that each school personnel member can ventilate his emotions, gain support and understanding from colleagues, and bolster up his defenses for returning to his students. Although mixing business with pleasure can be a cardinal professional sin, these informal consultations, or "gripe sessions," are a key source for invaluable information regarding behavioral problem children. In this setting the classroom teacher and other educational personnel can lower their defenses and admit that they too cannot "control" or "understand" the behaviors of every child (this is not meant to suggest that anyone should expect that he can or should control or understand all the behaviors of every child). The school counselor (and all educators), therefore, can gain valuable opinions from his colleagues that may be put to use at a later and more appropriate time.

The school counselor has, of course, responsibility for certain aspects of the detection and referral of behavioral problem children. His activities in this connection are varied. He will accept referrals from the classroom teachers, based on their belief that he is the most appropriate person to help the child (which he may or may not be). He should exert effort to become acquainted with the daily behavioral tone of the classrooms and use this as a seeking-out or detection technique. As a counselor he will undoubtedly encounter numerous children with social, emotional, educational, and/or vocational problems through teacher referrals and self-referrals (by the students themselves). And he must be prepared and willing to go beyond this: he must become a real detective—a behavior detective. The school counselor must be constantly aware of information given by students, teachers, administrators, and parents that might lead to detecting a child who has behavior problems and who is in need of professional help, whether it be help that he, the school counselor, can furnish or whether it be help available from some other professional source within or outside of the school.

Part of the foregoing discussion on the role of the school counselor is a bit idealistic. Since this responsibility to behavior problem children crosses all grade levels and since there are undeniably unmet student needs at both the elementary and secondary levels, it is lamentable that the majority of school counselors are assigned to service only secondary school students. In fact, elementary counseling is essentially nonexistent in many states. There is definitely a great need for elementary school counselors. Until there are such specialists, it is probable that many of the responsibilities herein attributed to school counselors will apply primarily to the secondary school level, and the related functions on the elementary school level will have to be fulfilled, as well as possible, by classroom teachers, school psychologists, school social workers, child development specialists, and other educational personnel.

It is somewhat regrettable that school counselors, with such an integral role in the psychoeducational services offered in the school systems, are not trained more adequately in behavioral disorders. All too often the recognition, assessment or diagnosis, and methods for modifying the behavior problems are considered to be outside of the school counselor's theoretical and technical capabilities, and are left to the school and clinical psychologists, if anyone. This is not meant to suggest that a school counselor with a limited amount of training in guidance can provide the same services as a more highly trained school or clinical psychologist, but it does mean that the generic position of the school counselor could feasibly include these services, albeit to a varying degree. It is interesting to note that many of these services are recognized as being appropriate for the counseling psychologist, a position which involves essentially an extension in training beyond the school counselor (American Psychological Association, 1956; Super, 1955). One cannot help wondering whether this restricted role in behavioral modification for school counselors is realistic, or whether it is the product of unrealistic concepts of training, community-social expectations, educational philosophy, professional insecurity, or theories of counseling; obviously this question cannot be answered at the present time, but subsequently a position will be set forth as to what the school counselor can do in the modification processes for behavioral problem children. Nevertheless, there are some specific services that are unquestionably justifiable, ethically and professionally, for the school counselor to assume within his realm of pupil personnel services; this is especially true at the detection and referral stage.

Several techniques for detection that are applicable to school counselors have already been presented in this and the previous section; let us now consider the school counselor's involvement in the referral process. Not only will he probably receive referrals, but he must also make referrals. The referrals that he makes might include students whom he detected during the course of his counseling duties, or they might include students who were referred to him. In regard to the latter, there is no reason to assume that the school counselor can or should be able to cope with all children referred to him; there will be many who have problems that are inappropriate for him to try to handle, and he must be willing to admit that he is not omnipotent and be prepared to refer these children to someone else. Therefore, many of the same guidelines set forth earlier for classroom teachers are equally applicable to school counselors and, for that matter, to all other psychoeducational staff members. For example, the school counselor must be familiar with referral sources and be willing to assume the responsibility for making a referral.

In summary, the role of the school counselor in the detection and referral of behavioral problem children is basically the same as that designated for classroom teachers. But in addition, the school counselor must facilitate communication with the classroom teachers regarding behavioral problem children. The school counselor should be available, through keeping a reasonably flexible schedule, to consult with teachers and other personnel; and it behooves the school administrator to make schedule flexibility possible for all staff members. The teacher-counselor consultations may be formal or, more likely, informal. By working outside of the classroom, the school counselor is in a good position to help create improved programs or services for the behavioral problem children. That is, his role and duties are not as restricted as those of the classroom teacher (admittedly an unwarranted restriction for the role and duties of the teacher); and consequently he should be able to foster in-service training programs, better administrative cooperation, and improved community understanding. Although the school counselor is not trained to be a psychological diagnostician like the school psychologist and is not trained to be a psychotherapist like the counseling or clinical psychologist, there are beneficial services that he can provide. For example, he can aid in attaining an efficient referral system for the school; he might assume the responsibility for setting up an in-service training program to discuss behavioral problem children, or for creating an anecdotal record program, or for bringing in consulting professionals from other disciplines and other agencies that serve behavioral problem children.

Each of these visiting consultants might help the school faculty improve their own understanding of the factors inherent in helping behavioral problem children.

Since training programs for school counselors differ and since there are great differences between individuals, the precise functions of the school counselor are unique to the particular counselor. In other words, some counselors may be able to use clinical intuition about the behavior of a child and thereby bypass certain referral sources, while others may not feel capable of doing this or may not be trained for it. For example, a specific unacceptable behavior pattern by a child in a classroom may lead one school counselor to realize that the child is in need of help far different from what he, the school counselor, or other educational personnel, such as the school psychologist, can provide; and he will take action to refer that child to a clinical psychologist at the local child guidance clinic. On the other hand, another school counselor may, quite frankly, not be adequately trained or may not be personally able to recognize the severity of the difficulty and may thus choose to refer the child, if he takes any referral action at all, to the school psychologist or school social worker.

THE SCHOOL PSYCHOLOGIST

One of the primary duties of the school psychologist is to provide diagnostic services for behavioral and educational problems; this task will receive special attention in the next chapter. An equally important and major function for the school psychologist is to serve as a consultant (Gray, 1963). The consultation may be with parents, educational personnel, or professionals in other community agencies. In this case, as with the school counselor, the school psychologist should: first, make himself available to other educational personnel, especially the classroom teachers (accessibility is directly related to effectiveness); second, actively seek relationships with all types of educators that will allow for formal and informal consultations; and third, realize that he, the school psychologist, needs the other persons as much as or more than they need him to perform acceptably their respective functions (as history will attest, it is quite likely that the classroom teacher can function with relative success without the services of the school psychologist, but it is very unlikely that the school psychologist can function effectively without the services of the classroom teacher).

For the school psychologist, establishing the proper relationships and percepts about his role in school activities is essential to all aspects of his work. This seems especially true of his detection, referral, and diagnostic responsibilities. White and Harris (1961) state:

Consultation with school personnel is a vital step in the diagnostic process for a school psychologist, because a school offers the unique opportunity for many observers to report on a pupil's functioning. In comparison to clinic practice, where firsthand historical data are usually obtained only from the child and his family, the school situation offers a wealth of observation on which the psychologist should capitalize. Much can be learned of a child's social problems, for example, by listening to the reports of his teachers and his counselors. Some psychologists who neglect the importance of listening carefully to what the school staff has to say will draw all kinds of inferences from what the parents say. Both types of reports are valuable, particularly because they cross-validate each other, or point up areas where the pupil presents two totally different pictures, which is probably significant in itself.[2]

In other words, it is unsound for the school psychologist to attempt to pass from the detection and referral stage to the diagnostic stage, regardless of how many tests are included in the diagnostic battery, without consulting with classroom teachers, school counselors, other educational personnel, and the parents involved about their dealings with a specific behavioral problem child. The observations of behavior made by persons in different settings, with different skills, and with different relationships with the child are especially important, and the results will be of reciprocal value.

The school psychologist, because of the level and type of specialized academic training that he has received and the status accorded to him in the educational-administrative hierarchy, has the responsibility of trying to improve the detection, referral, diagnostic, and treatment services available to behavioral problem children (and, for that matter, to all exceptional children). Like the school counselor, the school psychologist can and should take the initiative in promoting and developing detection procedures, obtaining records of behavioral observations, facilitating referrals to the appropriate sources, and encouraging and organizing in-service training programs. He is also in an excellent position to communicate with administrators about needed curricular and personnel changes. And his psychological training prepares him to work toward a beneficial relationship between the school system and other professions, such as medical physicians and members of clinic staffs, within the community. All of these activities facilitate detection and referrals.

Thus the school psychologist may detect a behavior problem during the course of his regular duties, such as when providing diagnostic serv-

2 From Mary A. White and M. W. Harris, THE SCHOOL PSYCHOLOGIST (New York: Harper & Row, 1961), p. 238. Reprinted by permission of Harper & Row, Publishers, Incorporated.

ices, and he is involved with and responsible for detection and referral aspects through cooperating with other educational personnel. Further, he must be prepared to refer from his own cases the children that are inappropriate for him to deal with. Although the school psychologist will have a major contribution to make to the diagnostic and treatment or behavioral modification stages, as will be elaborated on at subsequent points in this book, he also has the important function of seeking the teachers' help through consultations about students. In other words, it should be emphasized again that each educator, regardless of position, is dependent to some degree upon the others to achieve optimum efficacy of his own functioning; and the school psychologist is no exception. It is requisite that all educators, and especially those in the specialized roles, accept the fact that professional reciprocity is a necessary component of high-quality education.

THE SCHOOL ADMINISTRATOR

It is an obvious fact that school administrators usually have less direct contact with individual children than do educators in other roles. Even principals are frequently almost totally removed from helping individual students with problems; instead, they follow the role of being administratively involved with the students as a group, and even these activities may allow only limited encounters with the students themselves. Probably most administrators would agree that this is an unfortunate paradox: the administrators plan and control and assume the responsibility for the provision of services to the students, yet they have few firsthand dealings with the children. Even more paradoxical is the fact that the more important or the more far-reaching the effects of a specific administrative role, the less the personal contact with students. And when school administrators do come in contact with students, it is usually under circumstances where the students do not feel free to behave spontaneously. Our society has created an authoritarian aura around school administrators. When the principal walks into the classroom, even if he is a former teacher of that particular group of students, backs suddenly stiffen and behavior becomes controlled and unspontaneous—even the behavior of the teacher.

The school administrator, therefore, finds that he is not afforded the opportunity to *detect* behavioral problems, but only to *deal* with them after the fact. And, alas, many administrators (and teachers) believe that the only way to deal with behavioral problem children is with coercion and discipline. As will be revealed when behavioral modification is discussed later, punishment can be used to change behavior, but when it is used it must be part of a total program to change the behavior and should not be used just as an isolated incident of punishment for a behavior that has gone unnoticed or has been coped with differently in the past.

Regardless of these seemingly constricting influences because of role and social expectations, there are ways in which the school administrator can be involved, and in fact must be involved, in the helping processes for behavioral problem children, even at the detection and referral stage.

The school administrator is, by far, in the best position to facilitate all phases of helping the behavioral problem child. His role in detection may not be as directly involved as the classroom teacher's role, at least in the sense of observing the behavior of the children, but it is certainly as basically important. The school administrator can best help the behavioral problem child by helping the other types of educators help the students. Granted, this may seem like an indirect means of helping, but without cooperation and facilitation from the school administration, the efforts of the other educators would be futile and short-lived. The school administrator should use his position to help each of the other professionals fulfill their respective responsibilities; this is the administrator's responsibility to the behavioral problem child.

This involvement of school administrators can take several forms. The school administrator might dismiss school early on occasion to allow the faculty to meet to discuss one of the aspects of detection, such as how to record behavioral observations, or to consider the question "What is a behavioral problem child?" Or he might make an effort to arrange funds to bring in resource consultants, such as psychiatrists or clinical psychologists, to increase the understanding of the psychology of behavioral problem children. Or he could take steps to assure that the school system is equipped with both materials and personnel for coping with these problems; that is, he will make sure, for example, that the school psychologist has time to consult with teachers and is not bogged down with diagnostic activities only or is not required to test a certain number of students each week to keep in the good graces of the administration (a practice that unfortunately exists in many school districts). Or, finally, he might make sure that each educator in the school system recognizes his responsibilities to behavioral problem children, and check to make sure that lines of communication are open and that there has been adequate delineation of specific responsibilities (for example, exactly who in the school should get in touch with the child guidance clinic).

Just as with educators in other positions, the school administrator must foster communicative relationships with all personnel in the system. The classroom teacher must feel free to let the principal know when the services of the school psychologist are needed, and the principal must feel that he can talk with the school counselor or school psychologist without being concerned about showing his own lack of psychological knowledge. The general administrative atmosphere should never approach that in the following true situation: A classroom teacher felt so threatened by the administration, because promotions and salary increments depended on student achievement as measured on a standardized group achievement test, that he reported to the principal that he had no behavioral problem children; and he actually changed some of the students' answers on the achievement test to prove to the administration what an outstanding teacher he was. Obviously, there are several unusual factors in this example, such as the questionable practice of evaluating teachers on the basis of the students' achievement on a group test and the general mental health of the teacher in question, but it does serve to illustrate how poor relationships between teachers and administrators can affect the well-being of the children. (Incidentally, this situation came to light only when the school psychologist wondered why referrals had been received from every teacher in the school but one.) The point is that there must be mutual respect and cooperation.

School administrators and teachers alike must realize that certain types of exceptional children constitute a minority of the total school population, and although it may seem administratively imprudent to devote funds and personnel to the minority, the objective is to help not only the exceptional child, such as those with behavior problems, but the remainder or the majority of the total school population. The total school population benefits from special services to exceptional children; for example, it is apparent that changing the behavior of the disruptive student will not only help him, but also allow his peer group to improve their chances of learning in the classroom.

The school administrator is, therefore, very much involved in the detection and referral stage of helping behavioral problem children. He facilitates the roles of other educational personnel in the detection and referral processes by coordinating and administrating the numerous factors that might restrict their effectiveness. No matter how many or what the quality of the parts, the educational machine cannot work without someone to turn it on and keep it running.

OTHER PSYCHOEDUCATIONAL PERSONNEL

The intended boundaries for the format of this book are such that only scant attention can be given to other professionals who are employed within the school system and who will definitely be involved with behavioral problem children. These persons might include school social workers, speech and hearing therapists, reading specialists, itinerant teacher-consultants, school nurses, and school medical physicians. An extensive discussion of the roles of each professional directly or indirectly related to the schools is not justified. But it should be acknowledged that each of these professionals, and possibly others (including some non-professionals in the schools), may have a responsibility in the general detection and referral of behavioral problem children.[3] Brief comments are, however, merited for the roles of three of these other psychoeducational personnel: the speech and hearing therapist, the school social worker, and the reading specialist and some types of teacher-consultants.

The speech and hearing therapist is generally responsible for recognizing, diagnosing, and treating problems related to language development, speech patterns and habits, and hearing ability. Many of these therapists begin servicing children at the preschool or nursery school level, and their services continue on into university and adult outpatient clinics. As is potentially true with almost any human problem, there may be overt behavioral correlates to speech and hearing problems. For example, a child with a speech disorder may, because of this problem, resort to certain behaviors as a means of compensating, masking, or counteracting the presumed effects of the speech difficulty. Similarly, the presence of a hearing deficit or faulty language development could be the basis for compensatory behaviors, and some of these behaviors could easily be unacceptable, and consequently the child would be considered a behavioral problem child. It is, therefore, imperative that speech and hearing therapists fulfill the detection and referral tasks associated with problem behaviors. From their samplings of a child's behavior, they will have the opportunity to recognize behavior problems, or perhaps more importantly, they can prognosticate the possibility of unacceptable behavior on the basis of the observations that are directly related to language, speech, and hearing.

The school social worker is also very much involved with behavioral problem children; in fact, some might argue that any book on behavioral problem children should give primary attention to the activities of the school social worker. The school social worker carries on different activities in different educational settings. In some the school social worker does mainly social case work; in others the emphasis may be on direct counseling or psychotherapy with children. The diversity of functioning makes it a bit difficult to generalize, but it seems that regardless of role

[3] Any veteran educator will attest to the potential value of nonprofessionals for helping children. Frequently the maintenance man or the cook in the school has better rapport and a better opportunity to achieve emotional openness with students than the best trained professional. It would seem, especially in view of recent research that supports the value of lay counselors (Carkhuff, 1966), that perhaps education is missing an opportunity to capitalize on available pupil personnel workers when it neglects the relationships that are possible between nonprofessionals and students.

differences, the school social worker, like the other members of the psychoeducational staff, has the opportunity and the responsibility for using his professional skills to help the behavioral problem child at all stages—detection, referral, diagnosis, and treatment.

The reading specialist and some educators who are labeled teacher-consultants are involved with helping children with a particular educational problem. In the case of reading, the specialist may work with a child separately or in a group. In this context, the reading specialist or the teacher-consultant is exposed to psychosocial behaviors, and these behaviors may well be the keys to understanding the child's motives for areas other than the one receiving special attention. And, as will be pointed out in Chapter 4, there is research evidence to support the belief that educational achievement, or more correctly the lack of it, may be directly related to the probability of behavior problems. Here again is a professional role, that of the reading specialist or the teacher-consultant, that necessitates involvement in the detection and referral stage of helping behavioral problem children.

The foregoing few paragraphs should not be interpreted as meaning that children with speech and hearing disorders, faulty language development, reading difficulties, or other educational problems will be behavioral problem children; this is not the case. What should be emphasized is that children with these problems, like many children without these problems, may develop unacceptable behaviors. And there is reason to believe that these types of difficulties can, in some instances, foster behaviors that will prove to be socially unacceptable.

PROFESSIONAL UNITY

Although there are differences between theories and techniques espoused by the disciplines of psychology, social work, education, speech pathology, and medicine, the responsibility for helping the child in need of service serves as a common bond to draw these professions together. Too many interdisciplinary conflicts are perpetuated because of the still-developing status of the disciplines; professional ideology, which may really be professional jealousy or insecurity, may curtail the effectiveness of efforts to help behavioral problem children. This must not be allowed to happen.

No attempt will be made to provide specific summarizing statements on the responsibility for each specific discipline or professional role that is found in the school system; rather it seems more prudent and logical to issue a plea for unity of the helping professions. Many, if not most, of the considerations set forth in this chapter for classroom teachers, school counselors, and school psychologists are equally applicable, at least in essence, to school social workers, speech and hearing therapists, reading specialists and teacher-consultants, child development specialists, and school nurses and medical physicians. An interdisciplinary acceptance of what each respective profession and/or discipline can add to the psychoeducational services for behavioral problem children is the goal to strive for. The status of each profession and each role or position will be more enhanced by interdisciplinary cooperative services than by independent services.

REFERENCES

Allport, G. W., and Odbert, H. S. Trait-names: a psycho-lexical study. *Psychological Monographs,* 1936, 47:1-171.

American Psychological Association, Committee on Definition, Division of Counseling Psychology. Counseling psychology as a specialty. *American Psychologist,* 1956, 11:282-285.

Beilin, H. Teachers' and clinicians' attitudes toward the behavior problems of children: a reappraisal. *Child Development,* 1959, 30:9-25.

Beller, E. K. *Clinical process: the assessment of data in childhood personality disorders.* New York: Free Press of Glencoe, 1962.

Bower, E. M. *Early identification of emotionally handicapped children in school.* Springfield, Ill.: C. C Thomas, 1960.

Bower, E. M. *Technical report: a process for in-school screening of children with emotional handicaps.* Princeton, N.J.: Educational Testing Service, 1966.

Buros, O. K. (Ed.). *The sixth mental measurements yearbook.* Highland Park, N.J.: Gryphon Press, 1965.

Carkhuff, R. R. Training in the counseling and therapeutic practices: requiem or reveille? *Journal of Counseling Psychology,* 1966, 13:360-367.

Cooper, S., Ryan, W., and Hutcheson, B. R. Classroom screening for emotional disturbance. *American Psychologist,* 1959, 14:341.

Dayton, C. M. *Technical manual: Pupil Classroom Behavior Scale,* College Park, Md.: University of Maryland Research Center on the Interprofessional Research Commission on Pupil Personnel Services, 1967.

Dayton, C. M., and Uhl, N. P. *Relationship between Holland Vocational Preference Inventory and performance measures of high school stu-*

dents. Cooperative Research Project #5-0581-2-12-1. College Park, Md.: University of Maryland Research Center of the Interprofessional Research Commission on Pupil Personnel Services, 1966.

Eaton, M., Weathers, G., and Phillips, B. N. Some reactions of classroom teachers to problem behavior in school. *Educational Administration and Supervision,* 1957, 43:129-139.

Fitzsimons, Marian J. The predictive value of teachers' referrals. In M. Krugman (Ed.), *Orthopsychiatry and the School.* New York: American Orthopsychiatric Association, 1958, 149-153.

Goldfarb, A. Teachers' ratings in psychiatric case-finding. *American Journal of Public Health,* 1963, 53:1919-1927.

Gough, H. G. The Adjective Check List as a personality assessment research technique. *Psychological Reports,* 1960, 6:107-122.

Gray, Susan W. *The psychologist in the schools.* New York: Holt, Rinehart and Winston, 1963.

Haworth, Mary R., and Menolascino, F. J. Video-tape observations of disturbed young children. *Journal of Clinical Psychology,* 1967, 23:135-140.

Kessler, Jane W. *Psychopathology of childhood.* Englewood Cliffs, N.J.: Prentice-Hall, 1966.

Kleinmuntz, B. *Personality measurement: an introduction.* Homewood, Ill.: Dorsey Press, 1967.

Lambert, Nadine M., and Bower, E. M. *A process for in-school screening of children with emotional handicaps: manual for school administrators and teachers.* Princeton, N.J.: Educational Testing Service, 1961. (a)

Lambert, Nadine M., and Bower, E. M. *A process for in-school screening of children with emotional handicaps: technical report for school administrators and teachers.* Princeton, N. J.: Educational Testing Service, 1961. (b)

Novick, J., Rosenfeld, Eva, Bloch, D. A., and Dawson, D. Ascertaining deviant behavior in children. *Journal of Consulting Psychology,* 1966, 30:230-238.

Richardson, S. A., Dohrenwend, Barbara S., and Klein, D. *Interviewing: its forms and functions.* New York: Basic Books, 1965.

Rivlin, H. N. Classroom discipline and learning. In M. Krugman (Ed.), *Orthopsychiatry in the School.* New York: American Orthopsychiatric Association, 1958, 113-118.

Rutter, M. A children's behaviour questionnaire for completion by teachers: preliminary findings. *Journal of Child Psychology and Psychiatry,* 1967, 8:1-11.

Sarason, S., Davidson, K., and Blatt, B. *The preparation of teachers.* New York: John Wiley and Sons, 1962.

Scarr, Sandra. The Adjective Check List as a personality assessment technique with children: validity of the scales. *Journal of Consulting Psychology,* 1966, 30:122-128.

Super, D. E. Transition: from vocational guidance to counseling psychology. *Journal of Counseling Psychology,* 1955, 2:3-9.

Warters, Jane. *Techniques of Counseling* (2nd ed.). New York: McGraw-Hill, 1964.

White, Mary A., and Harris, M. W. *The school psychologist.* New York: Harper and Brothers, 1961.

Wickman, E. K. *Children's behavior and teachers' attitudes.* New York: The Commonwealth Fund, 1928.

4

Psychoeducational Diagnosis

Much of the foregoing material has pointed the way to one of the most crucial stages of helping behavioral problem children: psychoeducational diagnosis. It is crucial because it is from this evaluation stage that the plans for helping the child are derived.

Like so many of our contemporary terms, the word "diagnose" may be traced back to Latin and Greek antecedents. A lexical review would reveal such definitions as "to discriminate," "to distinguish," "to know," "to have a thorough understanding," and "to recognize and identify." Several diagnostic steps are necessary if one is to achieve thorough understanding. According to Beller (1962), these steps involve "observation, description, a delineation of causation or etiology, classification, prediction or prognosis, and control-modification or treatment plan" (p. 109). Much more is involved than merely categorizing the individual. The diagnostician would not be making a diagnosis if he stated only that the test results indicated that the child was mentally retarded or emotionally disturbed; such a statement would be the classification step, and that is but a part of a diagnosis. In accord with the various steps cited above, there are three requirements that must be fulfilled in a diagnosis: *the present functioning or characteristics should be evaluated and described; possible causative factors or etiology should be posited; and a prognosis should be made and a treatment approach recommended.*

The latter two requirements are frequently neglected in the psycho-educational diagnostic services provided in schools. All too often, tests are administered, scored, and the results entered (it is to be hoped) in the cumulative folders. This is not enough. The diagnostician must also express a clinical opinion as to what may be the causes of the conditions, what can be expected of the child, and what can be done to help him. In regard to the last requirement, for example, the school psychologist frequently finds it difficult to set forth a prognosis about a child's learning ability, and it is even more difficult for some to set forth recommendations for treatment that are practical and meaningful for educational personnel. This is one reason why psychologists employed by school systems must be acquainted with certain factors which seem to be non-psychological, such as curriculum development and teaching techniques and materials. In other words, the recommendations for treatment must take into consideration the facilities, personnel, and setting that will influence the treatment services; what may theoretically seem the best (and might be the best for a clinical setting) may not be the most practical for the school setting. The school diagnostician should, of course, strive to merge the theoretical-best with the practical-best, in order that the child may receive the optimum opportunity for help.

Previously it was stated that in trying to determine the possible causes for behavior problems, the delineation would be influenced by the level of explanation or degree of refinement of explanation that was necessary; this is also true of diagnosis. Chapter 2 presented the example of a teacher forming an opinion about the cause of a boy's behavior that was very different from the opinion that would be formed by a school psychologist in regard to the same boy. This situation applies also to diagnosis. A classroom teacher might make a statement incorporating the three diagnostic steps outlined above and would, therefore, be making a "diagnosis." However, someone in a different position, with other professional skills and another theoretical orientation, might find the teacher's "diagnosis" completely inadequate for his purposes; for example, the school psychologist might require considerably more refinement for his "diagnosis." The point is, *diagnoses from different sources need not contain exactly the same material and ideas.* This is the basis for the belief that a comprehensive diagnosis should be interdisciplinary; there should be diagnostic statements from professionals with varying theoretical and technical capabilities. And, as will later be shown, there is research evidence to support that the multifactor and/or multidiscipline diagnosis is far superior to the single-factor and/or single-discipline diagnosis.

THE SCHOOL DIAGNOSTICIAN

Theoretically any professional educator could be, and perhaps should be at some point, a "school diagnostician." That is, every educator could, in theory, set forth a "diagnosis" within his professional role, but as was just mentioned, there would be great differences in the degree of explanatory refinement between these diagnoses. In some cases, the title "school diagnostician" is limited to those educators who are assigned responsibilities for psychoeducational evaluation. And carrying out these responsibilities usually involves the use of psychological and/or educational tests. As an aside, even the administering of tests can be done by persons at all levels of technical competence. One of the best examples is the current trend to involve subprofessionals in the assessment procedures; their work is, of course, done in conjunction with a professional diagnostician. For example, Allerhand (1967) successfully trained parents of Head Start children to administer tests, but the interpretations were made by a professional.

There are several assumptions that are made about the diagnostician's fulfilling these psychoeducational diagnostic responsibilities and employing tests in the assessments. Newland (1963) lists six assumptions: (1) that the diagnostician is adequately trained and skilled in the use of the appraisal techniques; (2) that the sampling of behavior on which the appraisal is based is representative of the child's general behavior; (3) that the child has had experiences which are comparable to those of children who comprise the standardization sample for the technique or test; (4) that there will always be some amount of error present; (5) that the measurement is of present behavior only; (6) that the prognosis is an inference, not a proven fact. These principles are applicable to essentially all psychoeducational assessments, whether they be made by the teacher, the school counselor, or the school psychologist.

Before considering the roles that the various types of educators should play in psychoeducational assessments, it might be advisable to clarify some of the key terms (Ross, 1959). Historically, the terms "psychometrics" and "testing" were commonly used but gradually received less prominence because they applied mainly to instruments that yielded specific scores (thus eliminating those techniques based mainly on clinical judgment); and to some professionals the terms connoted a limited level of competency. The term "examination" fell into disfavor because it carried the connotation that there were passing and failing levels of performance; this term seemed especially inappropriate for certain clinical objectives. "Evaluation" was eventually seen as violating the nonevaluative role that professionals, particularly psychologists, endorse (that is, not making value judgments). The word "assessment" seemed more acceptable, but it too carries connotations that are sometimes objectionable (for example, the idea of determining the amount and value of a given thing). Ross concludes that the word "survey" is the most appropriate and points out that the definition of this word includes:

. . . an act of critical inspection to provide exact information with respect to certain conditions and prevalences; a comprehensive view; and the finding and describing of contours, dimensions, and positions. . . . We are, after all, exploring a patient's personality not with a view to evaluating or judging him but in order to find his conflicts and resources. (p. 35)

It does not seem that undue restrictions should be placed upon the use of any of these terms, especially since each seems to communicate some aspect of the relevant processes and since many of the objections are based more on subjectively perceived (and sometimes status-rooted) connotations rather than on concrete grounds. In this book such terms as "examination," "evaluation," "assessment," and "survey" will be used in a synonymous, interchangeable manner.

The Classroom Teacher

With adequate training in tests and measurements, classroom teachers may make some psychoeducational evaluations. Their activities are, however, usually limited to the administration and interpretation of group mental abilities and achievement tests. With the trend toward school guidance and counseling and school psychology, the classroom teacher has less direct involvement with the administrative aspects of testing today than would have been true a few years ago. The teacher does, however, have a very direct complementary involvement with psychoeducational diagnostic services, in that he is the implementer of the results of the services provided by the other school diagnosticians; that is, the more specialized diagnosticians, such as the school counselors and school psychologists, provide the psychoeducational data that the classroom teacher will use to structure his teaching services for the child. But it should also be recognized that classroom teachers make numerous "assessments" everyday that are psychoeducational appraisals, although on a lower level of refinement.

The School Counselor

The school counselor is definitely a school diagnostician when he provides testing services and when he subjectively appraises clients in counseling. Testing services are, however, only one facet of the counselor's many duties. Many school systems seem to start their guidance and counseling programs as a testing service and, as the program develops, eventually relegate testing to a less time-consuming, but still important role. In other words, the comprehensive school counselor should not be considered exclusively a diagnostician. He may provide diagnostic services, such as administering tests, for both counseling and noncounseling reasons (Goldman, 1961), but this should be done as an adjunct to the total pupil personnel services program.

The School Psychologist

The person primarily responsible for psychoeducational diagnostic services is most often the school psychologist; he may also have the title of "school psychometrician" or "school psychometrist," or "school psychological examiner," or "school diagnostician."

In many communities, the school psychologist may be the sole person available who can offer actual diagnostic services, with perhaps the exception of a local medical physician. But in more comprehensive psychoeducational programs the school system may have indirect or direct arrangements for augmenting the school psychology program with consulting or outpatient services from a child guidance clinic, a mental health department, or a private consulting clinical or counseling psychologist, psychiatrist, neurologist, pediatrician, or electroencephalographer.

School psychologists, like all professionals, differ in capabilities; moreover, school systems, both on the state and local levels, differ in the responsibilities that are assigned to the school psychologist. One school psychologist may be quite skilled in the use of personality measures, while another may be completely untrained; one may be able to use mental abilities tests that will accommodate specific physical and mental handicaps, such as intelligence test to be administered to a blind student, whereas another may not be familiar with these more specialized instruments. Thus the diagnostic procedures used by the school psychologist will be greatly dependent upon his professional preparation and his personal skills and characteristics.

Local and state regulations may also influence what diagnostic services the school psychologist provides. For example, some states allow school psychologists to work only with children who are believed to be mentally retarded, while other states allow them to work with any child enrolled in the schools. And there have been numerous newspaper accounts describing the turmoil that resulted from a school psychologist's attempt to use a clinical tool, such as a test, that was found to be unacceptable to the lay public; for example, one school district had quite a problem when members of the community protested against the school psychologist's use of a projective test that provided data regarding the psychosexual development of children. On this latter point, some school administrators are unfortunately almost as uninformed as the lay public on aspects of school psychology. They are unable or unwilling to present to their board of education or local parent group the rationale or justification for ethical uses of clinical diagnostic techniques in school psychology; thus they cannot come to the support of school psychologists in crisis situations.

Because of the incomplete understanding of psychoeducational diagnosis possessed by some educators and some members of the community, one of the basic activities that the school diagnostician must perform is to provide an understandable explanation of exactly what his role, duties, and functions encompass. Obviously, a thorough academic under-

standing is not necessary for the receivers of the school psychologist's
services, the professional and lay members of the community, but they
should understand in principle what psychoeducational diagnosis and
school psychology are all about. There should be no mysticism attached
to psychological practices, something that has unfortunately been perpetuated in the past by a lack of knowledge and understanding. And
special care should be taken to eliminate ill-founded concerns about the
moral and ethical aspects of assessments via tests (Kleinmuntz, 1967).

DIAGNOSTIC PROCEDURES

Psychoeducational diagnosis should involve more than one diagnostic
technique; data or information from a single test or one interview
scarcely constitutes a comprehensive diagnostic program. Evidence within
this chapter will show that the best diagnosis and the most comprehensive
evaluation will be based on multifactor diagnostic procedures that are
obtained from multidisciplinary sources.

Although school psychologists, and in some cases other types of educators, will probably provide the core of psychoeducational diagnostic
services in the school, there are a number of other professional workers,
both within and outside of the school, who may become involved. And
there is a wide variety of diagnostic techniques that can be employed.
This chapter presents a brief review of the primary professional sources
of diagnostic services and a consideration of the diagnostic procedures
or techniques that are employed.

The specific procedures that are involved in psychoeducational diagnosis will depend, first, upon the needs of the particular child, and
second, upon the professional persons who are available. Thus what is
considered to be "comprehensive services" in one school system might
be different from what would be found in another school system. In
general, the diagnostic information comes from the social case history,
the psychological examination, and the services of ancillary psychomedical
diagnosticians; this latter group would include services from psychiatrists, neurologists, pediatricians, and electroencephalographers. In the
following discussion, emphasis will be placed on those procedures and
services that are the most closely related to educational settings, and particularly to the techniques that might be used by the primary school
diagnostician, the school psychologist.

The Social Case History

One of the initial sources of diagnostic information is the "social case history," or, as it is called in some settings, the "intake interview." In some situations a series of sessions is allotted for this purpose and may be called "diagnostic counseling."

The objective of this diagnostic source is to gain an understanding of the person, in this case the behavioral problem child, by obtaining a thorough knowledge of historical factors that could have influenced and may still influence his functioning. Information is obtained regarding such areas as the person's childhood, education, vocational interests and activities, recreational and social activities, sexual experiences, medical history, and aspirations. The information may be provided by the person who is actually to receive the services and who is being "diagnosed," the behavioral problem child, or it may be obtained from a closely associated person, such as the child's parents, siblings, or teachers; or they may all provide information. The main emphasis during the interviewing is on developmental influences, some of which could have been before the child's birth—for example, the prenatal history. These developmental influences may be compounded with environmental, social and familial, psychological and physiological, and experiential factors.

Information for the social case history can be obtained by any educator. There is, however, a training factor involved in this diagnostic technique, as there is in all of the other diagnostic procedures. In this case, special training in interviewing techniques, sociology and psychology, and counseling are known to increase the quality of the clinical information that is derived. That is, an untrained interviewer could obtain historical information about a child, but a trained interviewer could use certain informational cues to obtain additional information and then derive clinical impressions from the data.

The classroom teacher may and should keep a record of a child's developmental history, but this information would be of limited value without supplementation from a clinically oriented interview. Thus the social case history interview or diagnostic counseling interviews ("diagnostic" being used here in the true clinical sense of the word) should be provided by a trained interviewer: the school social worker, the school counselor, or the school psychologist. From their interviews with the child and other associated persons, they can derive clinical impressions about the child's characteristics and present functioning, inferences about the probable causes, and assumptions about what may be the most appropriate approach for helping the child.

A diagnosis based only on the social case history, regardless of how skilled the interviewer is, will be of questionable reliability and validity. In other words, the components of the diagnosis are based on the interviewer's *impressions,* which may or may not be accurate, and other diagnostic information is necessary to confirm or contradict these clinical or subjective opinions. Therefore, while the social case history is an invaluable adjunct to the other diagnostic services, it does not stand alone; it needs the collaboration of other diagnostic sources. In all probability the next source would be the psychological appraisal or survey.

The Psychological Survey

The psychological survey can involve a vast number of techniques. Perhaps the best example of the possible variety is found in the area of testing; perusal of any of the basic reference texts will reveal a multitude of published tests (for example, Buros, 1965). As might be expected, however, some tests and some techniques are more frequently used than others in psychological surveys. This section will focus on the general categories of procedures and the most frequently used techniques. The psychological diagnostic procedures may be grouped for practical purposes herein into measures of academic achievement, mental abilities, personality, and psychomotor skills.

Consideration should be focused first on the training standards necessary for the appropriate use of many of the psychological assessment procedures. For example, it is quite easy to read an instruction manual for a test, to administer and score the instrument, and perhaps even to interpret the results to some degree; but to use the test appropriately, the examiner or diagnostician must have academic training in testing. This training involves an academic understanding of general psychology, specific knowledge of the statistical and technical aspects of testing, and experience in using the tests under the guiding supervision of a trained specialist. Therefore, although some diagnostic instruments—for example, group-administered academic achievement tests—may be used by educators with only limited special training in testing, most of the procedures discussed in this section require the user or examiner to have training on the graduate level. Usually it is assumed that a school diagnostician, regardless of job title, has at least a master's degree in psychology or its equivalent in education or sociology, and some of the procedures require training on an even more advanced level. This assumption does not apply to those assessment duties carried on in the course of classroom teaching.

Measures of academic achievement

Learning difficulties constitute one of the biggest problem areas for educators. The problem is further complicated by the fact that the educator's judgment of a child's learning is, in part, a reflection of his own teaching quality. This section will not go into exhaustive detail about how learning difficulties develop, but rather will emphasize the assessment of academic achievement. Briefly, however, learning difficulties might be placed in three categories (Ross, 1967):

1. Learning dysfunctions, where manifest perceptual disorders interfere with school performance without disrupting the over-all intellectual abilities;
2. Learning disorders, where neurotic learning inhibitions are present; and
3. Learning disabilities, where the ability to perform in the school is disrupted or impaired by psychological disorders that are essentially not learning-focused or educationally aligned—for example, childhood schizophrenia, infantile autism, and traumatic reactions.

Ross (1967) further subdivides these categories, exemplifies their characteristics, and presents possible treatment approaches.

It will become increasingly evident to the reader that learning difficulties are frequently given behavioral attributes. A word of caution is in order, however, because at times these attributes are derived from clinical assumptions rather than from empirical research. As one example, it is often stated that minimally brain-damaged children are more distractible than non-brain-injured children; that is, distractibility due to minimal dysfunction interferes with learning. Browning (1967) developed an experiment to test this assumption and found that the distractions influenced both minimally brain-damaged and non-brain-damaged children, and on occasion the distractions interfered with the learning of the non-brain-damaged children but did not have the same effect on those with brain damage. And when intelligence level was controlled statistically, the performance differences between brain-damaged and non-brain-damaged groups were no longer significant. This study readily exemplifies how some assumptions are basically unproven. But there are certain indications that learning difficulties do indeed reflect factors that could be part of a potential psychobehavioral problem; thus assessment of academic achievement is important.

For educators, one of the most accessible measures of a child's functioning is in the area of academic or educational achievement. Comparative measures may be obtained in a number of ways: standardized individual and group tests, objective and subjective quizzes and examinations assigned by the teacher, and general oral and written performances in the classroom. Each of these means provides data to the teacher about how well the child is achieving.

All children do not, of course, achieve at the same rate. Thus within a given classroom, even though the children may be relatively comparable in chronological age and general maturation, there will be individual differences that will affect the learning rates and academic achievement levels. Mental ability or intelligence is one of the primary determinants of academic achievement; therefore, an *overachiever* would be one who achieves above and beyond the levels expected from his chronological age and mental abilities, and conversely the *underachiever* would be one who achieves below these levels.

When a child deviates from the norm, either being above or below it, there is reason to believe that there may be behavioral correlates; that is, his discrepant achievement may result, either directly or indirectly, in behaviors that are different from those he would exhibit if his achievement were normal. All of these achievement-related behaviors need not, of course, be problem behaviors, but it is possible that some may be.

The relationship between a child's behavior and his learning style, as perceived by the classroom teacher, is undeniable. Gordon and Thomas (1967) found that teachers' judgments of their students' intelligence were significantly distorted by the teachers' perceptions of certain factors intrinsic to the behavioral patterns or temperament of the children. Other studies to be subsequently cited will lend support to the assumption that the way a teacher perceives behaviors in the classroom is, to some extent, dependent upon the given child's mode of learning.

In view of the critical relationship of academic achievement to the criteria that are frequently used to assess the efficacy of educational practices, it is not surprising that there has been a wealth of research in this area. Differences in research designs and other factors make comparisons of these studies inconclusive (Farquhar, 1963). There are, however, several factors that seem to be positively related to the child's level of academic achievement: the ability to handle or cope with anxiety, feelings of self-worth, conformity to the demands and requirements of authority figures, social acceptance by members of his peer group, the degree of conflict due to needs for independence and dependence, involvement in activities related to academic interests, and the realism of goals (Taylor, 1964). And in regard to underachievers, Kessler (1966) concludes that their differentiating characteristics are: they are predominantly males; there are detrimental socioeconomic and familial factors; their mental abilities are usually relatively high and there are distinct patterns of mental abilities; they have more negative self-concepts; and their aspiration levels are unrealistic.

From the data presented in Chapter 2, it is apparent that behavioral problem children frequently present such characteristics as poor reading skills, poor concentration or attention, and other traits that would seemingly have an effect on the academic achievement of the child. And other studies have similarly indicated that behavior problems, regardless of etiology, do in fact affect academic achievement. But there is also the question of "Which came first, the chicken or the egg?" That is, did the behavior affect the achievement, or did the achievement affect the behavior?

There is relatively consistent support from the research literature for the belief that behavioral problem children, whether their problems stem from social-emotional disturbances or organicity, will have achievement correlates; but there is not a clear-cut answer as to which influences the other. Fitzsimons (1958) made the generalization that children in her study who needed psychological or psychiatric services were characterized as not performing educationally at the level their mental abilities suggested. In a study of first-grade children in the Minneapolis Public Schools, Olson (1930) found that the lower the achievement, the higher the problem tendencies and the higher the achievement, the lower the problem tendencies; this finding seems especially relevant to the materials in this book. In comparing reading and arithmetic levels, Bower (1960) found that the emotionally disturbed children ranked significantly lower than the other children in the class; the difference between the two groups was greater in arithmetic than in reading, and the older the emotionally disturbed child became—that is, the higher the grade—the greater the difference. Tamkin (1960) found a high percentage of educational disability among emotionally disturbed children, but his analysis of the data possessed some limitations. Consequently, Stone and Rowley (1964) replicated parts of Tamkin's study, and they too found that emotionally disturbed children did not achieve commensurately with either their chronological ages or their mental ages.

Although many of the research studies mentioned above were conducted with emotionally disturbed children, there is also evidence that the neurologically impaired child or the child with inferred minimal brain dysfunction, such as those presenting the hyperkinetic behavior syndrome, may have achievement deficits. For example, Lawrence (1960) concluded that many learning problems in the public schools reflect minimal brain damage. Frierson and Barbe (1967) present a rather comprehensive collection of research relevant to learning disorders evolving from social-emotional, neurological and more specific factors.

On the basis of the above-mentioned studies as a rationale, a group of thirty-five behavioral problem boys were matched with a group of thirty-five well-behaved boys from the same classrooms (Woody, 1964, 1968a). The boys were between the chronological ages of eight years and twelve years and eleven months. The following variables were controlled: referring teacher's definition of the terms "well-behaved" and "behavioral problem," sex and race (all were Caucasian males), grade placement, chronological age, referring school district, geographical area, and general physical condition. Although several other hypotheses were tested and will be presented later in this chapter, in regard to academic achievement it was found that the well-behaved boys scored significantly higher than the behavioral problem boys in both reading achievement and arithmetic achievement (Woody, 1964, 1968a).

There seems to be strong evidence for the belief that poor academic achievement or educational disability characterizes the behavioral problem child. There will, of course, be exceptions to this generalization. Although further replication would be advantageous, there is evidence that the degree of deficiency in achievement may correspond to the probability of behavior problems, and the causes may be either social-emotional or organic factors (or a combination). It is impossible, at this point in our knowledge from research, to answer absolutely the question as to which influences the other—that is, whether behavior problems cause the achievement discrepancy or vice versa. Subjectively, it seems that both answers are possible; for example, the former may be found with a behavioral problem child who does not study or apply his mental abilities to learning and thus develops an achievement deficit; and the latter may be illustrated by the child who has a maturational lag that influences his learning so that he is not developmentally ready to learn to read when most of his peers are, and consequently compensatory problem behaviors occur.

Regardless of which influences the other, there seems little doubt of a positive correlation between behavior and achievement. It is therefore important that this area of functioning be included in the psycho-educational evaluation; Powell and Chansky (1967) provide an overview of the evaluation of academic disabilities. Numerous group and individual achievement tests (covering such areas as reading, arithmetic, and general academic knowledge) are available. And, in general, the administration and scoring of these tests are uncomplicated and well within the scope of the classroom teacher's abilities and responsibilities.

Measures of mental abilities

While academic achievement is one of the most accessible areas for measurement, the area of mental abilities or intelligence is one of the most elusive. Controversy has continued for years, and in all likelihood will continue on into the ages, about what factors constitute general intelligence, what mental abilities should be measured, and how definitions for the key terms may be established. But the relationship between mental abilities and learning activities makes it imperative that psycho-educational evaluations include some measurement of mental abilities.

The use of mental abilities or intelligence tests, with the exception of a few group-administered tests of general intelligence, requires that the administrator have special training in theories and techniques of assessment. Because of this requirement, the responsibility for the meas-urement of mental abilities is usually assigned to the school counselor or—and more probably—the school psychologist; but, as previously sug-gested by the Allerhand (1967) study, it is possible to engage trained technicians for this assessment process.

There are two types of mental abilities or intelligence tests: those that can be used in groups and those that are administered individually to one child at a time. In general, the group-administered tests provide an over-all estimate of the child's functioning and are quick and easy to administer and score, but unfortunately they do not discriminate as finely as individually administered tests. Most psychoeducational diagnoses of behavioral problem children should, therefore, rely on the more powerful approach, the individually administered test of mental abilities. This approach, because of its diagnostic usefulness, will be treated in greatest detail in this discussion.

Logically, the primary purpose of this type of instrument should be to provide an estimate or measure of specific mental abilities and over-all level of mental functioning. Often the main concern is with obtaining an intelligence quotient (IQ), but this concept actually has relatively little value. For example, it is well known that two children may have the same IQ, but be functioning mentally in very different ways. The reason for this is that the IQ is a gross estimate of the average level of functioning, and it is composed of a variety of specific mental abilities. Thus one child may be high in one mental ability and low in another, while a second child may be low in the first mental ability and high in the second; they are functioning differently, although an average of the abilities might produce the same quotient. For this reason every edu-cator would do well to forget about intelligence quotients and give pri-ority to mental abilities scores. If a parent asks what his child's IQ is, it might very well be stated, but in turn the parent should be asked to explain to the diagnostician what the IQ means; when he tries to explain (and in most cases the parent will admit that he does not know what it means), the diagnostician should make clear the meaninglessness of an intelligence quotient and then interpret the child's mental abilities (in terms of highs and lows).

A relevant example comes to mind of a college student beginning his directed teaching. On his first day in the school, the supervising teacher showed him the intelligence quotients penciled in beside each student's name in the roll book and said something to the effect that "if they have a low IQ we overlook certain things." This practice is certainly question-able; the IQ alone is a pretty limited means of estimating a child's ability in a specific class, since what really matters is the strength of mental abilities that are especially relevant for the subject matter of the particular class. There is no reason why a child with an IQ of 100 should merit a perceptual set from the teacher any different from that for a child with an IQ of 120—especially in, as was the case in point, a music class.

Although the primary purpose of the measurement of mental abili-ties is to estimate functioning in different intellectual areas, clinical usage and subsequent research have revealed several other diagnostic possibilities. It appears that mental abilities scores are sensitive, in some cases, to specific disorders or types of problems. For example, there seem to be several signs of emotional disturbance that can be derived from mental abilities data (Kissel, 1966; Wechsler and Jaros, 1965). Thus, the profile of mental abilities can be used as a means of positing the causes of a particular behavior, and of distinguishing one type of disorder from another; this is referred to as *differential diagnosis*. It is only fair to point out that this inferred sensitivity—that is, the possibility of using mental abilities profiles to diagnose emotional problems—is widely dis-puted by psychologists. In the following discussion, emphasis will be placed on some of the clinical diagnostic techniques that are practical and that are based on mental abilities data. Obviously this type of usage is complex, and cannot be appropriately done unless the interpreter is a well-trained school diagnostician; these types of techniques are most appropriate for school, counseling, and clinical psychologists, and even then care must be exercised because, as will be pointed out, there are many potential sources of error in this approach.

In regard to making a differential diagnosis from mental abilities data, it should be emphasized that the results from research are not con-clusive. Two of the most frequently used tests, the Wechsler Intelligence Scale for Children and the Stanford-Binet Intelligence Scale, have been subjected to much research (Himelstein, 1966; Littell, 1960), but results regarding differential diagnosis have offered only limited encouragement for this type of usage. There are, however, some specific areas that merit consideration. These are: differentiating neurologically impaired and emotionally disturbed children, the relationship of over-all intellectual functioning to problem behaviors, the significance of differences between verbal and nonverbal (or performance) mental abilities, and profile analysis of mental abilities.

Neurological impairments. A number of research sources provide evidence that psychological tests, and particularly mental abilities and psychomotor tests, are capable of distinguishing persons with neurological impairment or brain injury (Gutman, 1950; Harris, Miller, Muench,

Stone, Teuber, and Zubin, 1950; Laufer and Denhoff, 1957), but it seems that the tests vary greatly in degree of success (Yates, 1954). This positive viewpoint is contradicted by others, primarily on the grounds that the use of tests in this manner is unreliable (Pond, 1960; Woody, 1964, 1967).

The main problem in using psychological tests in the diagnosis of brain damage is their inability to differentiate. Test data may indicate that there is an area of disturbance, but a question arises as to whether it is due to organic brain damage or to social-emotional disturbances (Beck, 1961). Just as observable behavior problems are unreliable indicators of the etiology of the problem, the same thing seems true of the use of psychological test data. It appears that psychological test data, such as might be derived from a mental abilities test, are of great potential value, but their value is very dependent upon the clinical skills of the examiner. Consequently, it is logical that while the diagnosing of neurological damage might well involve the use of psychological test data, other diagnostic procedures, such as an electroencephalographic or a neurological examination, should also be used.

Emotional disturbances. There are studies which indicate that mental abilities tests, as well as other more specialized psychological tests (particularly those that purport to measure factors related to personality), can be used to distinguish persons who are socially and emotionally disturbed. Several specific diagnostic signs will be reviewed later; in general, it can be stated that certain types of mental abilities are believed to reflect personal adjustment, and certain types of profiles of mental abilities are believed to reflect social and emotional problem areas.

Over-all level of intelligence. In view of the influences of behavior problems, it might be hypothesized that behavioral problem children will reflect mental functioning lower than normal children—that is, children whose behaviors are acceptable and would be considered well behaved. In other words, it may be that behavior problems interfere with the development of intellectual factors and thereby lower mental abilities.

Although many behavioral problem children, whether socially and emotionally disturbed or brain-damaged, have average or higher intelligence, most studies indicate that a sample of these children will have a lower mean intelligence level than a sample of controls or normal children. As compared to general or nonabnormal samples, research supports that scores on intelligence or mental abilities tests will be lower for emotionally handicapped (Bower, 1960), brain-damaged (Beck and Lam, 1955; Lezak and Dixon, 1964; Reed and Fitzhugh, 1966; Reitan, 1959; Ross, 1958; Young and Pitts, 1951), and behavioral problem children

(Rogers, Lilienfeld, and Pasamanick, 1954). And in the study mentioned earlier which matched pairs of behavioral problem and well-behaved boys (Woody, 1968a), it was found that the well-behaved boys scored significantly higher than the behavioral problem boys in all three intelligence quotients derived from the Wechsler Intelligence Scale for Children (WISC): Verbal Scale IQ, Performance Scale IQ, and Full Scale IQ. But there are contradictions; for example, Vane, Weitzman, and Applebaum (1966) found that problem and nonproblem children had essentially the same mean intelligence quotients on the Stanford-Binet Intelligence Scale.

On the basis of this impressive amount of research, it seems relatively safe to conclude that behavioral problem children, whether because of social-emotional or neurological causes, typically have a lower level of over-all mental functioning, as might be reflected in an intelligence quotient, than normal (nonproblem) children. Since there are children who do not conform to this position, low intelligence alone cannot, obviously, be used as a hard and fast sign of behavior problems, but it does serve to show that there is definitely an interrelationship between mental abilities and behavior.

Differences between verbal and performance abilities. Another assumption often made in the psychoeducational diagnosis of the behavioral problem child is that a difference between verbal and nonverbal (or performance) scores is a valid indication of abnormality. This belief is supported by several experimental studies. In their study with mentally handicapped subjects, Beck and Lam (1955) found that the organic group and the group of subjects who were possible organics had mean intelligence quotients on the WISC Performance Scale lower than their mean intelligence quotients on the Verbal Scale, while the nonorganics scored higher on the Performance Scale than on the Verbal Scale. Similarly, Denhoff, Laufer, and Holden (1959) believe that a Performance Scale intelligence quotient at least ten points lower than the Verbal Scale intelligence quotient on the Wechsler Intelligence Scale for Children (WISC) with children over eight years old is a good indicator of neurological impairment; but Schulman, Kaspar, and Throne (1963) caution that while this verbal-performance difference in either direction seems to be supported by research for adults, these findings may not be directly transferable to children.

Wechsler (1958) has indicated that a significant Performance Scale minus Verbal Scale pattern is frequently found with "acting-out" persons. This assumption was investigated by Fernald and Wisser (1967); in a study of juvenile delinquents, they found that the Performance-minus-Verbal score was not significantly related statistically to the degree of acting-out behavior.

Obviously there is controversy about the significance of a difference between verbal and nonverbal factors. Further complicating evidence is found in a study using electroencephalographic findings as the criteria for disturbance (that is, probable neurological impairment); the results revealed that there was no significant relationship between the abnormality of the electroencephalogram and the degree of difference between the WISC Verbal and Performance Scales with behavioral problem and well-behaved boys (Woody, 1967). Thus it appears that this diagnostic sign is still of questionable validity; it may eventually prove to be valid and of value in psychoeducational diagnosis, but further research is necessary before this can be safely assumed.

Profile analysis of mental abilities. Profile analysis of mental abilities data is assumed to be another diagnostic technique. That is, there is evidence that a mental abilities test profile, such as that of the Wechsler Intelligence Scale for Children, will provide a valid and reliable means of differential diagnosis. In regard to distinguishing persons with neurological impairments, some researchers believe that this profile analysis technique is of value (Haynes and Sells, 1963), some believe that it is of lesser value (Balthazar, 1963; Haines, 1954), and some believe that it is still unexplored (Strauss and Kephart, 1955). As will be brought out in the subsequent discussion, research has failed to ascertain the value of this diagnostic technique.

For those who support this technique, the basic assumption is that persons with particular problems will score in a unique manner on the series of mental abilities subtests. Let us briefly review a few of the supporting studies. Morris and Dozier (1961) concluded that behavioral problem children generally fall below their mean level of ability on five subtests of the Wechsler Intelligence Scale for Children—arithmetic, digit span, block design, object assembly, and coding; the most frequent combination of subtests revealing the lowest scores was: arithmetic, digit span, and block design; and they also suggest that arithmetic and digit span, with either object assembly or coding, might constitute another diagnostic grouping of subtests. Young and Pitts (1951) found that Negro congenital syphilitics had significantly different scores from the Negro controls on the following WISC subtests: information, vocabulary, coding, similarities, and object assembly. As is evidenced by these few studies, different combinations of subtests for particular conditions are supported by research, and other studies have made item and subtest analyses that provide still more possible diagnostic signs (Altus, 1956; Bakwin and Bakwin, 1960; Denhoff, Laufer, and Holden, 1959; Wunderlin and McPherson, 1962).

To summarize at this point, some researchers believe that behavior disorders, particularly those that are caused by neurological conditions, can be detected in the profile of mental abilities subtests. But it must be acknowledged that there are numerous contradictions and inconsistencies as to which subtests reflect or suggest which specific abnormal conditions. In a comparison of behavioral problem and well-behaved boys (Woody, 1967), it was found that the mean scores for the two groups were not significantly different on the following subtests of the Wechsler Intelligence Scale for Children: comprehension, picture arrangement, object assembly, and coding; but that there was a significant difference between the mean scores for the following subtests: information, arithmetic, similarities, vocabulary, digit span, picture completion, and block design (Woody, 1968a). It seems especially notable that the groups were not significantly different on the comprehension subtest, a subtest that purportedly measures the child's social-logical reasoning ability; in other words, it might be expected that behavioral problem boys would score significantly lower than well-behaved boys on this subtest, but that was not the case.

In view of the contradictions among research studies, it appears that the diagnostic assumption involving profile analysis has yet to be adequately validated. Moreover, the school or clinical diagnostician's practice of making a profile analysis by merely visually scanning the scores and then formulating a clinical opinion is highly subjective and vulnerable to error. The reliability, not to mention the validity of the underlying assumption, of this technique is certainly questionable.[1]

A similar technique has to do with the amount of variance among subtests. Some diagnosticians believe that a great deal of variance among subtest scores suggests that the child is emotionally disturbed or may have behavior problems. In the comparison of behavioral problem and well-behaved boys, there was no significant difference in median variances of Wechsler Intelligence Scale for Children subtest scores for subjects judged to have normal or borderline electroencephalograms and median variances for subjects judged to have mildly abnormal or abnormal electroencephalograms; thus it seems doubtful that subtest variance reflects neurological abnormalities (Woody, 1967). Moreover, Vane, Weitzman, and Applebaum (1966), studying matched groups of white and Negro children and matched groups of problem and nonproblem children, concluded that test scatter or subtest variance was not conclusive; although

[1] Two terms will be frequently used in this chapter: *validity* and *reliability*. *Validity* refers to how well the instrument or method does in fact measure what it purports to measure. *Reliability* refers to the consistency of the measurement; that is, whether essentially the same score would be obtained on two different administrations of the test to the same sample, with no intervening variables to influence the subjects' functioning. Reliability will be of special importance in this chapter when interpretation of diagnostic data is considered. In this situation there are two forms of reliability: *intrajudge* and *interjudge*. The first refers to how well the judge or diagnostician can duplicate his ratings or interpretations, and the second refers to how well several judges or diagnosticians agree with each other.

problem children had more scatter than nonproblem children, as much scatter was also found in certain culturally defined groups. It would appear that subtest variance or scatter may be indicative of conditions other than behavior problems and their causes, and that this technique is thus not a sensitive diagnostic sign. The technique might, however, gain additional support from further research.

To summarize the use of mental abilities test data in the psychoeducational diagnosis of behavioral problem children, there seems to be ample support for the belief that mental abilities are influenced by behavior problems, and it is crucial that some measures of mental abilities should be included in the psychoeducational survey. But, as research examples have indicated, care must be exercised to avoid going beyond what the mental abilities test is known to measure validly and reliably. In the hands of a skilled clinician even the techniques that were deemed of questionable value may be put to beneficial use, but the success of these techniques is definitely less certain than the primary objective of measuring mental abilities. Mental abilities test data, then, are extremely valuable in psychoeducational assessments, and, in fact, it is desirable to have data of this kind for almost every type of problem encountered in school psychology; but this one source of diagnostic information should not be used as the sole means of differential diagnosis.

Measures of personality

Recent years have brought increased professional interest in, and public awareness of, the assessment of personality factors. It has become the popular conception that knowledge of one's personal characteristics can be the key to improving his functioning in numerous areas. On this basis, personality assessment has been accorded a place in industrial, personnel, educational, psychological, social, and medical services. There are times, however, when one wonders whether too many persons jumped on the personality bandwagon before it was properly constructed. Personality assessment seems to be potentially valuable to professional helping processes, but it lacks empirical support for some of the relevant practices and techniques.

For most diagnosticians, both in schools and in clinics, personality assessment occupies a prominent position in their vocational duties. Although legal definitions of the role of psychologists, and the responsibilities of a given type of psychological position, such as that of the school psychologist, may to some extent delimit the types of diagnostic procedures used, personality assessment may be used in psychoeducational diagnostic services.

It should be recognized early in this discussion that attitudes and opinions toward personality assessment, and more specifically toward certain of the instruments used, are quite diversified. Some professionals feel that these techniques are extremely valuable, while others maintain that these techniques, particularly those that are projective in rationale and subjective in interpretation, are perhaps both invalid and unreliable.

Basically there are two approaches or types of instruments used in personality assessment: objective or self-report and projective. Objective or self-report instruments are standardized, much in the same manner as intelligence or achievement tests; sampling procedures reveal the distribution of given personal characteristics or personality factors in the general population. Representatives of this group might include the Edwards Personal Preference Schedule (Edwards, 1959), the Eysenck Personality Inventory (Eysenck and Eysenck, 1963), the Junior Eysenck Personality Inventory (S. Eysenck, 1965), the Maudsley Personality Inventory (Eysenck, 1959a), the Minnesota Multiphasic Personality Inventory (Hathaway and McKinley, 1951), the Sixteen Personality Factor Questionnaire (Cattell, Saunders, and Stice, 1957), and (according to some theoretical viewpoints) the Tennessee Self Concept Scale (Fitts, 1965).

Projective techniques are not statistically standardized, but various research studies have revealed what specific responses and what types of responses are common or "popular" for a particular test stimulus. In view of the professional interest in and usage of projective techniques, special attention will shortly be focused on them. Suffice it to say at this point that personality assessment by projective procedures, even when a quantitative scoring procedure is used, is much more subjective or clinical in nature than assessment by the objective or self-report instruments. Projective instruments include the Children's Apperception Test (Bellak and Bellak, 1949), the Thematic Apperception Test (Murray, 1943), the Blacky Pictures (Blum, 1950), the Rorschach ink blots (Rorschach, 1951), and many others. The essential difference between these two approaches seems to be the question of whether personality assessment should be based on clinical or statistical prediction.

Even the diagnostic methods that provide permanently recorded, quantifiable data, and are labeled "objective," actually involve subjectivity when the results are interpreted. The process of clinically interpreting so-called objective measures of any personal characteristics introduces the possibility of subjectivity and consequently the possibility of varying degrees of reliability due to the judgmental processes, which are not quantifiable.

Projective methods of assessing personality characteristics or, more correctly, methods of deriving *inferences* or *assumptions* about personality characteristics are currently receiving wide attention and acceptance. The rationale for projective methods is that the subject, such as a behavioral problem child, will, when presented with nebulously defined or unstructured stimuli, react perceptually in a manner that will convey or reveal his underlying personality factors. For example, the Rorschach method employs a series of ink blots which do not reflect any exact item or theme, although there are popular or fairly common perceptual responses to specific aspects of each blot; the subject's verbal response to what he perceives in the whole or part of the blot will be a projection of his personality composite. Similarly, the Thematic Apperception Test (TAT) presents the subject with a series of pictures of scenes or of persons engaged in some activity, but the pictures are not clearly defined. For example, it might not be clear whether the persons in the picture are males or females, whether they are young or old, or whether they are behaving in an affectionate or hostile manner. Thus the subject's perceptions of the figures in the pictures, their actions, their relationships, and numerous other factors are used by the skilled clinician to draw inferences about the subject's personality.

One of the primary problems in using projective techniques is that methods of interpretation vary. There are often several scoring procedures for the same test, and there are usually several possible theoretical positions for making clinical or subjective interpretations. With the Thematic Apperception Test, Murray (1943) seems to emphasize the characteristics of the central figures, the forces acting on them, and the outcomes of the stories; Arnold (1949) categorizes the data according to the interpersonal relationships reflected in the subject's responses; and there are numerous other variants for interpretation (Anderson and Anderson, 1951; Murstein, 1963, 1965). Basically, the methods for evaluating responses to a picture-type projective instrument might be divided into the categories of nonquantitative and quantitative. Nonquantitative evaluation is exemplified by Murray's (1943) system; his analysis is content-oriented, focusing particularly on the characteristics of the hero in the story, the needs of the hero, the environmental forces, the outcomes, the interplay of themes within a story, and the interests, sentiments, and relationships (Kleinmuntz, 1967). Murstein (1963) and Wyatt (1947) provide a more complete overview of nonquantitative, content-oriented approaches. When quantitative procedures are used, numerical ratings are made of the presence of specific factors within the stories. For example, Eron (1950, Eron, Terry, and Callahan, 1950) makes ratings of the emotional tone in the stories, and McClelland (1958) places major emphasis on rating the achievement motive within the stories. Normative data have been collected for most of these systems—for example, Eron (1950).

Two of the projective instruments that are frequently used with behavioral problem children are the Children's Apperception Test (CAT) and the Blacky Pictures. Both of these instruments employ a series of pictures of animals representing family figures, and they are designed to elicit the thematic content of fantasies regarding the child's perceptions of familial relationships. The child's perceived feelings of his own family's structure and dynamics will be reflected, via projection, in the content of the stories that he tells about the family groups of animals in the pictures. For example, if a behavioral problem child who is being tested places emphasis on the way that the central animal, which will probably be the animal nearest to the age or family position of the child, receives poor treatment or negative attitudes within the animal family, an inference might be drawn that the child perceives himself to be placed below one or more of his siblings in the preferential treatment or esteem received from the parents, or that he is not receiving an adequate amount of affection and security. If this type of inference proves to be valid, then the diagnostician will have derived some valuable guidelines from the psychoeducational assessment that will aid him in his attempts to help the behavioral problem child.

On the basis of the rationale for the Thematic Apperception Test, Solomon, Klein, and Starr (1966) have begun work on the School Apperception Method (SAM). This method involves a collection of pictures depicting ambiguous school scenes, designed for children, and requiring that the child make up a story about each picture. The method has continued to be developed and revised (Solomon and Starr, 1967), and normative and validation data are being obtained. At this point, the procedure could be used only for subjective content analyses, but if and when experimentation validates its components, it may be very useful for assessing personality and learning difficulties of behavioral problem children.

The use of projective techniques in the assessment of personality requires that the diagnostician be highly trained in general psychology, theories of normal and abnormal personality, and clinical procedures. These techniques are not within the realm of the classroom teacher, and in most cases will not be included in the academic training of school counselors; in fact, not all school psychologists will be academically prepared to use these techniques, although they will be more likely to have the necessary training than classroom teachers or school counselors. Although training is equally important for the proper use of all measures of personality factors, including the objective instruments, the skills of the diagnostician are especially crucial in the use of projective instruments. These skills are strongly related to the reliability of the method and the interpretation procedures and to the validity of the principle of projection (Beller, 1962; Wallen, 1956).

Although there are many disciples of projective techniques, there are also those who maintain that projective instruments and methods are unreliable and lacking in validity. Indeed, Eysenck (1959b) holds that there is such adequate evidence regarding the lack of validity and the poor reliability of projective tests that their use, except in research, cannot be defended. At present, however, this position seems to represent

one end of the continuum of opinions about projective personality assessment procedures, while at the other end of the continuum are those who
believe that these techniques are infallible and can provide almost every
type of information that could be clinically useful to the diagnostician—
even to measuring intelligence! It seems that projective techniques, like
so many diagnostic techniques, are still unproved. There is evidence that
they do provide the talented clinician with a means for gaining diagnostic
information, but likewise there is evidence that suggests that the usefulness is a function of the clinician's skills and not of the instrument.

In conclusion, one must reemphasize that the appraisal of personal
characteristics or personality factors involves a very demanding set of
processes. There are so many pitfalls within personality assessment that it
cannot be taken lightly; it is a complex task, and the results can have
extreme importance to all concerned. If properly performed, however,
the assessment of personality can provide some of the most valuable diagnostic information that it is possible to derive, and this information can
be used to great benefit in the services for behavioral problem children.

Other psychological tests

Tests of achievement, mental abilities, and personality have been
cited as possible contributing sources of information for the psychoeducational diagnosis. There are also, however, tests for a number of other
areas of mental functioning. These include instruments to measure vocational interests, manual dexterity, values and attitudes, aptitudes, and
psychomotor ability.

All of these areas, and other areas not named here, are of potential
value to the psychoeducational diagnosis. Their appropriateness depends
upon the specific needs of the child being evaluated. One paramount
recommendation is: Do not adhere strictly to a set number of diagnostic
instruments. As the psychoeducational evaluation progresses, use cues
from the foregoing procedures to determine which other diagnostic procedures should be used; and always keep the plan flexible and subject to
change. In other words, the exact components of a psychoeducational
evaluation should depend upon the referral comments for the beginning
of the appraisal, but the total appraisal format will evolve as the survey
progresses. There are school systems and school diagnosticians that always
hold to a specific set of tests. Although this practice may serve to screen
the children—that is, to identify the ones who may most need further
diagnostic services—this type of administrative rigidity hardly allows for
making the assessment an individually structured service.

One other major group of diagnostic techniques merits consideration: visual-motor tests. Although there are many tests in this category,

two examples seem to be the most notable for our purposes: the Bender Visual-Motor Gestalt Test and the human-figure drawings.

Most visual-motor tests are designed primarily to estimate one particular perceptual skill. The perceptual skill being measured does, however, involve psychological processes, so in most cases other, secondary diagnostic signs may also be derived from the instrument being used. From this single perceptual factor, with its secondary factors, the diagnostician makes an assumption about the subject's mental functioning and, in some instances, his neurological development.

One of the best-known and most frequently used visual-motor tests is the Bender Visual-Motor Gestalt Test (Bender, 1938), and it has proven to be successful in differentiating various types of disorders. Its efficacy has been supported by many studies (for example, Goldberg, 1959; Inglis, Colwell, and Post, 1960; Throne, Kaspar, and Schulman, 1964), and some even believe that it is probably the best supporting test for the diagnosis of organicity or neurological damage (Lawrence, 1960).

Essentially, the Bender Visual-Motor Gestalt Test might be described as follows: the child is asked to draw a series of designs, presented to him on individual cards; from the way in which the child draws the designs, the diagnostician, using clinical judgment, makes diagnostic assumptions. Research has shown that the way in which the designs are placed on the page, the sequence, the accuracy of each design, and numerous other signs can be used as clinical clues to the child's visual-motor, perceptual, and neurological development, and some clinicians even believe that this type of test is sensitive to emotional instability, intelligence, and personality factors (Murstein, 1965). This type of instrument, even though there are several possible scoring procedures, is subjective in nature, and the interpretation of the child's reproductions depends greatly upon the clinical competency of the diagnostician. Therefore, this instrument is a clinical tool that is usually appropriate only to psychologists who have had the type of relevant training that would allow a realistic understanding of its capabilities and limitations. Used properly, however, it may indeed be a beneficial adjunct to the psychoeducational evaluation, particularly for estimating visual-motor perceptual development. In addition, there are a number of other, similar single-factor visual-motor tests or perceptual tests which have relatively strong research support for their clinical usefulness, especially for the drawing of inferences regarding neurological impairments.

Human-figure drawings constitute another type of psychological test. Depending upon the basic administrative procedure to be used, the subject is requested to draw a person, and sometimes other objects involved with the person, such as a house and tree, to allow the noting of the way the child sees a "person" in relation to other objects in his immediate environment. Although various investigators have originated individual names—such as Draw-A-Man (Goodenough, 1926)—this type of test will be referred to generically as human-figure drawings.

The procedure—asking the child to draw a picture of a person—is simple enough; the complexity comes with the interpretation. Originally, emphasis was on using these drawings as a means of estimating the over-all intellectual functioning level, and in fact intelligence quotients can be derived by noting what details the child includes in the drawing and comparing them and their quality to the productions made by the stand-ardization sample subjects; by finding what mental age the child's draw-ing is compatible with and comparing that with his chronological age, an estimate of intelligence can be made (Goodenough, 1926).

Vane (1967) has pointed out that the different versions of this method do not have the same amount of reliability and validity; for example, she found that the correlations between the Harris (1963) version and the Stanford-Binet Intelligence Scale were lower than the correlations be-tween the Goodenough (1926) version and the same intelligence scale.

As the human-figure drawing test has gained in acceptance, research has expanded its uses. Now many psychologists believe that the drawings can be interpreted in much the same way as would a response to a projec-tive personality instrument. And indeed studies have shown that distinct valid emotional indicators can be derived from human-figure drawings to separate different types of children, such as emotionally disturbed or behavioral problem children from well-adjusted children (Koppitz, 1966a) and shy children from aggressive children (Koppitz, 1966b); but it is also known that these indicators vary in reliability (Hammer and Kaplan, 1966).

Thus there is evidence to support the claim that a child's drawings of human beings and possibly other objects can be used to make assumptions about his intellectual abilities and personality. This requires, however, that the assessor be familiar with a method of appraisal; for example, how detailed a drawing must be to be compatible with a child's chronological age and what certain aspects attributed to the drawing by the child might suggest about his psychosocial adjustment.

Watson (1967) found that impressions based on human-figure draw-ings can, depending upon the skill or sophistication of the diagnostician, correlate significantly with clinicians' over-all diagnostic impressions; but he concludes that psychologists may tend to overestimate the extent to which drawing distortions are useful. As with other psychomotor tests, the human-figure drawing method can, in the hands of a well-trained clini-cian, be beneficial as one *component* of the psychoeducational assessment.

This is a good time to emphasize that single-factor tests, such as the Bender Visual-Motor Gestalt Test and the human-figure drawing test, can be accurate in a differential diagnosis, but there are many impending considerations. In general, it is believed that the multi-factored test, such as the Wechsler Intelligence Scale for Children, has a stronger capacity for accurately differentiating; that is, the multi-factor test includes measures from several psychological sources and thereby allows for a more comprehensive view of the person's functioning (Haynes and Sells, 1963; Yates, 1954).

Ancillary Psychomedical Diagnostic Services

A school diagnostician will initially see many children for an evaluation who will need referral to another diagnostician, perhaps to someone who is outside of the school system. In making these referrals, one practical question will be: What services are available? In some communities referrals to another diagnostician might be limited to the local general medical practitioner, someone who is typically quite minimally prepared to contribute greatly to a *psychological* assessment. But there are other medical services that can prove to be invaluable to the school diagnostician, and referral to them must definitely be administratively possible. The primary sources of psychomedical diagnostic services that would be potentially useful for behavioral problem children include psychiatrists, neurologists, pediatricians, and electroencephalographers.

The psychiatric examination

The psychiatrist is one of the foremost collaborators with psycho-educational diagnosticians. And his involvement is especially important for the diagnosis and treatment of behavioral problem and emotionally disturbed children. Although the psychiatrist's functions are in many ways similar to those of the psychologist, and particularly those of the clinical psychologist, there is one major difference: the psychologist is a behavioral scientist dealing with psychological problems, and when he holds a doctorate it is a Doctor of Philosophy degree; the psychiatrist is a medical physician dealing with psychological problems, and he holds a Doctor of Medicine degree.

Since he is a medical physician with advanced training in psychiatry, the psychiatrist is the best person for combining medicine and psychology. Although the psychotherapy conducted by psychiatrists and psychologists is remarkably similar in content (Strupp, 1955), the psychiatrist has the added responsibility of the total medical care of the person and may, therefore, prescribe drugs or some other type of medical service that will benefit the psychiatric treatment of the patient.

In the diagnostic stage, however, there is a common ground between psychiatrists and psychologists, and in many cases they will work together on the diagnosis. For example, the psychiatrist would conduct a psychiatric interview and formulate several diagnostic hypotheses; next the person would be seen by the psychologist for a psychological examination, perhaps involving some of the tests described earlier; and then the psychiatrist and the psychologist would compare their findings. In this last process, the psychiatrist would present his judgments based on the psychiatric interview and the psychologist would present the psychological test data and his clinical impressions. This interchange would allow for confirmation or contradiction of the psychiatrist's and psychologist's initial diagnostic hypotheses and might well lead them to create new hypotheses; and it might then be necessary to secure even more diagnostic information from other professional sources.

One thing that should be emphasized is that psychiatrists and psychologists are in no way competitive. They each have their own professional skills, and for either to assume that he is capable of performing the others' duties is unjustified. As most community mental health programs will attest, it is commonly accepted that both the psychiatrist's and the psychologist's roles can be enhanced and made more effective by cooperation and collaboration. It is on this basis that many psychiatrists and psychologists are in private practice together or provide interdisciplinary services in a mental health unit. Since psychiatric services are of critical importance, an increasing number of school systems are arranging for a psychiatrist to serve as a consultant with the psychoeducational personnel, or a close liaison is formed between the schools and the local community mental health center.

The neurological examination

The neurologist is also a medical physician; he holds a Doctor of Medicine degree and has had advanced training in neurology. His primary concern is with the neuroanatomical structures and their influences on the organism and on behavior. Thus, if a behavioral problem child reveals behavioral signs or produces responses during the psychological survey or has a medical history compatible with neurological impairment or brain damage, referral to a neurologist would serve as a source for validating this diagnostic possibility.

The pediatric examination

The pediatrician is another medical physician, holding a Doctor of Medicine degree, who has received advanced training in pediatrics. His services are especially valuable with children who seem to have developmental difficulties. In his examination, the pediatrician investigates the physiological aspects of developmental patterns and functioning, and with this information he is in a position to make recommendations regarding diagnosis and treatment of the child. For example, certain children who reflect the hyperkinetic syndrome (as described in Chapter 2) might be referred to the pediatrician, and on the basis of his examination they might be placed on a medication that would help control their behaviors in school. Although medications can readily effect physiological changes that will result in observable behavioral changes, in many cases the medication will have to be supplemented with other therapeutic procedures. Some medications control but do not cure, and such medically induced controls might only be appropriate for a given period of time; in the meantime efforts should be made, perhaps by behavioral modification techniques, to develop nonmedical behavioral controls.

As one might gather from the last statement, the services of the pediatrician are frequently most effective when they are part of an interdisciplinary program. Thus it is quite common to have, for example, a pediatrician, a school psychologist, and a school social worker all working together to help a behavioral problem child.

The electroencephalographic examination

The clinical examination by electroencephalography, usually called EEG, may be provided by a medical physician or a psychologist or some other type of scientist. That is, some electroencephalographers are psychiatrists or neurologists or some other medical specialists and hold a Doctor of Medicine degree, but others may be psychologists, physiologists, or neuroanatomists and hold a Doctor of Philosophy degree. But they have all had postdoctoral training in electroencephalography. The services are usually available from a centrally located hospital, and referrals typically must come from the child's family medical physician.

There is much research to document the statement that clinical electroencephalography is very valuable in the diagnosis of behavioral problem children with all types of etiological backgrounds. It seems particularly appropriate for detecting neurological impairments, such as might be present in a child with minimal brain dysfunction.

Electroencephalography is a procedure for recording the electrical activity of the brain. This technique was first described by Canton in 1875, when he detected the spontaneous electrical activity in the brains of rabbits and monkeys, but since that time there have been many theoretical modifications and technical refinements which, when combined with the vast amount of research that has been generated, have led to a well-established scientific procedure for use with humans. The electroencephalogram is the printed record of this measurement; it is in the form of numerous channels or rows of wavy and jagged lines that, to the trained electroencephalographer, are representations of neurological activities. The interpretation of the electroencephalogram is based on four factors: the amplitude or height of the waves, which is referred to as voltage or potential; the frequency, whether fast, medium, or slow; the regularity or irregularity; and the symmetry or asymmetry of the record. Maturation may have a significant influence, but a relatively stable, well-organized EEG measurement may be achieved by the age of eight or ten years. Distinctive patterns are believed to reflect particular conditions of the brain, such as an epileptic or convulsive condition; and special stimuli —for example, light, sound, or drugs—may be used to elicit activity that cannot be recorded when the brain is at rest. Artifacts or false (invalid) signs may be produced in the record by extraneous sources of stimuli, such as gritting the teeth, snapping fingers, or noises outside of the room; but the skilled electroencephalographer can readily recognize these in the record (Glaser, 1963).

Although there is a trend toward using computers or electronic analyzers for interpretation, for all practical purposes much of the value of electroencephalography is dependent upon the clinical judgment of a single electroencephalographer. Since subjectivity is intrinsic to clinical judgment, intrajudge reliability and, moreover, interjudge reliability are two significant factors. In the case of intrajudge reliability, the question is: Does the electroencephalographer judge the EEG the same way twice, or are the data ambiguous enough and his skills unstable enough to produce differences in his interpretations? And with interjudge reliability we might ask: Would two or more electroencephalographers read or interpret the same electroencephalogram in the same manner? Unfortunately, there are very few systematic investigations of reliability in clinical electroencephalography. It has been found that a single electroencephalographer does indeed seem to vary in the way he views an EEG record (Woody, 1966), and a study of interjudge reliability revealed that several electroencephalographers may differ in their judgments of a variety of factors that constitute the bases for a diagnostic interpretation of an electroencephalogram; for example, when asked to classify the EEG's as either "normal" or "abnormal," a group of three electroencephalographers had complete agreement for only 53 percent of the records (Woody, 1968b). In other words, there is evidence that intrajudge and interjudge reliabilities may vary according to the factors being judged in electroencephalography. This research does not suggest that electroencephalography is of no value; on the contrary, it may be of great value in differential diagnosis. But it does seem that unless reliabilities and, furthermore, the validity of some of the cues or signs for interpretations are checked for a given study, the results are of questionable value. In the case of the individual diagnosis, such as with a behavioral problem child,

the interpretation of the child's electroencephalogram by one electroencephalographer should be viewed as a subjective judgment of the record, which may or may not agree with the interpretations of other electroencephalographers.

Numerous studies support the view that electroencephalography is
an important adjunct to the diagnosis of behavioral problem children.
Bakwin and Bakwin (1960) estimate that 60 percent of children with behavior disorders have abnormal EEG's, whereas only about 12 percent of
the general population have EEG's that would be classified outside of the
normal range. Kennard (1959), in a study of children admitted to a mental hospital, found that 83 percent of the children with a history of and
behavior patterns suggesting organicity revealed a strong positive correlation with EEG abnormality; 47 percent of the suspected organics had
abnormal EEG records; and only 29 percent of the nonorganics had EEG
abnormalities. Aird and Yamamoto (1966), in a study of behavior disorders in childhood, found that 49 percent of the behavioral problem subjects had abnormal EEG's. And in a study of brain-injured and hyperactive children, Cruickshank, Bentzen, Ratzeburg, and Tannhauser (1961)
found that, of the thirty-five children who received EEG examinations,
60 percent had abnormal EEG records. Glaser (1963) believes that the
over-all research suggests that children exhibiting behavior disorders
show a high incidence of EEG abnormality, varying from 40 to 75 percent; but Henry (1944) cautions that there is a need for more precise
definitions of what is meant by "abnormal" waves and records in research
dealing with behavioral problem and delinquent children.

Although these studies have found a higher percentage of EEG
abnormality with behavioral problem children than with the general
population of children, one area of contradictory research should be
noted. There are studies that show that persons with no evidence of any
kind of neurological abnormality will have abnormal EEG's, with the
percentages running from 10 to 15 percent of normal persons (Bucy, 1947;
Ford, 1960). And Gibbs, Rich, Fois, and Gibbs (1960), in a study of mentally retarded subjects, suggest that although the individual may be abnormal in some clinical aspect, his EEG will not necessarily be abnormal.
In other words, electroencephalography may not always be sensitive to
the over-all condition of an individual; perhaps this is due in part to
factors related to the reliability of the interpretations, as discussed earlier,
or perhaps it is due in part to the lack of sensitivity of electroencephalography to certain conditions or components of human functioning.

In a research project with thirty-five behavioral problem boys
matched with thirty-five well-behaved boys, the coded electroencephalograms were judged to be in one of the following categories: normal,
borderline, mildly abnormal, abnormal, and markedly abnormal (Woody,

1964, 1967).[2] It should be noted that this five-category approach allows much more refinement than the simple dichotomy of normal and abnormal. Table 4–1 shows the rather unexpected results; the well-behaved

TABLE 4–1. EEG Ratings

Group	Normal	Border-line	Mildly Abnormal	Abnormal	Markedly Abnormal
Well-Behaved	4	11	12	8	0
Behavioral Problem	4	11	12	8	0

and behavioral problem groups contributed identical numbers to each category on the EEG rating scale. The fact that there was no significant difference in EEG abnormality between the two groups certainly raises a question about the validity of the belief that behavioral problem children have more abnormal EEG's than the general population of children; this is especially true since these studies employed more controls within the research design, such as checking the reliability of the electroencephalographer's interpretations, than some of the other studies that have provided the bases for this questionable diagnostic belief.

In summary, clinical electroencephalography as a diagnostic technique is extremely valuable in the assessment and diagnosis of behavioral problem children, especially those thought to have neurological impairments—that is, minimal brain dysfunction. Therefore, school diagnosticians should be prepared to initiate referrals, usually through and in cooperation with a medical physician, for an electroencephalographic examination; this is a diagnostic source that must not be neglected. However, the diagnostician must also be prepared to use the electroencephalographic findings as just one of the components of the diagnosis; that is, the fact that electroencephalography appears to be an impressive scientific and medically aligned diagnostic procedure should not blind the diagnostician to its limitations. As with other diagnostic techniques, electroencephalography can make a real and meaningful contribution to the diagnosis of behavioral problem children, but it does not provide an infallible criterion.

[2] The electroencephalograms were coded and randomly stacked. Thus the electroencephalographer knew only the recording procedure, the chronological age, and the sex; he did not know the reasons for the children's referrals nor whether they were well-behaved or behavioral problem children.

DIAGNOSIS IN PERSPECTIVE

In the first four chapters, consideration was given to several stages: definitions of behavioral problem children, characteristics and causes, detection and referral, and psychoeducational diagnosis. As we approach the discussion of actual means for modifying unacceptable behaviors, it seems appropriate to recapitulate some of the ideas set forth in the previous chapters, and particularly to place their culminating point, psychoeducational diagnosis, in its proper perspective.

In considering the definition of behavioral problem children, it was stated that such a child was one who had adjustment difficulties in regard to the socially acceptable norms for behavior, and that these difficulties would in turn influence his own and his peers' academic progress and interpersonal relations. It is important to stress that behavioral problem children should not be thought of as an absolute, permanently determined group of children; rather, every child has problems at some time in his life, and it is quite likely that the problems will be manifested in overt behaviors that may, in part, be unacceptable and fulfill the definition of "behavioral problem children." In other words, the use of the term "behavioral problem children" is for purposes of setting the boundaries of discussion and providing a common frame of reference; it is not meant to convey that behavioral problem children should be permanently placed in the category of exceptionality. Further, in the discussion on behavioral characteristics and the possible causes for problem behaviors, there was evident extreme variance in professional opinions and the results of research; this led to the conclusion that observable behaviors alone could not be used to diagnose problems.

The processes of psychoeducational assessment and diagnosis are important for understanding the child and for developing guidelines for helping him. In view of the research evidence cited in this chapter, it seems appropriate to make the following recommendations:

1. Psychoeducational assessments and diagnoses necessitate special advanced training for diagnosticians. Except for contributing relevant materials obtained in the classroom (such as from a group-administered achievement test), the teacher will not usually have the responsibility of psychoeducational assessments and diagnoses; this responsibility will fall on the school psychologist and, to some degree, the school counselor.

2. A comprehensive psychoeducational assessment should usually be interdisciplinary in nature. Thus the behavioral problem child might be seen at the diagnostic stage by the school social worker, the school counselor, and the school

psychologist (and perhaps by other school personnel, such as the speech and hearing therapist), and may then, on the basis of inferences derived from the diagnostic information obtained by school personnel, be referred to some other professional person who provides specialized diagnostic services. Such referral sources could feasibly include: clinical psychologists, psychiatrists, neurologists, pediatricians, and electroencephalographers.

3. The parents of the child should at all times be involved in the planning of diagnostic services; their cooperation is imperative. Moreover, the parents must be provided with a thoughtful and meaningful interpretation of the diagnostic results. The diagnostic services are of little value if the parents are not able, through lack of understanding, to support the psychoeducational recommendations in their relationships with their children. And the child should be given an understandable orientation to the proceedings.

4. The diagnostic techniques, procedures, or tests that constitute the survey should be determined on an individual basis. A set test battery should not be the exclusive source for diagnostic information. Rather, after initial diagnostic impressions have been formulated from screening procedures, the ensuing composite diagnostic techniques, the survey, should be based upon what appear to be the needs of that particular child.

5. It should be recognized that single-factor tests are designed to measure but one factor. Certain clinical practices have extended the purposes of this type of test—to the making of differential diagnoses, for example—but research evidence suggests that this is an unreliable procedure. It seems that multi-factor tests provide a much stronger basis for a differential diagnosis.

6. It must be remembered that diagnostic data, even from the most reputable of techniques and the most highly trained diagnosticians, are not infallible. There is the possibility of error in virtually every diagnostic procedure. When clinical judgment of a diagnostician is involved in the interpretation, the matter of reliability is especially crucial.

7. Diagnostic data should be used for descriptive purposes, not for permanently categorizing a child. In other words, the informational data derived from various diagnostic procedures are measures of the child's functioning at that particular time, and indeed the measurements are usually of a specific type or types of functioning and generalization of these results to the child's over-all functioning is based on assumptions, not indisputable facts.

8. Diagnostic data should not be used exclusively to determine the treatment program of the child. The diagnostician and the other cooperating personnel, when deciding what approach or what technique should be used in trying to help the child attain more satisfactory behavior, should employ the diagnostic data as guidelines, but professional opinions and ideas based on other information (such as what services the parents prefer that the child be offered and what is practically available) must be incorporated in the treatment program.

9. Diagnosis should be an on-going process. Regardless of how many diagnostic procedures have gone into the psychoeducational evaluation, it is necessary to continually assess the child's condition, and a reassessment might lead to a modification of the previously determined treatment program that would provide the child with even better services.

10. To be complete, the psychoeducational assessment must not only describe the child's functioning at that particular point in time, but must also state the possible causes of the conditions and set forth recommendations for improving the child's functioning. Further, it may be helpful to make a prognosis regarding the probable outcome of treatment, but this is always only learned speculation and should be subject to being proved wrong.

These ten recommendations are necessarily general, but adherence to them should result in relatively effective psychoeducational diagnostic services.

Ensuing chapters will consider means of modifying problem behaviors. The psychoeducational assessment and diagnosis play an important part in the over-all quest to help behavioral problem children. The data collected in the survey can be used to posit what behaviors should be coped with first and what secondary ramifications might be present that would influence the treatment service. As might be inferred from the ten recommendations given above, assessment practices are not the ends in themselves; they serve the function of adding scientific clarity to the assumptions on which treatment efforts are based. Assessment techniques can also contribute to estimating the effects of a particular treatment. Greenspoon and Gersten (1967) elaborate on psychological testing from the point of view of the final goal—behavioral modification.

As the reader moves now to the second part of this book, which is devoted to theories and techniques of behavioral modification, he should have a fairly solid understanding of the psychology of behavioral problem children. Obviously, there is still much that needs to be said, and this book alone can hardly guarantee a comprehensive knowledge of the subject. The contents of Part I should, however, provide the platform on which to build, and should give adequate support for actions to help the behavioral problem child at the various stages. Efforts for detection, referral, and diagnosis would be of little value if they were not allowed to culminate in the provision of services to help the child attain more acceptable behaviors; thus we progress to the processes of behavioral modification.

REFERENCES

Aird, R. B., and Yamamoto, T. Behavior disorders of childhood. *Electroencephalography and Clinical Neurophysiology*, 1966, 21:148-156.
Allerhand, M. E. Effectiveness of parents of Head Start children as ad-

ministrators of psychological tests. *Journal of Consulting Psychology,* 1967, 31:286-290.

Altus, Grace T. A WISC profile for retarded readers. *Journal of Consulting Psychology,* 1956, 20:1955-1956.

Anderson, H. H., and Anderson, Gladys L. (Eds.). *An introduction to projective techniques.* Englewood Cliffs, N.J.: Prentice-Hall, 1951.

Arnold, M. B. A demonstration analysis of the TAT in a clinical setting. *Journal of Abnormal and Social Psychology,* 1949, 44:97-111.

Bakwin, H., and Bakwin, Ruth M. *Clinical management of behavior disorders in children* (2nd ed.). Philadelphia: W. B. Saunders, 1960.

Balthazar, E. E. Cerebral unilateralization in chronic epileptic cases: the Wechsler object assembly subtest. *Journal of Clinical Psychology,* 1963, 19:169-171.

Beck, H. S. Detecting psychological symptoms of brain injury. *Exceptional Children,* 1961, 28:57-62.

Beck, H. S., and Lam, R. L. Use of the WISC in predicting organicity. *Journal of Clinical Psychology,* 1955, 11:154-158.

Bellak, L., and Bellak, Sonya S. *Manual: Children's Apperception Test.* New York: C. P. S. Company, 1949.

Beller, E. K. *Clinical process: the assessment of data in childhood personality disorders.* New York: Free Press of Glencoe, 1962.

Bender, Lauretta. *A visual motor gestalt test and its clinical use.* Research Monograph No. 3. New York: American Orthopsychiatric Association, 1938.

Blum, G. S. *Manual: the Blacky Pictures.* New York: Psychological Corporation, 1950.

Bower, E. M. *Early identification of emotionally handicapped children in school.* Springfield, Ill.: C. C Thomas, 1960.

Browning, R. M. Effects of irrelevant peripheral visual stimuli on discrimination learning in minimally brain-damaged children. *Journal of Consulting Psychology,* 1967, 31:371-376.

Bucy, P. C. The clinical use of electroencephalography. *Journal of Neurosurgery,* 1947, 14:442-447.

Buros, O. K. (Ed.). *The sixth mental measurements yearbook.* Highland Park, N.J.: Gryphon Press, 1965.

Cattell, R. B., Saunders, D. R., and Stice, G. *Handbook: Sixteen Personality Factor Questionnaire.* Champaign, Ill.: Institute for Personality and Ability Testing, 1957.

Cruickshank, W. M., Bentzen, Frances A., Ratzeburg, F. H., and Tannhauser, Miriam T. *A teaching method for brain-injured and hyperactive children.* Syracuse, N.Y.: Syracuse University Press, 1961.

Denhoff, E., Laufer, M. W., and Holden, R. H. The syndromes of cerebral dysfunction. *Journal of the Oklahoma State Medical Association,* 1959, 52:360-366.

Edwards, A. L. *Manual: Edwards Personal Preference Schedule* (rev. ed.). New York: Psychological Corporation, 1959.

Eron, L. D. A normative study of the Thematic Apperception Test. *Psychological Monographs,* 1950, 64, No. 315.

Eron, L. D., Terry, Dorothy, and Callahan, R. The use of rating scales for emotional tone of TAT stories. *Journal of Consulting Psychology,* 1950, 14:473-478.

Eysenck, H. J. *Manual: Maudsley Personality Inventory.* London, Eng.: University of London Press, 1959. (a)

Eysenck, H. J. Personality tests: 1950-1955. In G. W. T. H. Fleming (Ed.), *Recent progress in psychiatry.* London, Eng.: J. & A. Churchill, 1959, 118-159. (b)

Eysenck, H. J., and Eysenck, Sybil B. G. *Manual: the Eysenck Personality Inventory.* San Diego: Educational and Industrial Testing Service, 1963.

Eysenck, Sybil B. G. *Manual of the Junior Eysenck Personality Inventory.* London, Eng.: University of London Press, 1965.

Farquhar, W. W. *A comprehensive study of the motivational factors underlying achievement of eleventh grade high school students.* Office of Research and Publications, Michigan State University, Cooperative Research Project No. 846, Office of Education, U. S. Department of Health, Education and Welfare, 1963.

Fernald, P. S., and Wisser, R. E. Using WISC Verbal-Performance discrepancy to predict degree of acting out. *Journal of Clinical Psychology,* 1967, 23:92-93.

Fitts, W. H. *Manual: Tennessee Self Concept Scale.* Nashville, Tenn.: Counselor Recordings and Tests, 1965.

Fitzsimons, Marian J. The predictive value of teachers' referrals. In M. Krugman (Ed.), *Orthopsychiatry in the schools.* New York: American Orthopsychiatric Association, 1958, 149-153.

Ford, F. R. *Diseases of the nervous system: in infancy, childhood, and adolescence* (4th ed.). Springfield, Ill.: C. C Thomas, 1960.

Frierson, E. C., and Barbe, W. B. (Eds.). *Educating children with learning disabilities: selected readings.* New York: Appleton-Century-Crofts, 1967.

Gibbs, E. L., Rich, C. L., Fois, A., and Gibbs, F. A. Electroencephalographic study of mentally retarded persons. *American Journal of Mental Deficiency,* 1960, 65:236-247.

Glaser, G. H. (Ed.). *EEG and behavior.* New York: Basic Books, 1963.

Goldberg, L. R. The effectiveness of clinicians' judgments: the diagnosis of organic brain damage from the Bender-Gestalt Test. *Journal of Consulting Psychology,* 1959, 23:25-33.

Goldman, L. *Using tests in counseling.* New York: Appleton-Century-Crofts, 1961.

Goodenough, Florence L. *Measurement of intelligence by drawings.* Yonkers-on-Hudson, N.Y.: World Book, 1926.

Gordon, E. M., and Thomas, A. Children's behavioral style and the teacher's appraisal of their intelligence. *Journal of School Psychology,* 1967, 5:292-300.

Greenspoon, J., and Gersten, C. D. A new look at psychological testing: psychological testing from the standpoint of a behaviorist. *American Psychologist,* 1967, 22:848-853.

Gutman, Bridgette. The application of the Wechsler-Bellevue Scale in the diagnosis of organic brain disorders. *Journal of Clinical Psychology,* 1950, 6:195-198.

Haines, Miriam S. Test performance of preschool children with and without organic brain pathology. *Journal of Consulting Psychology,* 1954, 18:371-374.

Hammer, M., and Kaplan, A. M. The reliability of children's human figure drawings. *Journal of Clinical Psychology,* 1966, 22:316-319.

Harris, D. B. *Children's drawings as measures of intellectual maturity.* New York: Harcourt, Brace, and World, 1963.

Harris, R. E., Miller, J. G., Muench, G. A., Stone, L. J., Teuber, H. L., and Zubin, J. *Recent advances in diagnostic psychological testing.* Springfield, Ill.: C. C Thomas, 1950.

Hathaway, S. R., and McKinley, J. C. *The Minnesota Multiphasic Personality Inventory manual* (rev. ed.). New York: Psychological Corporation, 1951.

Haynes, J. R., and Sells, S. B. Assessment of organic brain damage by psychological tests. *Psychological Bulletin,* 1963, 60:316-326.

Henry, C. A. Electroencephalograms of normal children. *Monographs of the Society for Research in Child Development,* 1944, 9, Serial No. 39.

Himelstein, P. Research with the Stanford-Binet, Form L-M: the first five years. *Psychological Bulletin,* 1966, 65:156-164.

Inglis, J., Colwell, Catherine, and Post, F. An evaluation of the predictive power of a test known to differentiate between elderly "functional" and "organic" patients. *Journal of Mental Science,* 1960, 106:1486-1492.

Kennard, Margaret A. The characteristics of thought disturbances as related to electroencephalographic findings in children and adolescents. *American Journal of Psychiatry,* 1959, 115:911-921.

Kessler, Jane W. *Psychopathology of childhood.* Englewood Cliffs, N.J.: Prentice-Hall, 1966.

Kissel, S. Schizophrenic patterns on the WISC: a missing control. *Journal of Clinical Psychology,* 1966, 22:201.

Kleinmuntz, B. *Personality measurement: an introduction.* Homewood, Ill.: Dorsey Press, 1967.

Koppitz, Elizabeth M. Emotional indicators on human figure drawings of children: a validation study. *Journal of Clinical Psychology,* 1966, 22:313-315. (a)

Koppitz, Elizabeth M. Emotional indicators on human figure drawings of shy and aggressive children. *Journal of Clinical Psychology,* 1966, 22: 466-469. (b)

Laufer, M. W., and Denhoff, E. Hyperkinetic behavior syndrome in children. *Journal of Pediatrics,* 1957, 50:463-473.

Lawrence, Margaret M. Minimal brain injury in child psychiatry. *Comprehensive Psychiatry,* 1960, 1:360-369.

Lezak, Muriel D., and Dixon, H. H., Jr. The "brain-injured" child in a clinic population: a statistical description. *Exceptional Children,* 1964, 30:237-240.

Littell, W. M. The Wechsler Intelligence Scale for Children: review of a decade of research. *Psychological Bulletin,* 1960, 57:132-156.

McClelland, D. C. Methods of measuring human motivation. In J. W. Atkinson (Ed.), *Motives in fantasy, action, and society.* Princeton, N.J.: D. Van Nostrand, 1958, 7-42.

Morris, D. P., and Dozier, Elizabeth. Childhood behavior disorders: subtler organic factors. *Texas State Journal of Medicine,* 1961, 57:314-318.

Murray, H. A. *Manual: Thematic Apperception Test.* Cambridge, Mass.: Harvard University Press, 1943.

Murstein, B. I. *Theory and research in projective techniques.* New York: John Wiley and Sons, 1963.

Murstein, B. I. (Ed.). *Handbook of projective techniques.* New York: Basic Books, 1965.

Newland, T. E. Psychological assessment of exceptional children and youth. In W. M. Cruickshank (Ed.), *Psychology of exceptional children and youth* (2nd ed.). Englewood Cliffs, N.J.: Prentice-Hall, 1963, 53-117.

Olson, W. C. *Problem tendencies in children: a method for their measurement and description.* Minneapolis: University of Minnesota Press, 1930.

Pond, D. Is there a syndrome of "brain damage" in children? *Cerebral Palsy Bulletin,* 1960, 2:296-297.

Powell, H. F., and Chansky, N. M. The evaluation of academic disabilities. In J. F. Magary (Ed.), *School psychological services in theory and practice: a handbook.* Englewood Cliffs, N.J.: Prentice-Hall, 1967, 523-555.

Reed, H. J., and Fitzhugh, Kathleen B. Patterns of deficits in relation to severity of cerebral dysfunction in children and adults. *Journal of Consulting Psychology,* 1966, 30:98-102.

Reitan, R. M. The comparative effects of brain damage on the Halstead Impairment Index and the Wechsler-Bellevue Scale. *Journal of Clinical Psychology,* 1959, 15:281-285.

Rogers, M. E., Lilienfeld, A. M., and Pasamanick, B. *Prenatal and paranatal factors in the development of childhood behavior disorders.* Baltimore: Johns Hopkins University Press, 1954.

Rorschach, H. *Psychodiagnostics.* New York: Grune and Stratton, 1951.

Ross, A. O. Brain injury and intellectual performance. *Journal of Consulting Psychology,* 1958, 22:151-152.

Ross, A. O. *The practice of clinical child psychology.* New York: Grune and Stratton, 1959.

Ross, A. O. Learning difficulties of children: dysfunctions, disorders, disabilities. *Journal of School Psychology,* 1967, 5:82-92.

Schulman, J. L., Kaspar, J. C., and Throne, Frances M. The brain damage behavior syndrome: a clinical-experimental study. Unpublished manuscript. Chicago: Children's Memorial Hospital, 1963.

Solomon, I. L., Klein, M. I., and Starr, B. D. The School Apperception Method. *Journal of School Psychology,* 1966, 4:28-35.

Solomon, I. L., and Starr, B. D. New developments in the School Apperception Method. *Journal of School Psychology,* 1967, 5:157-158.

Stone, F. Beth, and Rowley, V. N. Educational disability in emotionally disturbed children. *Exceptional Children,* 1964, 30:423-426.

Strauss, A. A., and Kephart, N. C. *Psychopathology and education of the brain-injured child, Vol. II. Progressive theory and clinic.* New York: Grune and Stratton, 1955.

Strupp, H. H. Psychotherapeutic technique, professional affiliation, and experience level. *Journal of Consulting Psychology,* 1955, 19:97-102.

Tamkin, A. S. A survey of educational disability in emotionally disturbed children. *Journal of Educational Research,* 1960, 53:313-315.

Taylor, R. G. Personality traits and discrepant achievement: a review. *Journal of Counseling Psychology,* 1964, 11:76-82.

Throne, Frances M., Kaspar, J. C., and Schulman, J. L. Performance time and brain damage ratings. *American Journal of Mental Deficiency,* 1964, 68:656-659.

Torres, F. Electroencephalography in general practice. *Lancet,* 1962, 82:22-26.

Vane, Julia R. An evaluation of the Harris revision of the Goodenough Draw-A-Man Test. *Journal of Clinical Psychology,* 1967, 23:375-377.

Vane, Julia, Weitzman, J., and Applebaum, A. P. Performance of Negro and white children and problem and nonproblem children on the Stanford-Binet Scale. *Journal of Clinical Psychology,* 1966, 22:431-435.

Wallen, R. W. *Clinical psychology.* New York: McGraw-Hill, 1956.

Watson, C. G. Relationship of distortion to DAP diagnostic accuracy among psychologists at three levels of sophistication. *Journal of Consulting Psychology,* 1967, 31:142-146.

Wechsler, D. *The measurement and appraisal of adult intelligence.* Baltimore: Williams and Wilkins, 1958.

Wechsler, D., and Jaros, Eugenia. Schizophrenic patterns on the WISC. *Journal of Clinical Psychology,* 1965, 21:288-291.

Woody, R. H. The use of electroencephalography and mental abilities tests in the diagnosis of behavioral problem males. Unpublished doctoral dissertation, Michigan State University, 1964.

Woody, R. H. Intra-judge reliability in clinical electroencephalography. *Journal of Clinical Psychology,* 1966, 22:150-154.

Woody, R. H. Diagnosis of behavioral problem children: electroencephalography and mental abilities tests. *Journal of School Psychology,* 1967, 5:116-121.

Woody, R. H. Diagnosis of behavioral problem children: mental abilities and achievement tests. *Journal of School Psychology,* 1968, 6:111-116. (a)

Woody, R. H. Inter-judge reliability in clinical electroencephalography. *Journal of Clinical Psychology,* 1968, 26:251-256. (b)

Wunderlin, R. J., and McPherson, Marion W. Sensitivity to imbalance in normal and anoxic damaged children. *Journal of Clinical Psychology,* 1962, 18:410-413.

Wyatt, F. A. The scoring and analysis of the TAT. *Journal of Psychology,* 1947, 24:319-330.

Yates, A. J. The validity of some psychological tests of brain damage. *Psychological Bulletin,* 1954, 51:359-379.

Young, Florence M., and Pitts, Virginia A. The performance of congenital syphilitics on the Wechsler Intelligence Scale for Children. *Journal of Consulting Psychology,* 1951, 15:239-242.

Part two

BEHAVIORAL
MODIFICATION

5

Influencing and
Modifying Behavior

The term "behavioral modifica-
tion," although used in its generic sense in the first part of this book,
actually denotes a specific theoretical position in regard to changing behaviors. Krasner and Ullmann (1965) prefer the term "behavior influence" for the generic sense and reserve "behavioral modification" to
refer to an approach to treatment that is based, at least in part, on learning theory; this will be the practice in subsequent sections of this book.
The distinction is that sources for "influencing" behavior can be quite
diverse, such as guidance or counseling or psychotherapy, but sources for
"modifying" behavior in the special sense of the word are only those that
are derived from theories of learning. Behavioral modification sources are
generally referred to as *behavior therapy* or *conditioning therapy*. These
terms will become increasingly clear as this chapter progresses.

APPROACHES TO BEHAVIORAL CHANGE

There are several possible approaches to changing behavior. Just as
there are numerous professional sources for services that can influence
behavior, there are numerous theoretical frameworks on which to base
influencing and modifying efforts. Each theoretical position has its own
components and endorsed techniques. As will become evident, theoreticians often emphasize the uniqueness of their espoused theory and
point out the differences between it and other theoretical positions.
There are, however, many points in common between theoretical positions; and often the differing techniques, upon analysis, prove to be quite
similar in certain respects. The theoretical position that will be set forth
in this chapter is eclectic; it stresses the common elements and the potential value of drawing from several theoretical positions and using diverse

119

techniques, with the criterion for selection depending upon the needs of the particular child being served.[1]

Before offering ideas on a theoretical approach to influencing and modifying behavior, it is advisable to emphasize that efforts to change behavior may come from several professional sources, much in the same manner as efforts to recognize and diagnose behavior problems may come from different sources. Because of disciplinary alignment, these different sources may each have a somewhat different general theoretical orientation. This orientation can also be influenced by role definitions and administrative boundaries for a given profession. Thus there will be some types of influencing and modifying practices that seem more appropriate for certain types of educators than for others, and one of the goals for presenting a theoretical position is to develop one approach that is applicable to educators in general. Because of differences in professional skills and personal characteristics, certain technical aspects will be somewhat restricted; but the over-all theoretical framework for behavioral modification to be proposed will be applicable to all professional educators to some degree.

The professional sources for influencing and modifying behavior might be designated by the title of their position or by the type of services that they provide. But since titles vary according to the individual setting, it seems most appropriate to classify the sources according to the types of services that they can feasibly offer. Although the categories may be somewhat arbitrary, for our purposes the following four divisions best

---

1 Throughout this book it is emphasized that the client is influential in determining the goals for the psychoeducational services offered to him. This assumes that the child or client is able to recognize the need for the services and is voluntarily involved. There may be, of course, variations of this matter. For example, there may be some children who, because of lack of intelligence and/or insight or because of the severity of their emotional or behavioral disturbance, do not become cognizant of the reasons why a professional is working with them. In most of these instances the child's parents will assume the responsibility for seeking out and supporting the services; and in other instances, especially those within the context of the school, a significant adult, e.g., a classroom teacher or school counselor, will have to assume responsibility. This type of situation is related to the discussion on referral presented in Chapter 3, but it also has further implications: there will be behavioral problem children who are disruptive to the educational environment or who are psychologically or physically destructive (toward other children or themselves) for whom "mandatory" psychoeducational services will be necessary. It is hoped that the parents, in these cases, will be supportive and involved, but it is feasible that the mandate of responsibility for the development of children given to the schools by the public will have to be the basis of the educators' requiring that services be accepted. This could obviously influence, e.g., hamper, the processes, especially in therapy, but a certain amount of such resistance would have to be tolerated in view of the circumstances. It is probable that most "involuntary" clients will not present such extreme conditions, but will rather be children who violate school norms and who do not appreciate the value of having special services; and in the majority of these cases the parents will be accepting and cooperative, so that the involuntary nature of the situation is but a percept due to the lack of understanding possessed by the child.

serve to illustrate the sources of behavioral influence and modification: guidance, counseling, psychotherapy, and behavior therapy.

Guidance

Guidance can be provided by virtually any person, whether he be professionally trained or untrained, adult or child. Anyone with whom an individual interacts can be a source of guidance. For example, the behavioral problem child might be guided in his behavior, and consequently might change his behavior in some manner, by the comments and activities of his parents, siblings, relatives, classmates, educators, or public figures. In other words, guidance in the broad sense is the influencing of the person's thoughts and ideas; and because of this there may be changes in behavior.

Guidance within the school system is usually a much more professionally defined set of processes. In this professional sense of the word, which will be the primary usage in this book, *guidance encompasses services from educators that are based on a psychoeducational understanding of the development and behavior of children.* Any educator is a potential source of guidance in this sense, and indeed every educator has the responsibility of fulfilling this guidance service.

Guidance counselors or school counselors are usually trained on an advanced level in the guidance and counseling processes, but involvement by other educators and particularly classroom teachers is tantamount to effective guidance services. In fact, the majority of guidance should emanate from within the classroom. This intraclass guidance takes many forms: it can be relatively formal, such as individual sessions with a child about specific problems; or it can be group-centered and less structured, such as providing information (perhaps even in a didactic manner) to the class of children about potential problem areas that might influence their behavior. Guidance, therefore, can include the dispensing of information, advice-giving, suggestions, persuasions, or any other type of response that is designed to influence the child. It is presumed that the guidance person, such as the teacher, is offering this guidance to help the child and because he (the teacher) is supposedly in a position, because of maturity and training, to make better judgments than the child. In true guidance, however, it is essential that there be a component of *permissiveness;* that is, the guidance is offered and the recipient, the child, is free to assess and accept or reject the contents of the guidance as he sees fit.

It is not the purpose of this book to provide a comprehensive analysis of guidance services. Suffice it to say, when guidance is offered in the schools, there should be cooperation between educators. Therefore, guidance might be provided within the classroom by the teacher, but the school counselor or school psychologist might also be helping the teacher in a consulting capacity. Through professional sources, guidance can be performed in a wide variety of circumstances and can use diverse techniques both within and outside of the classroom (Peters, Shertzer, and Van Hoose, 1965).

Counseling

Although the term "counseling" is frequently linked with "guidance," the two terms have individual meanings; they are not synonymous. Although the processes of counseling do involve certain aspects of guidance, they also encompass certain concepts and principles that are outside of the previously stated definition for guidance. It is these concepts and principles that we will consider in detail.

Definitions of counseling are about as numerous as the writers in the area. Almost everyone who has written in the area of counseling has chosen to offer his own definition. Since definitions have been well reviewed elsewhere (Arbuckle, 1965), this discussion can be limited to generalizations derived from the definitions.

One of the first distinctions that must be made is that *counseling is similar to but different from psychotherapy;* more on this will be said in the section on psychotherapy. In counseling, the person receiving the service is usually called a "counselee" or a "client"; he has adjustment problems, but he is not considered to be "mentally ill." The counseling is focused on the present and future, rather than on an analysis of the past; and in most counseling theories the emphasis is on helping the client achieve understanding of or "insight" into why he thinks, feels, and behaves the way that he does. McGowan and Schmidt (1962), in considering definitions of counseling, conclude:

Counseling can be characterized by the following: (1) It is a social learning interaction between two people, the methods and purposes of which range between the extremes of simple advising and intense long-term psychological treatment; (2) the recipients of counseling services are generally called clients; (3) concern typically is with normal or "usual" persons rather than those who exhibit abnormal or extreme modes of adjustment; (4) clients typically may be expected to be upset or frustrated at the beginning of counseling but not usually psychologically disabled or disintegrated; (5) counseling functions aim toward helping clients to understand and accept what they are and in light of this awareness to realize their potential, if necessary through some alteration or modification of their attitudes, outlook, or behavior; (6) although listening and talking are the primary methods, psychological tests, social and biographical histories, outside resources, and other psychological or sociological instruments or materials are usually employed; (7) attention is paid to extracounseling as well as intracounseling events and changes; and (8) more emphasis is given to the positive and obvious than to the negative and unconscious in the counseling process. (pp. 3-4)

In another survey of definitions of counseling, Gustad (1953) offers the following consensus-type definition:

Counseling is a learning-oriented process, carried on in a simple, one-to-one social environment, in which a counselor, professionally competent in relevant psychological skills and knowledge, seeks to assist the client by methods appropriate to the latter's needs and within the context of the total personnel program, to learn more about himself, to learn how to put such understanding into effect in relation to more clearly perceived, realistically defined goals to the end that the client may become a happier and more productive member of his society. (p. 17)

And finally, Brammer and Shostrom (1960) view counseling and psychotherapy as being on a "therapeutic psychology" continuum; that is, counseling starts the continuum at one end and progresses to a point where it overlaps with psychotherapy and then ceases as psychotherapy progresses on further into therapeutic services. They state:

Counseling is characterized by the following words: educational, supportive, situational, problem-solving, conscious awareness, emphasis on "normals," and short term. Psychotherapy is characterized by: supportive (in a more particular sense), reconstructive, depth emphasis, analytical, focus on the unconscious, emphasis on "neurotics" or other severe emotional problems, and long term. (p. 6)

There seems to be relative compatibility between these three definitions. The concept of a *counseling-psychotherapy continuum* is especially pertinent and will be frequently cited in later sections.

Although there are differences between counseling and psychotherapy, these differences seem to be determined more by the types of goals for the treatment than by the theoretical components. Smith (1967) acknowledges the profusion of theoretical and technical elements that counseling and psychotherapy have in common and concludes that the justification for separate terms lies in association: "therapy" is associated with psychiatry and clinical psychology, whereas "counseling" is a more acceptable term for situations in the schools. Albert (1966) takes the position that, with perhaps the exception of strictly information-giving types of academic and vocational advisement—that is, guidance—no form of counseling can be restricted to the conscious, rational layers of personality; the counselor may and should be able to delve into the realm of personality, which is typically the province of psychotherapy. Similarly, Patterson

(1966a, 1966b) maintains that counseling and psychotherapy are two terms for the same functions, and that the school has the responsibility of fulfilling the need for counseling broadly conceived. Thus support is given for the belief that "therapeutic" procedures, as will be shown later, are within the areas of responsibility of the school (Patterson, 1966a; Smith, 1967).

There are several issues relevant to counseling that researchers do not agree upon. Many of these will become evident in later chapters. For now, two of these issues might be used as examples. First, certain theoretical approaches to counseling maintain that the counselor's values and morals should be divorced from the counseling relationship; others claim that this is impossible and that while he may not and should not impose his values and morals on the counselees or clients, he must hold them in awareness and admit that they are present in the relationship (Blocher, 1966; London, 1964; Patterson, 1958). Second, some theoretical positions state that the primary product of counseling should be *insight* and that counseling can be successful without changes in behavior. Other positions state the opposite, that the primary product of counseling should be behavioral change: that is, counseling cannot be successful unless the problems that brought the client to counseling are alleviated or eliminated, and if there is a problem behavior it is necessary to change it (Krumboltz, 1965; London, 1964).

The professional school counselor should have advanced training in counseling and guidance, and in general it is believed that this means holding a master's degree in counseling or its equivalent; increasingly, two years of graduate-level study are being required for the master's degree. Many states have already instituted certification standards for school counselors which typically involve both academic and experiential factors. But it is likely that many counselors will be both teachers and counselors; that is, they may spend several periods a day in a counseling capacity and also teach several sections of students.

Professional counselors may be employed in a variety of settings. Although our main concern here is with school counseling as a source for changing behaviors, it should be pointed out that counselors are also trained to work in rehabilitation, social service, medical, and mental health settings; thus it is quite possible that behavioral problem children might be serviced by a counselor in other than the school setting. Similarly, there are other professional disciplines that provide "counseling" services. Most notable would be social work, speech and hearing therapy, special education, and various subspecialties in medicine and psychology.

Counseling psychology is essentially an extension both in training and in responsibilities beyond that of school counseling. The counseling psychologist is similar in many ways to the clinical psychologist, especially in that both have training beyond the master's level (usually holding a doctoral degree) and both provide psychodiagnostic and psychotherapeutic services (American Psychological Association, 1956). Perhaps the best distinction is that clinical psychologists are primarily concerned with psychopathology, the abnormalities of their clients, whereas counseling psychologists are primarily concerned with the hygiology, the normalities of their clients (even when dealing with abnormal persons); but there are many more common elements than differences between these two psychological specialists (Super, 1955).

Psychotherapy

As stated previously, there is reason to believe that there is a *counseling-psychotherapy continuum* (Brammer and Shostrom, 1960). This continuum is readily demonstrated when content analyses are made of therapeutic sessions conducted by counseling psychologists. They may begin "counseling" for a very specific problem area, but in the course of the sessions the processes progress from a content level to a deeper level of emotional involvement, and the sessions evolve into psychotherapy. In general, psychotherapy does not stop with helping the client achieve better adjustment, as does counseling, but progresses on into personality change.

There are many theoretical approaches to psychotherapy. One of the best-known is *psychoanalysis,* as originally developed by Sigmund Freud. From Freud's early works there have been a number of deviations; these are labeled neoanalytic or neo-Freudian or social psychological theories. These analytically oriented theories have continued to change and have evolved to the contemporary ego-analytic theories. Another major group of theoretical positions has developed from the works of Carl R. Rogers (Rogers, 1951, 1961). This position, which was initially termed *nondirective therapy* but eventually became better known as *client-centered therapy,* has had a tremendous impact on psychology, and especially upon counseling services. There are numerous other theories, each of which purports to have developed a unique approach to counseling and/or psychotherapy, but in many cases theories have actually borrowed from other existing theories (Ford and Urban, 1963; Harper, 1959; Patterson, 1966b).

London (1964) deals with the similarities among the theories of counseling and psychotherapy. Structurally, there must be three elements in a system of psychotherapy:

(1) a theory of personality, which addresses itself to the nature of man and behavior, (2) a superordinate moral code, usually a social philosophy, which addresses the organization of society and the relationship of individuals to it, and

(3) a body of therapeutic techniques, which are deliberate means of manipulating or influencing behavior. (p. 25)

And Ford and Urban (1963), in a comprehensive comparative analysis of systems of psychotherapy, state that an analysis of a theoretical position should consider what the position maintains for the normal course of behavior development, the development of behavior disorders, the goals of therapy, the conditions for producing behavior change, and the means of evaluating behavior change. In viewing the rather diverse spectrum of psychotherapeutic theories, there does seem to be one common bond: *theories of psychotherapy attempt to help the person achieve insight— that is, an understanding of why he believes, thinks, feels, and acts the way he does; and changes in behavior are probably secondary to the goal of insight.* The question of goals will arise again shortly when psychotherapy and behavior therapy are compared.

It is obviously difficult to establish a specific definition for the term "psychotherapy" without adhering to one distinct school or theory, and it is even more difficult when one wishes to honor the assumed continuum between counseling and psychotherapy. In regard to the latter point, it seems that "counseling" implies adjustment, while "psychotherapy" implies personality change, regardless of theoretical position. But a general definition of psychotherapy must include several points: there has to be a continued interpersonal relationship; one of the persons involved must be specially trained (that is, the therapist); one (or more) of those involved must feel dissatisfied with his personal or interpersonal adjustment; psychological procedures must be used; there must be a formal underlying psychological theory for the specific aspects intrinsic to the purposes of the relationship; and the objective must be to ameliorate the problems that brought the participants, the therapist and the client, together (Eysenck, 1965b; Winder, 1957). The original definition for this position, set forth by Winder (1957), was intended to apply primarily to clinical psychology, but it is apparent that these criteria for psychotherapy are quite compatible with the definitions set forth earlier for counseling; and it will become evident later that these criteria also apply to certain aspects of behavior therapy.

Psychotherapy may be a source for changing the behaviors of school children. In many cases there will be no one within the school staff who can provide this highly demanding service, and the services will have to be obtained outside of the school, such as from a child guidance clinic or a private practitioner. There are, however, school systems where school counselors and school psychologists (and possibly even school social workers) will be capable of conducting psychotherapy. But as was previously stated, changes in behavior may or may not be intrinsic to the goals of counseling and psychotherapy. Despite the possibility that behavioral change will not be a primary goal, counseling and psychotherapy are probably uppermost in the minds of most professionals when they consider the sources for treating behavioral problem children.

Psychotherapy may be conducted in numerous forms. Smith (1967) differentiates three types of therapy: *supportive, re-educational,* and *reconstructive.* Supportive procedures are directed at helping the client gain better control of his impulses, ego strength, and interest in the acceptance of reality. The techniques might include information-giving, persuasion, suggestion, reassurance, modification of the environment (such as in school), environmental manipulation (such as in the home and school), group activity, and tutoring. Re-educative approaches strive for insight into relatively conscious conflicts for the purpose of changing factors intrinsic to self-concepts, goals and aspirations, motivations, and, to some extent, behavioral symptoms. The previously cited client-centered theory of Rogers and other theories that rely heavily on a therapist-client relationship would be aligned with re-education. This form deals primarily with current adjustment. Reconstructive approaches attempt to help the client achieve insight into both conscious and unconscious conflicts, and the primary objective is a restructuring of the personality. Analytically oriented theories typify this form.

Play therapy provides a medium for children who are too young to fulfill the requirements for adult-style counseling and psychotherapy. On the counseling level, Nelson (1966) points out how play in counseling can facilitate the child's attempts to learn means of functioning in social situations, help him test various behavioral roles, and help him more aptly express and cope with his frustrations and concerns. As opposed to play therapy with its analytically oriented interpretations, play in counseling relies on reflections and summarization of feelings and attitudes. Axline (1947) presents a relatively nondirective approach to play therapy that is neither planned in advance nor interpretative; rather it relies upon the relationship between child and therapist. There are a number of approaches to play therapy, with goals ranging from releasing emotions to interpreting conscious and unconscious conflicts to building a meaningful therapeutic relationship. Ginott (1961) provides a practical description of methodology for conducting therapy with groups of children. Hammer and Kaplan (1967) present a collection of treatises on the use of analytically oriented techniques with children. And Kessler (1966) synthesizes the variety of psychotherapeutic approaches to childhood problems.

As might be inferred from the foregoing discussion, therapy and counseling can be provided individually or in groups. Group counseling or therapy seems to have special merit for several reasons: it is time-saving, since the therapist can deal with more clients in a given time than in the individual format; it seems especially effective with mild emotional problems and behavior problems; it provides a microcosm of a controlled social environment where clients can solve relationship problems and try out new coping behaviors; it offers a catalytic effect, since being involved with others who are trying to change behaviors provides each member with a strong incentive to change his behavior (Smith, 1967). Over all, it seems unwise to claim that group procedures are best, but they certainly qualify for consideration in many therapeutic circumstances.

The relationship between therapist and client has been mentioned several times. Although it will receive more extensive consideration later, clarification is required at this point. In the forms of counseling and psychotherapy that place emphasis on the relationship, the assumption is that the conditions between the therapist and the client may, in and of themselves, have therapeutic value. Rogers (1961) posited that these conditions were unconditional positive regard, empathic understanding, and congruence; more recently, Truax and Carkhuff (1967) have labeled these nonpossessive warmth, accurate empathy, and genuineness. Since these conditions will be enlarged upon later in this chapter, suffice it to say that the research evidence seems to show that the success of counseling and psychotherapy depends to a major degree on the development of the conditions between therapist and client. Although the conditions might be given different names and differing degrees of importance, and perhaps even secondary conditions might be added, depending upon the particular theory of counseling and psychotherapy, the significance of the relationship is undeniable.

In the position to be endorsed and presented in this chapter, counseling and psychotherapy are deemed of value in aiding the behavioral problem child; but special consideration is also given to the specific goal of changing unacceptable behaviors. The treatment services are geared to helping the child both to understand or gain insight and to achieve relief from the conditions that are causing him to be unhappy, to be ineffective in his learning, to suffer socially and psychologically, and to behave in an unacceptable manner. Success of the treatment necessitates behavioral change—that is, relief for the client from the problems that brought him to treatment; and insight may occur as a secondary goal.

Behavior Therapy

Behavior therapy has become increasingly popular and the subject of much scientific research during recent years; in fact, few of the most prominent behavior therapy sources can be traced back beyond about one decade. But there is evidence that some of the techniques have been used for years and that theories developed during the past half-century have contributed to the current theoretical status of behavior therapy (Breger and McGaugh, 1966).

It should be noted that, despite their similarities, behavior therapy is distinguished by professionals from psychotherapy. Eysenck (1960) favors this distinction, but Wolpe (1963) has assumed the position that behavior therapy is part of the all-encompassing psychotherapy, and he states that since there is reason to think

that most neuroses are primarily conditioned habits of autonomic response, and it is really only through inadvertent effects on these habits that the mind-therapists obtain any favourable results, it seems gratuitous to resign to them this well-known and convenient term. Despite its etymology "psychotherapy" should continue to designate the whole field. . . . (p. 23)

In this book, the term "therapy" is used generically and denotes any activity of any theoretical orientation that can be used to influence systematically, but the terms "psychotherapy" and "behavior therapy" will be distinguished.

There are several definitions of behavior therapy that merit citation. Wolpe (1964) states:

These methods stem from the conception that neuroses are persistent unadaptive habits that have been conditioned (that is, learned). If this conception is correct, the fundamental overcoming of neurosis can consist of nothing but deconditioning—or undoing the relevant habit patterns. (p. 9)

He continues:

Learning theory predicts that *unless* there are intervening events that directly recondition neurotic reactions, recovery from neurosis that is radical . . . will be lasting. . . . (p. 13)

Eysenck (1965a), in contrasting psychoanalysis with behavior therapy, indicates that in learning theory, the basis of behavior therapy, the therapists are

dealing with unadapative behaviour conditioned to certain classes of stimuli; no reference is made to any underlying disorders or complexes in the psyche. . . . Behaviour therapy concentrates on actual *behaviour* as most likely to lead to the extinction of the unadaptive conditioned responses. (p. 402)

Psychoanalysis maintains, as do essentially all theories of psychotherapy, that *neurotic* behaviors reflect underlying motives, whereas

Learning theory does not postulate any such "unconscious causes," but regards neurotic symptoms as simple learned habits; there is no neurosis underlying the symptom, but merely the symptom itself. *Get rid of the symptom and you have eliminated the neurosis.* (Eysenck, 1965a, p. 401)

In summary, behavior therapy might best be described as an approach to treatment that is based on learning theory or principles of conditioning; and its primary objective is to modify the unacceptable behaviors that brought the client to treatment—that is, to eliminate his problem behaviors. Moreover, this position denies that behavior problems reflect an underlying neurosis or conflict. Counseling and psychotherapy are based on the assumption that behavior problems are the manifestations of underlying conflicts and that the conflicts must be resolved through insight before the problems can be eliminated; but behavior therapy is based on the assumption that behaviors are simply maladaptive habits and that if the behaviors are changed, the problems will be permanently removed because the behaviors have been unlearned.

Behavior therapy, or techniques of behavioral modification, have proved to be successful in combating a wide variety of problem behaviors, such as might be encountered with behavioral problem children in the schools (Woody, 1966). And from the basic position of behavior therapy there have evolved applications to counseling, usually called "behavioral counseling," and uses in the classroom (Woody, 1968a). The success of this learning theory approach for helping behavioral problem children seems undeniable, and supporting evidence for its efficacy will be presented later. From this approach it seems that educators can derive some of the most effective means for helping behavioral problem children. But one should emphasize that behavioral modification techniques in isolation are not necessarily the most appropriate means; rather an integrated or eclectic approach, an approach that draws from both the counseling-psychotherapy continuum and behavior therapy, justifies endorsement.

The remainder of this chapter will clarify the frameworks for the counseling-psychotherapy continuum and for behavior therapy, give special attention to the theoretical and technical boundaries of behavior therapy and the efficacy of this approach, and then draw counseling-psychotherapy and behavior therapy into a *psychobehavioral* or *integrative* therapeutic approach. This eclectic approach seems to be especially suited for the services offered within a school system; that is, although an individual theoretical approach might be more effective in another setting, such as a psychological clinic or hospital, the philosophical and practical characteristics of the school setting necessitate the incorporation or integration of the most appropriate aspects of all available theories. And there is evidence that this integration is quite feasible; research data and professional statements indicate that these different theoretical positions are already quite interwoven.

ACTION AND INSIGHT SYSTEMS

It is not possible to consider in depth all theories of counseling and psychotherapy for bringing about changes in behavior. As has been mentioned, the goals for treatment vary with the theory; and there are theories that place little, if any, emphasis on having actual changes in behavior as a therapeutic goal. In such theories the goal of the treatment is not to change the observable behavior, even if it is socially unacceptable and is causing the person to experience difficulties; rather the primary goal is the development of personal understanding of why the person behaves in the manner that he does.

London (1964) has divided systems of therapy into the dichotomy of *insight* and *action*. This dichotomy readily exemplifies the role of observable behavior in the goals of counseling and psychotherapy. Insight theories include those schools of or approaches to treatment that attempt to help the person, or more correctly to help the person help himself, gain understanding of why he behaves the way he does, the psychological meaning of his behavior, and how these motives can aid him in acquiring personal acceptance of his behavior. If a change in behavior results, it is secondary in importance to the gaining of self-understanding. The insight therapies include systems such as Carl Rogers' client-centered approach, Sigmund Freud's psychoanalysis, Alfred Adler's individual psychology, and a number of others representing seemingly diverse approaches. According to London, however, these systems do not differ as much as they allege. For example, each relies upon verbal communication as the main instrument of therapy, the counselor or therapist tends to remove his personal factors from the relationship, and the client is essentially responsible for the process of therapy. Technically, although client-centered counselors *reflect* and psychoanalysts *interpret,* they all assess and elaborate:

Rogerians limit the therapeutic attack to the exposure of feelings in whatever connection they are presented to the therapist, while Freudians, though similarly interested in dealing with feelings, are concerned with identifying their sources as well. (London, 1964, p. 48)

In other words, London indicates that the differences in techniques or devices serve to satisfy the theoretical preferences of the therapist, but produce little variation in effects on the clients. Indeed, research has revealed that therapists, regardless of orientation, are in relative accord about the concept of the ideal therapeutic relationship (Fiedler, 1950) and about the types of responses that they make during treatment (Strupp, 1955).

The action therapists are generally termed "behaviorists." They believe that behavior essentially reflects the results of learning and does not solely reflect underlying motives. Thus neuroses or emotional problems are the mechanical results of learning. Behaviorists tend to view psychological disorders as being only casually related to behavior problems, and insight as being only peripherally or incidentally related to the eliminating of these behavior problems. The action therapists treat by manipulating the learning opportunities. Much of their theoretical rationale for treatment is derived from experimental studies with both animals and humans. The therapist has more responsibility for the treatment sessions, the outcome of the treatment, and whatever changes take place (London, 1964).

Perhaps the biggest difference between action and insight systems occurs in the recognition of symptoms. There is agreement on the definition of a symptom, but disagreement over the relevance of the symptom to the treatment. The actionists are indifferent to the origin of the symptoms and strive to eliminate or alleviate the discomfort (that is, social, psychological, and physical discomforts) that the client is experiencing because of the symptoms. Thus the actionists maintain that the primary criterion for assessing the clinical status or usefulness of a method should be related directly to the well-being of the client, and the secondary criterion should be related to the amount of time and effort required by the therapist and the cost of the treatment to the client (London, 1964). And systematic improvement, that is, relief for the client from his discomforting problems, is the only criterion for improvement of neuroses (Wolpe, 1964). On the other hand, the insightists are not primarily concerned with alleviating the problems—that is, symptomatic improvement; they want the client to understand why he behaves the way he does and to gain acceptance of what he is as a person. Likewise, the concept of economy is not considered; in general, the amount of time and effort required of the insight therapist and the cost of the treatment to the client are regarded as insignificant.

The differences between the insight and action systems may be exemplified by the following situation: Let us consider the case of a homosexual who has been arrested several times, is losing his job, and is suffering from his sexual preferences. He could choose either insight or action treatment. If he chooses action treatment, the goal would be to rid him of the social, vocational, and psychological discomforts, even though he enjoys being a homosexual and perhaps even consciously accepts the fact that he is a homosexual; he would be treated so as to change his behavior permanently into heterosexual behavior and thereby eliminate his symptoms or sources of discomfort. But if the same homosexual chooses insight treatment, the goal would be to promote an empathic understanding, accepting, or interpretive relationship with the therapist, to help the client understand why he is a homosexual, and to discern the value of this type of behavior to the inner man; and if the homosexual behavior should change, it would be as a result of changes in understanding of self, not from a conscious attempt to alleviate the discomfort.

It is apparent that if one accepts the thesis that changes in behavior should be one of the definite goals of helping behavioral problem children in the school and that the treatment efforts are to achieve the goal of behavioral change readily, there must be some alignment with an action system.

Such dichotomizing of theories into action and insight is, of course, gross. In any theory there are many nuances that are not adequately described by simple labels. In fact, it is probable that most therapists would not accept a polarity for existing theories. But for expository purposes, this dichotomy has meaning. Specifically, it distinguishes the assumed origin of the problem (neurotic conflict or maladaptive behavior) and the approximate therapeutic goal (self-understanding or symptom removal). The dichotomy is used here only for purposes of discussion, not as a comprehensive theoretical model for analysis.

As we progress to consideration of certain theoretical and technical aspects of behavioral modification, it should be pointed out that while research may be cited that took place in a setting other than a regular classroom, such as in an experimental school for emotionally disturbed children or a child guidance clinic, there are common factors in these special settings and the schools; one of the primary criteria for the selection of the research references throughout this book was that the materials or contents be applicable to the psychoeducational services offered in the schools. Therefore, when terms such as "client," "therapy," or "treatment" are used, this does not imply that all educators will become "therapists" (although in one sense of the word the educator is in fact an "educational therapist"), nor that the behavioral problem child should be thought of as a "client" or "patient." Rather the terminology of psychology is used, and lexical transpositions must be made for each of the types of educators: the classroom teacher may attempt to modify a "student's" unacceptable behavior, while a school counselor or a school psychologist may provide "counseling" or "therapy" to influence or modify a "client's" behavior, while a psychologist in a mental health clinic may attempt to change the personality and behavior of a "patient."

EFFICACY OF PSYCHOTHERAPY AND
BEHAVIOR THERAPY

Although Wolpe (1963) has stated that behavior therapy "is in no sense a new cult or 'school,' " others believe that cultism is present and that behaviorists are not different from psychoanalysts, client-centered therapists, or members espousing any other approach when it comes to dogmatism and rigidity in the belief that their approach is the best (Breger and McGaugh, 1965). Part of this separation seems to be due to the fact that each theoretical approach must substantiate its value, and the method of support often ends up as a defensive one. The defense is usually built around a comparison of a particular theory's applied results with those of another theory. This has been especially true of behavior therapy; for example, Eysenck's critiques of psychotherapy have become famous (or infamous, depending on the point of view) for disparaging the value of psychotherapy, and particularly psychoanalysis (Eysenck, 1952, 1965b). It seems doubtful that a theoretical position can be substantiated by a comparison of gross outcomes, especially since the goals are different among theories; indeed, the goals differ even among seemingly similar theories (Mahrer, 1967). But since behavior therapy constitutes a major basis for the techniques that will be presented in this book, it behooves us to consider the behaviorist's point of view regarding the relative efficacy of psychotherapy and behavior therapy.

The evaluation of such a nebulous entity as counseling or psychotherapy, with rather ambiguous criteria for success or failure, is indeed a difficult task. Few professionals have been willing to attempt a critique of all or even most of the existing systems of psychotherapy. The many pitfalls inherent in this type of evaluation give the researchers ample reasons for relying upon the efforts of others, which seldom materialize.

One of the most recent and seemingly comprehensive critiques has been made by Eysenck (1965b). Eysenck (1952) had previously issued an evaluation of the effects of psychotherapy that raised the ire of psychologists and psychiatrists espousing numerous theoretical approaches to psychotherapy. Essentially, in the earlier critique, Eysenck summarized the available evidence and concluded that "there was little support for those who believed in the efficacy of psychotherapy," since the few truly experimental studies available revealed that there was as much recovery due to spontaneous remission of problems (that is, recovery without treatment) as there was recovery known to be due (or believed to be due) to psychotherapy. It should be recognized that in 1952, Eysenck's challenging conclusion was made not in an attempt to eliminate popular approaches to psychotherapy, but rather to stimulate better and more worthwhile research in an area that had obviously been neglected. This neglect of empirical investigation of the efficacy of the different approaches to psychotherapy certainly seems incompatible with the methods necessary for a "science," and if psychotherapy is to be considered a scientific procedure, the purported neglect is indefensible.

It was because of this rather controversial historical foundation that Eysenck's review and critique of the research literature in 1965 was received with great interest by the mental health professions. In the 1965 evaluation, Eysenck draws eight conclusions, three of which merit special attention for our purpose, that of creating a frame of reference for considering the use of learning theory principles in modifying behavior in a school setting. Eysenck (1965b) states:

Children suffering from emotional disorders and treated by psychotherapy recover and improve to approximately the same extent as children not receiving psychotherapy.[2]

He further states:

Neurotic patients treated by means of psychotherapeutic procedures based on learning, improve significantly more quickly than do patients treated by means of psychoanalytic or eclectic psychotherapy, or not treated by psychotherapy at all.[3]

Finally, he states:

With the single exception of the psychotherapeutic methods based on learning theory, results of published research with military and civilian neurotics, and with both adults and children, suggest that the therapeutic effects of psychotherapy are small or non-existent, and do not in any demonstrable way add to the non-specific effects of routine medical treatment, or to such events as occur in the patients' everyday experience.[4]

With these pointed statements, Eysenck proceeds to urge psychologists and psychiatrists to acknowledge that current psychotherapeutic procedures "have not lived up to the hopes which greeted their emergence fifty years ago."

It is only fair to state that these critiques of Eysenck's have not gone undisputed. For example, Kiesler (1966) convincingly points out that

[2] H. J. Eysenck, The Effects of Psychotherapy, *International Journal of Psychiatry*, Vol. 1 (1965), p. 135.
[3] *Ibid.*
[4] *Ibid.*, p. 136.

Eysenck's critiques are based on rather uncertain grounds. Nevertheless, it seems that there is reason to question the concrete value of counseling and psychotherapy, but this question is raised primarily because of *the lack of agreement in regard to what should be the criteria for determining success or failure or value.* As mentioned previously, psychotherapy and behavior therapy differ in their goals, and so it is logical that the criteria for assessing their value should also differ. It is not within the scope of this book to debate the value of each respective form of psychotherapy. In view of research evidence (and the lack of it), it seems that the best position to maintain is that the true value of counseling and psychotherapy has yet to be determined.

An impressive array of documentary research has been and is being compiled for behavior therapy—that is, the therapeutic procedures based on learning theory. This seemingly successful documentation or survival of experimentation is due in part to the clearly determined criterion for success: *the elimination of the problem.* If the problem is gone, the behavior therapy has been successful; if the problem remains, the behavior therapy has failed. Let us consider briefly some of the research studies that purport to measure the efficacy of behavior therapy.

Wolpe (1964), in three series of results between 1952 and 1958, reports that out of 210 neurotic patients "nearly 90 percent . . . were rated as either apparently cured or much improved after an average of about 30 therapeutic interviews" (p. 12). Wolpe's cases were unselected; that is, any person diagnosed as neurotic was included.

Schmidt, Castell, and Brown (1965) made a study of adult psychiatric patients. Of the patients treated with behavior therapy, discounting dropouts, 75 percent made some improvement, as assessed by the psychologist and the psychiatrist concerned with the case. In a follow-up assessment approximately one year after discharge from treatment, it was found that of the 32 patients who completed treatment, contact could be made with 19 (61 percent of the original treatment group); and "among the patients who had responded favourably to the treatment some improvement was maintained in 93 percent of the cases followed up" (p. 16).

One of the most often quoted studies related to the efficacy of behavior therapy is provided by Lazarus (1963). Having used behavior therapy with 126 patients who were considered to be severely neurotic, Lazarus summarizes the results:

. . . it was found that out of the total of 408 patients treated by the writer, 321 individuals (i. e., 78 per cent) appeared to derive definite and constructive benefit. Of the 126 patients, most of whom could be described as "extremely neurotic," 61.9 per cent were rated as "markedly improved" or "completely recovered" in a mean of 14.07 sessions. (p. 69)

In the follow-ups, Lazarus found only one patient who had relapsed, and he had remained well until he was involved in an accidental traumatic situation. Regarding symptom substitution (a problem frequently attributed to behavior therapy), Lazarus states that "only the most tenuous suggestions of possible 'symptom substitution' were encountered in two cases . . ." (p. 79).

Cooper, Gelder, and Marks (1965) compared psychiatric patients who had received behavior therapy with control patients who had received a wide variety of other (nonbehavior) therapeutic treatments. The over-all improvement rate at the end of behavior therapy was 61 percent, while only 44 percent of the control (nonbehavior) patients were improved; 29 percent and 22 percent respectively were rated as "much improved." After a one-year period, a follow-up revealed the groups to be essentially equal in improvement.

To show a comparison of the effectiveness of behavior therapy with other therapeutic approaches, such as psychoanalysis, Wolpe (1964) reviewed studies related to improvement or cure associated with psychoanalysis. Wolpe states:

. . . considering only the completely analyzed cases, it seems to be a controversion of the psychoanalytic theory of neurosis if 40 per cent of the analyses that were rated complete did not effect marked improvement, let alone complete recovery. (p. 9)

And subsequently he summarizes:

But even the figure of 60 per cent apparently cured or much improved (by psychoanalysis)—even then . . . the results do not show any definite superiority over the results obtained in hospitals and clinics or by psychotherapists employing the various conventional methods. The fact that so much effort, more than 600 hours . . . for each markedly improved case in the series, was needed to produce such undistinguished results raises the startling question whether psychoanalytic therapy introduces features that actually impede recovery! (p. 9)

In another evaluation of all forms of psychotherapy, Levitt (1963) made a review of twenty-two studies and found that the over-all improvement rate was 65.2 percent. Levitt states:

. . . the inescapable conclusion is that available evaluation studies do not furnish a reasonable basis for the hypothesis that psychotherapy facilitates recovery from emotional illness in children. (p. 49)

In a comparison of behavior rehearsal (a behavior therapy technique), nondirective therapy, and advice-giving, Lazarus (1966) found that the behavior therapy technique was the most effective. Similarly, Paul (1966) found desensitization (a behavior therapy technique) to be more effective than insight procedures. Paul (1967a) conducted a follow-up study on the effects of individual systematic desensitization, insight-oriented psychotherapy, attention-placebo, and no treatment (control group) two years after the treatment. In general, the therapeutic improvement had stayed about the same as it was at the time of termination; after two years, the improvement percentages were as follows: systematic desensitization, 85 percent; insight-oriented psychotherapy, 50 percent; attention-placebo, 50 percent; and no treatment (controls), 22 percent. Elsewhere, Paul (1967b) discusses the ramifications of assessing the outcomes of therapy and concludes that it is a possible but a rigorous undertaking. Paul and Shannon (1966) used behavior therapy and psychotherapy with groups of chronically anxious male college students; in general it seemed that behavior therapy contributed more beneficially to the problem of anxiety than did insight-oriented psychotherapy or attention-placebo. Lazarus (1961) found that group desensitization therapy (that is, behavior therapy) was more effective than group psychotherapy for treating phobias. Other reviews of the research relevant to the efficacy of behavior therapy, especially as compared to other therapeutic approaches, may be found elsewhere (Eysenck and Rachman, 1965; Wolpe and Lazarus, 1966).

Another factor related to the efficacy of behavior therapy is the number of treatment sessions required to achieve therapeutic success. As mentioned earlier, expenditure of time (both by the therapist and by the client) and money is seen as a primary concern in behavior therapy, but it receives scant attention in counseling and psychotherapy. Since there are a number of variables that could influence a measure of this factor, such as the severity and type of disorder being treated and differences in skills among therapists, this still remains an inconclusive point. But behavior therapists frequently point to the greater length of time required for insight-oriented systems as compared to the length of time for action-oriented systems. For example, Wolpe (1964) points out the long time necessary for psychoanalysis and the relative brevity of behavior therapy. In the case of counseling and psychotherapy, there is really no way of establishing the length of time needed for therapy; and, in fact, this time element or number of sessions receives little or no consideration in evaluating the outcome or the efficacy of the treatment. But in the case of behavior therapy, the therapeutic format always gives consideration to trying to bring relief, improvement, or cure in the shortest possible time. For example, in treating phobias, Wolpe and Lazarus (1966) report that the mean number of sessions for successful treatment was 11.2 (the median number of sessions was 10.0); and Cautela (1966a) says that behavior therapy studies successfully treat phobias in 10 to 20 sessions, as compared to the several months or years necessary to treat them by analytically oriented therapy. There seems to be little doubt that a comparison of number of sessions readily reveals that behavioral modification or behavior therapy requires much less time or fewer therapeutic sessions than insight-oriented systems. It must be acknowledged, however, that the theoretical criteria for success, as has been repeatedly emphasized, are different; and thus this time factor should not be accorded unquestioned importance. But it is logical that in some cases—for example, with a behavioral problem child who is severely disrupting the learning activities in the classroom—the immediacy of results may be important.

In summary, one should note that many behavior therapy researchers claim the improvement and cure percentages to be approximately 90 percent for behavior therapy and approximately 65 percent for other conventional forms of counseling and psychotherapy. And, as Eysenck indicates in his critiques of the effectiveness of psychotherapy (Eysenck, 1952, 1965b), the amount and degree of improvement due to conventional forms of psychotherapy (excluding behavior therapy) may not exceed that of spontaneous remission of the problems. Proponents of the other forms of psychotherapy have not, unfortunately, researched their efficacy so as to be able to contradict these assertions adequately.

It must be pointed out that the effectiveness of behavior therapy is still also questionable. Even the above-mentioned studies, which supposedly document the superiority of behavior therapy, are not without possible sources of bias. For example, "success" is frequently determined solely by the behavior therapist who provides the treatment or in some other manner that would allow observer biases. Moreover, many behavior therapy techniques are still based only on clinical case studies; and there have been few, if any, studies that adequately establish experimental control groups (Beech, 1963; Breger and McGaugh, 1965). Gelder (1965) has indicated that behavior therapy is still lacking in validation studies and that its value cannot be determined by over-all comparisons of rates of recovery for mixed groups of patients receiving incomparable treatments. And, of course, there are always studies, such as the one by Cooper, Gelder, and Marks (1965), which find that behavior therapy is no more effective than psychotherapy after a given period of time; that is, the beneficial results of behavior therapy may be more immediate than those of counseling and psychotherapy, but after a period of time their efficacy is equal.

But before setting forth a theoretically eclectic position for behavioral modification in the schools, let us briefly consider some of the controversial issues related to behavior therapy. An understanding and at least a partial resolution of these is necessary before a theoretical position can be adequately constructed.

CRITICAL ISSUES

Behavior therapy has had an undeniable impact on the field of psychology; and relevant aspects are rapidly finding their way into other fields, such as education, sociology, and medicine. In view of its prominence and its proponents' frequent confrontations and open disputes with theorists representing other positions, it is not surprising that several controversial points about behavior therapy have arisen and have been publicized by those professionals who are theoretically opposed to it.

Delimiting the most controversial points will obviously depend to some extent on personal opinion. Rachman (1963) believes that the major objections to behavior therapy are that it is superficial, that it is symptom-oriented and does not give adequate consideration to the underlying or "inner causes" of the neuroses relevant to the problem behaviors, that it produces only temporary benefits, and that in eliminating certain problems or symptoms it provokes new ones. In general, it seems that the major issues are: whether behavior therapy thoroughly eliminates the problem behaviors, an issue relevant to symptom substitution and permanence of benefits; the justification for the philosophical concomitants of a treatment approach that allows the therapist to make the decisions as to what are "right" and "wrong" behaviors; and the validity of the purported empirical bases of behavior therapy.

Perhaps the objection that is voiced most loudly is in regard to the elimination of a symptom, the seeming neglect of the inferred underlying neurotic conflict that caused the problem behaviors, and the possibility of the development of a substitute symptom. The concept of symptom substitution is exemplified as follows: insight-oriented psychologists believe that action therapies may eliminate a problem behavior, but do not eliminate the *cause* of the problem; therefore, a new but related substitute symptom will emerge. To put this into practical terms, the insight-oriented position would maintain that if behavior therapy techniques were used to stop thumb-sucking, which might be caused by an underlying neurotic conflict related to insecurity, the underlying neurotic conflict would not be resolved by the treatment. Therefore, in the absence of the thumb-sucking, there would emerge as a manifestation of the neurotic conflict a new or substitute symptom such as nail-biting, compulsive eating, or some similar oral means of security-giving compensation.

If the theoretical bases of the insight and action systems are considered, there is bound to be a dispute on this issue. Insight theories, in order to support their belief about the development of problem behaviors, must maintain the concept of symptom substitution. But, of course, such a concept is incompatible with the behavior therapy position on the development of problem behaviors; the latter maintains that unless the problem behaviors are relearned, elimination of the problem will be permanent (Wolpe, 1964). Thus the behavior therapist would claim that any new behavior that appeared to be a substitute symptom was not really caused by the same underlying etiological factors that caused the original problem behavior that was treated, but rather that the person had encountered conditions or stimuli (perhaps quite similar to those that had caused the initial problem) which had resulted in his being conditioned to a new problem behavior. That is, there was no substitution of symptoms; the client had merely, in the course of intervening events, *learned* a new unadaptive habit. It is quite feasible, from the viewpoint of behavior therapy, for a person to relearn an abnormal or unacceptable behavioral response and to display the same symptom for which he has already been treated; or a new behavior problem may emerge that resembles the original problem but really has absolutely no etiological relationship to it.

Through theoretical intricacies, it might be feasible to derive a basis for transfer of symptoms or symptom substitution; but, in general, behaviorists believe that this possibility has been greatly exaggerated (Lazarus, 1965; Rachman, 1963; Wolpe, 1958). It seems that the few cases of "symptom substitution" that are available are so designated more by the theoretical orientation of the diagnostician than by undeniable linking facts. A good example of a similar situation is in the use of clinical hypnosis; many critics believe that the use of hypnotic techniques to eliminate problems will result in new symptoms. Hilgard (1965) has pointed out that the aftereffects of clinical hypnosis (a technique of behavior therapy) are frequently misinterpreted and exaggerated; for example, he presents evidence that questions whether the undesirable aftereffects, or sequelae, when they do occur, are actually produced by the hypnotic induction, the hypnotic state, or perhaps are rather produced by the relationship of the subject with the therapist using hypnosis. Hilgard states:

. . . the interaction with the hypnotist as an authority figure is one thing; the consequence of having hypnotic experiences is perhaps another. (p. 56)

For all aspects of behavior therapy, the point is: what really caused the new problem behavior to develop? Are transfers of symptoms or symptom substitutions, if they should occur, the results of the behavior therapy or of *some other variables* that might be encountered in the person's environmental gestalt? Could symptom substitutions, if such could actually be determined, possibly reflect a culturally conditioned response? For example, communication media have fostered the popular conception that if you stop smoking through the use of a behavior therapy technique, such as by means of clinical hypnosis, you will end up biting your nails. Thus, if the person were treated in this manner, he might well then start biting his nails, because he had been previously conditioned to expect this!

In summary of the controversy of symptom substitution, there is little *empirical* evidence to support the belief that treatment by behavior therapy—that is, the elimination of the actual symptoms or problem behaviors—will result in symptom substitution. When a person who has been treated by behavior therapy does develop another problem, there is no concrete evidence that this is an aftereffect that can be attributed to the behavior therapy. But it is recognized that the over-all efficacy, in terms of its long-range value, has yet to be proved superior to other forms of treatment, such as counseling and psychotherapy. More on the long-term efficacy will be presented in the section on the empirical validation of behavior therapy.

The second controversial issue that should be considered has to do with the philosophical concomitants of a treatment approach that allows the therapist to make the decisions as to what are "right" and "wrong" behaviors. The basic philosophical question would be: Who has the right to make decisions about what is acceptable behavior? Since what is right for one person need not be right for another, and if personal worth and integrity are to be accorded to each man, is it not possible that only the individual can decide what is right for himself?

These are the questions that have been posed by many who dispute or distrust the philosophy of the behavior therapy approach. It is feared that a great deal of personal expression could be restricted and constricted by the behavioral norms of a person's society. It is a rather common belief among educators, psychologists, and philosophers that *creativity,* an essential for a productive person and society, necessitates individual freedom to explore, try, and develop thoughts, feelings, ideas, and behaviors. This idea has held an honored position in theories of counseling and psychotherapy, and is the basis for the therapeutic practice of letting the client assume the responsibility for the process of the counseling or psychotherapy and for determining when the treatment has reached a satisfactory point for termination (which, of course, could be reached without having changed the problem behavior that brought the client to treatment). And there have been numerous fictional treatises that have portrayed the stifling of the individual through conditioning techniques implemented by the governmental establishment. All of this has led to an outcry from many professionals when conditioning techniques began to receive application in psychology and psychiatry; that is, it was feared that behavioral controls might be the first in a series of steps toward forcing individual conformity to socially acceptable behaviors and denying the person the right to individuality of thinking, feeling, and behaving.

But mass human cybernetics is not the purpose of behavior therapy. Quite the contrary. The purpose is to help the person achieve the behavioral state that he desires, and to do so by the most effective means. Thus when long-term problems, such as chronic sexual disturbances, are treated so as to produce immediate effects by conditioning techniques, behavior therapy actually earns philosophical support. For example, in a psychiatric project that provided treatment to persons with sexual problems, such as transvestites, homosexuals, and persons with sexual fetishes, the persons voluntarily came and asked that these sexual activities be eliminated or controlled (Woody, 1967). In several cases the persons still derived satisfaction from the sexual deviations; but in weighing other factors, such as the wish to maintain their marriages and avoid hurting their spouse or children because of their sexual preferences, the patients had chosen to have a pleasurable behavior eliminated. It was their decision. It is likely that the philosophically minded would approve of this type of use. But paradoxically, if the person asked to be conditioned into a sexual deviation, such as wanting to become a homosexual through conditioning techniques, it is obvious that philosophers would question this; they would probably feel that the therapist should uphold the standards of society; and they would thus be placing limits on the right of the patient to decide what behaviors should be acceptable therapeutic goals. Behavior therapists are well aware of their responsibility to both the individual and society, and in the case where the person requests therapy to become something that is deviant to the social norms, the behavior therapist's social responsibility takes precedence; he would not provide treatment for these purposes unless there were extremely important extenuating circumstances.

The philosophical issue of whether the behavior therapist brings his own moral and value system and that of society's into the treatment is equally relevant to the roles of counselors and psychotherapists. It is undeniable that values and morals are involved in the treatments offered by counselors, psychotherapists, and behavior therapists. This is a crucial area that must be dealt with in the professional training of persons who will serve in a therapeutic role (London, 1964).

To summarize, it is apparent that behavior therapy can accord as much respect to the individual as any other theoretical approach; such respect is a function of the given therapist, not the theory. And the entire therapeutic program is designed to bring the person happiness and satisfaction through behavioral modification. He is helped to become the type of person who behaves in a manner that will bring him intrapersonal and interpersonal gratification.

The third controversial issue has to do with the empirical basis for behavior therapy. Proponents of behavior therapy have claimed superiority for their theory over other theories of psychotherapy because they have followed the "scientific method" for its derivation. That is, supposedly whenever a theoretical change is advanced, this is done because the theoretical principle has been subjected to experimentation; and this experimentation has involved comparing an experimental group of subjects (who have received the special treatment aspect under consideration) with a control group of subjects (who have not received the special treatment aspect). If the experimental and control subjects were properly matched (if, that is, the groups were essentially equivalent in basic characteristics), the differences between the two groups after treatment are assumed to be due to the specific treatment aspect being investigated. It is frequently asserted that other approaches to treatment, such as psychotherapy, are not derived from empirical experimentation, but in many cases are the products of "clinical" experimentation (that is, the opinions of professionals derived solely from subjective analysis of the clients with whom they have worked). For example, critics often state that psychoanalysis is based entirely upon the subjective judgments and opinions of Freud (in other words, "clinical" evidence); and consequently the validity of many of the underlying theoretical constructs has not been empirically determined.

One must grant, after perusal of the research in the area, that behavior therapy has drawn from experimentation, both with animals and with humans. But it is also readily evident that there are many clinical case studies; and many of the so-called "experimental" studies violate some of the assumptions for good, "tight" research designs. It seems, therefore, that the behaviorists who claim total immunity to subjectivity in their theoretical structure are actually subject to as much possible error as their counterparts who support insight-oriented psychotherapy on "experimental" grounds. Neither psychotherapy nor behavior therapy has achieved a truly empirical status. Admittedly, behavior therapists should be commended for attempting experimentation with experimental and control groups, something that some proponents of counseling and psychotherapy have not always followed as closely as would be possible. But still there are many potential sources of error in behavior therapy research. This matter will receive further attention in a later section of this chapter.

These loopholes in the theoretical structures of counseling, psychotherapy, and behavior therapy can only be plugged by continued, rigorous attempts at experimentation. The reality of the situation is, however, that pure research, such as would be conducted by the experimental psychologist in his animal laboratory, is not an easy accomplishment. When working clinically with a person in providing the day-to-day services, the practitioner holds the primary here-and-now responsibility of trying to help the individual within the administrative objectives of the setting in which he is employed. In other words, research is necessary; but in working with human beings, as opposed to laboratory animals, there are many research possibilities that cannot readily be investigated. It is possible that certain aspects might merit investigation and might provide a "plug" for a theoretical loophole if a certain study could be conducted, but the practical goal of helping the individual sometimes negates the actual implementation of a research study. In practice, there must be a preference for personal benefits over the purely experimental benefits. One cannot, of course, exist without the other. In subsequent chapters, the reader should be cognizant that some studies are "experimental" and some are "clinical" in design; and even some of the experimental studies are not beyond questioning.

TOWARD A PSYCHOBEHAVIORAL POSITION

The term "psychobehavioral position" is used, as might be surmised, to denote an integration of aspects from the insight-oriented counseling-psychotherapy continuum with aspects of behavior therapy. A suitable synonym might be "integration therapy." References to psychobehavioral therapy or integration therapy should not be interpreted as representing a new theoretical position; more than anything else, it probably represents a frame of reference for practice. It is not the purpose of this book to propose a new theory for modifying problem behavior; rather, the intention is to set forth practical techniques that can be used to change behaviors. It seems that most, if not all, theories of counseling, psychotherapy, and behavior therapy have at least some aspects that may effectively contribute to this task, and that a single theoretical approach does not have exclusive hold on the right way in which to deal with behavioral problem children. It is on this basis, therefore, that an integration of theories and techniques is proposed. This integrative approach is quite compatible with previously expressed reasons for eclectic psychology, such as have been cited by Thorne (1950, 1955, 1961).

There are at least three primary reasons why this integrative approach seems best for helping behavioral problem children in the schools. First, there are great differences between persons who are to be treated. The concept of individuality greatly influences the theory and techniques

used in the treatment. Not enough is yet known empirically about individual differences to assert unquestionably that one specific theory has
universal applicability. There are certain persons or even groups of
persons, with their unique composites of characteristics, for whom a
given theory might be quite appropriate; but the minute the theoretician
assumes complete coverage by the theory, an exceptional person will
appear. Consideration must be given to the possibility of exceptionality.

Second, techniques within a theoretical position vary in reliability
and validity. For example, there are certain techniques used by behavior
therapists that seem to be quite valid for a specific disorder, while another
technique within the same theoretical framework may not be valid. Similarly, some techniques can be effectively used by one professional, but
not by another; the reliability must be questioned.

Third, in the case of behavioral problem children in the schools,
there are some aspects that are peculiar to these particular children and,
moreover, to the setting in which the services will be provided. For
example, in treating children, certain techniques might not be as valuable as they would be with adults. But more specifically, the public educational institution has characteristics that might influence the theory of
techniques that are used. Thus a technique or theory might be readily
accepted in a mental health clinic, but receive a skeptical reception in
the school setting.

It would seem, therefore, that theories and techniques must be based
on individual needs—the "individual needs" being influenced by the
professional's characteristics, the client's or behavioral problem child's
individual characteristics, the problem behaviors being treated, and the
institutional setting in which the services are to be provided. The logical
conclusion is that an eclectic approach is undeniably necessary.

As stated previously, the results of behavior therapy with problem
behaviors that are commonly encountered in the school are impressive.
But there are also aspects of counseling and psychotherapy that seem
valuable. Of special significance is the fact that behavior therapy techniques are based on conditioning and are devoid, at least theoretically,
of many of the interpersonal factors that are associated with a warm,
helping relationship. Although some behaviorists would maintain that
behavioral modification can be effectively performed under laboratory
conditions—that is, by relying upon the instruments or apparatus rather
than on human elements—this does not appear to be the most appropriate
way to approach the changing of problem behaviors. As will be revealed,
there is evidence that even so-called "pure" behavior therapy is not
devoid of the interpersonal factors of the therapist-client relationship,
and indeed these human factors may well influence the outcome of the
behavior therapy; but this latter point has not been adequately researched
to allow the drawing of a definite conclusion. The position maintained

here is that behavior therapy techniques are not and should not be impersonal. There is value to be had from a warm, understanding relationship between the therapist and the client. This will receive further elaboration as the discussion progresses.

The relationship between the therapist and the client receives emphasis for its therapeutic values from essentially all of the insight-oriented approaches to counseling and psychotherapy. Each approach does, of course, have its own terms, concepts, and theoretical proclivities; but in the end there is accord for the belief that the components of the relationship influence the client's quest for insight.

Although each theory of counseling and psychotherapy could provide examples, the client-centered theory of Carl R. Rogers has made a tremendous impact on psychology and education, and it seems to serve as one of the best examples of the components of the therapist-client relationship that can be generalized to all helping relationships. Through the years, Rogers has set forth several treatises on his client-centered theory (1951, 1961), and it hardly does the theory justice to try to make a synopsis in a few sentences. The over-all hypothesis for client-centered therapy, according to Rogers (1961), is:

If I can provide a certain type of relationship, the other person will discover within himself the capacity to use that relationship for growth, and change and personal development will occur. (p. 33)

Subsequent research has provided evidence that this hypothesis is, in fact, true in general; but it has been found that there are persons who do not respond to this gross concept; and particularly that observable behavioral change, such as would be a primary goal in working with behavioral problem children, may or may not occur because of this type of relationship. The lack of guaranteed changes in behavior and, relative to this, the length of time necessary for behavioral change to occur, if it occurs at all, seem to justify rejecting this hypothesis as being the sole determinant of effective therapy. That is, the therapeutic relationship is extremely valuable for essentially any kind of therapy, but there are persons who will not respond immediately or, in fact, at all by making behavioral changes simply because of this relationship.

It is worthwhile, however, to consider briefly the components of the client-centered relationship, because although they are rather general in nature, there is reason to believe that their presence can beneficially influence behavioral modification efforts. The Rogerian position is that constructive personality change will occur if the therapist can communicate three attitudes to the client: unconditional positive regard, empathic understanding, and congruence. *Unconditional positive regard* is manifested by the therapist's caring for the client, but it is highly important

that the "caring" be nonpossessive, nonevaluative, and without reserva-
tions. In other words, the therapist (be he teacher, counselor, or psychologist) must communicate real concern and positive feelings without
imposing his own value system and without the reservation that he may
withdraw his regard if he evaluates the client's ideas, beliefs, or behaviors
in a certain way. *Empathic understanding* denotes the therapist's communicating to the client that he actually feels or senses what the client
is feeling, sensing, or experiencing at each moment. *Congruence* means
that the therapist must be himself; he must not role-play at understanding. He must be genuine; he must actually feel with the client. Just as an
actor strives to empathize with the character he is portraying, so does
the client-centered therapist try to move inside of the other person, the
client. But his empathic understanding must not be acting; it must be
real. These three attitudes must be communicated to the client, and the
client must perceive them if positive personality change is to occur.

As was mentioned earlier, Truax and Carkhuff (1967) have investigated the Rogerian conditions or attitudes and have consequently made
some revisions. Empathy has been changed to *accurate empathy*. It is believed that the therapist must be capable of more than sensing the
private inner world of his client. Accurate empathy

. . . involves both the therapist's *sensitivity to current feelings* and his *verbal
facility to communicate this understanding* in a language attuned to the client's
current feelings. (Truax and Carkhuff, 1967, p. 46)

Unconditional positive regard has been modified to the dimension of
nonpossessive warmth; these two terms designate essentially the same
attributes. Congruence has evolved to *genuineness.* The extensive research of Truax and Carkhuff has verified and clarified the significance
of relationship variables in counseling and psychotherapy, has provided
a much-needed empirical base, and has resulted in several methods for
estimating the degree to which the various relationship dimensions are
fulfilled.

It is obvious that attaining these three attitudes or factors is no
easy matter. It necessarily involves the personality attributes of the therapist. That is, if a therapist is unable to accept others, or if his own inner
problems lead him to sympathize instead of empathize, or if he cannot set
aside his own needs in order to deal with the client's needs, he will be
unable to be a sincere, effective therapist. Professional training, such as
is provided by graduate programs in counselor education, does facilitate
the development of these attitudes; but since the bases for the attitudes
are intrinsic to the therapist's personality structure, it frequently takes
more than academic understanding—it requires self-understanding. Self-
understanding on the part of the therapist will vary among professionals;

it may be affected by day-to-day experiences, maturity, or engaging in a systematic program to gain understanding.

This latter approach might include counseling or psychotherapy. It is generally accepted in training programs for psychologists and psychiatrists that part of their preparation, especially on the doctoral level, should include the experience of sitting on the client's side of the desk, of receiving counseling or psychotherapy. This is not seen as a mark against the would-be therapist; on the contrary, it is seen as a reflection of a serious, personal commitment to become a more effective therapist.

It should be apparent that the ideas expressed in the preceding paragraphs are incompatible with pure behavior therapy. Many behavior therapists place little value on the personal characteristics of the therapist and believe that the therapist's own preferences do not enter into the behavior therapy. But there is reason to disagree with this position. As will be documented shortly, the therapist's personality factors may very much play a part in even the most orthodox behavior therapy. Thus it is necessary for even behavior therapists to recognize their own values, to have self-understanding, and to control these personal factors in their therapeutic efforts. The concept of self-understanding is necessary for all therapists, regardless of theoretical orientation.

It should be noted that some behavior therapists have acknowledged the value of a "good relationship" between the therapist and the client (Lazarus, 1961; Lazarus, Davison, and Polefka, 1965; Wolpe and Lazarus, 1966). But others have repudiated the assumption of the importance of the relationship. For example, it has been stated that therapists may be changed during the course of behavior therapy without affecting the outcome of the therapy (Geer, 1964; Geer and Katkin, 1966; Lazarus, Davison, and Polefka, 1965); this switching of therapists would not, of course, be acceptable in the insight-oriented systems of counseling and psychotherapy. Furthermore, Eysenck (1960) has indicated that the therapeutic relationship is not necessary:

Personal relations are not essential for cures of neurotic disorder, although they may be useful in certain circumstances. (p. 11)

Unfortunately, Eysenck never clarifies when "they may be useful" or under what "certain circumstances."

In opposition to those behaviorists who do not fully endorse the value of the therapist's personal factors—that is, the relationship—research has indicated that these personal factors are very important to the outcome of behavior therapy. It has been found that the degree of interpersonal compatibility between the therapist and the client influences the effects of verbal conditioning (Sapolsky, 1960); and in behavioral counseling, which relies upon verbal reinforcement from counselors, it has been

found that counselors vary in reinforcing effectiveness (Ryan and Krumboltz, 1964). Wolpe and Lazarus (1966) make direct reference to capitaliz-
ing on the therapist-client relationship:

As in most systems of psychotherapy, the patient enjoys the nonjudgmental acceptance of a person whom he perceives as possessing the necessary skills and desire to be of service, but, in behavior therapy he receives, in addition, the
benefits of special conditioning procedures which have independent validity.[5]

This is, of course, the position proposed here: The therapist-client relationship is important, but it can be beneficially augmented by behavior
therapy techniques.

One might wonder whether the "nonjudgmental acceptance" contributed to the therapeutic effects in the same way as do the Rogers-
Truax-Carkhuff attributes of "nonpossessive acceptance" and "nonpossessive warmth." Not only is it possible that the effects of behavior therapy
are contaminated by unmeasured influences from the therapist-client
relationship and that certain behavioral techniques promote insight, as
was discussed previously, but there is also reason to wonder how much of
the effect is due to clinical suggestion or hypnosis. An illustration of this
point is found in the conflicting reports about the use of hypnosis in behavior therapy. Cautela (1966b) reports from a personal communication
that Wolpe uses planned hypnosis with 25 percent of his desensitization
cases, yet elsewhere Wolpe and Lazarus (1966) state that hypnosis is used
in 33 percent of the desensitization cases. Leaving this discrepancy aside,
it is interesting to note that the effects of behavior therapy are seldom, if
ever, attributed even in part to hypnosis or clinical suggestion. In view
of the striking similarity between hypnotic induction techniques and
the techniques used to induce relaxation for behavior therapy, the failure
of many behavior therapy studies to cite specifically the use of procedures
that might fall in the hypnotic spectrum, and the lack of clear-cut documentation to confirm or deny the possible influence of suggestion, a
healthy skepticism as to what really causes the desired therapeutic effects
is justified.

Although behavior therapists have been reluctant or unwilling to
acknowledge the influences of the therapist-client relationship, analysis
of their actual procedures reveals that these effects are present. In a case
study, Clark (1963) combined counseling with behavior therapy: he offered
advice and information about the problem areas to the client, counseled,
and used a reciprocal inhibition technique (which is within the realm of
behavior therapy) to treat the overt symptom. Various other case studies
have revealed the use of interpretation and positive-regard responses to

  [5] From BEHAVIOR THERAPY TECHNIQUES, J. Wolpe and A. A. Lazarus,
Pergamon Press, Oxford, 1967 (1966), p. 10.

promote insight about the problems; the use of discussions; and the use of other clinical procedures (such as a probing intake interview) that could very easily be classified as insight-oriented counseling or psychotherapy; yet the studies themselves have been labeled behavior therapy (Lazarus, 1961, 1964; Lazarus, Davison, and Polefka, 1965; Lazarus and Rachman, 1957; Rachman, 1959; Wolpe, 1960; Wolpe and Lazarus, 1966). This use in behavior therapy of aspects of counseling and psychotherapy, which is frequently unacknowledged or denied, has been described elsewhere in detail (Breger and McGaugh, 1965, 1966; Woody, in press).

There is practical evidence that behaviorally oriented and insight-oriented procedures can be used in combination. Katahn, Strenger, and Cherry (1966) employed combined group counseling and behavior therapy (relaxation and desensitization) with college students who had a high degree of test anxiety. A follow-up after eight treatment sessions revealed that there was a significant increase in grade point average and that the amount of test anxiety was significantly lower. Of special interest is the fact that the students typically attributed the overt changes in behavior to the relaxation training and desensitization—that is, to the behavior therapy; but all "invariably" felt that the counseling interaction was one of the most important (supportive?) aspects of the treatment. Similarly, Paul and Shannon (1966) used action and insight procedures with groups of chronically anxious males; the results suggested that desensitization (behavior therapy) in groups is about as effective as when used individually, and it seemed that group involvement itself may have contributed to the effects of treatment. Sipprelle (1967) provides a unique clinical approach that utilizes induced-anxiety, reciprocal inhibition (behavior therapy), stimulated recall via video tape recordings (action and insight), and insight procedures. Cooper (1963) has stated that behavior therapists can draw beneficially on the traditional forms of insight-oriented psychotherapy.

What is perhaps more significant than the practical aspects of combining insight and action systems is the fact that behavior therapy and the counseling-psychotherapy continuum may not be totally different in their theoretical bases. Marks and Gelder (1966) provide a comprehensive analysis of the theoretical aspects of psychotherapy and behavior therapy and conclude that there is much "common ground" between the two positions. Likewise, Mowrer (1966) concludes that Freudian psychoanalysis, Rogerian client-centered therapy, and behavior therapy have quite similar definitions for the origins of neurotic behaviors.

It is apparent that there is considerable research to contradict the belief that behavior therapy is entirely distinct from the counseling-psychotherapy continuum. There does indeed seem to be a common ground, both theoretically and technically. Since this interrelationship has frequently been uncontrolled in research studies on behavior therapy, it seems unjustified to conclude that the behavior therapy principles are solely responsible for therapeutic effects; some of these effects may have been due in part to aspects inherent in counseling and psychotherapy.

Beech (1963) states that the differing results obtained by behavior therapists seem to suggest that therapeutic success may be influenced by the patient-therapist relationship. Marks and Gelder (1966) believe that certain disorders require behavior therapy, others an insight-oriented form of psychotherapy, and others a combined approach.

Thus far, in support of a psychobehavioral or integrative approach, considerable research documentation has been presented for the belief that behavior therapy is not totally independent of aspects inherent in the counseling-psychotherapy continuum. Furthermore, it is suggested that the most effective form of treatment will be a planned combination of the two approaches (Woody, 1968b, in press). This assertion has yet to be adequately researched, but there is considerable evidence that any one technique is not applicable to all clients. Woody said the following:

A key concern of insight counselors and therapists, particularly those who rely on nondirective relationship factors, would be whether they could use a conditioning-oriented procedure without violating certain tenets of their theoretical position. Although there is insufficient research evidence to warrant a conclusive statement, it appears that if the insight counselor or therapist has a justifiable reason for resorting to a behavioral technique and the client understands the reason—and in most cases the client will have been the initiator of the reason—then there is justification for believing that a behavioral technique can be used. And in a study of psychologists who used hypnosis clinically, Woody and Herr (1965) found that many espoused a therapeutic theory that would customarily be incompatible with such a presumably directive technique as clinical hypnosis, yet they both used the techniques and maintained their theoretical position.

Determining guidelines for integrating psychotherapeutic and behavior therapy techniques depends to a large extent on the expertise of the therapist. This obviously paves the way for error, but the lack of relevant research negates any definitive guidelines. Thus, subsequent recommendations should be viewed as hypotheses in search of supporting or contradictory evidence, because they are derived from personal clinical experiences and interpretations of the research of others.

Regardless of subsequent therapeutic techniques that may evolve, the initial quest should be for an empathic, nonpossessive, sincere therapist-client relationship. Not only is there reason to believe that this is potentially a directly contributing source in behavioral change due to the acquisition of insight and sociopersonal learning from the therapist, but it also seems to facilitate behavior therapy or conditioning procedures. In a recent therapeutic project, insight psychotherapy was provided by one therapist concurrently with the administration of a program of aversive therapy (by means of electric shocks) by three behavior therapists; the subjective conclusions were that the clients formed a relationship with all therapists, including those who were administering painful electric shocks to them, and that the insight psychotherapy provided the clients with an opportunity to resolve, among other things, their conflicting feelings about their aversive-behavior therapists: this resolution of defensiveness or resistance appeared to facilitate the conditioning processes (Woody, 1967). These findings seem compatible with those of the previously cited study of Katahn, Strenger, and Cherry (1966).

When traditional verbal psychotherapy is being conducted, there are three specific problem areas that could be dealt with by integration of behavior therapy techniques:

1. *Facilitation and acceleration of therapy.* In this role, conditioning techniques can be used to eliminate the barriers to therapeutic progress that typically arise in psychotherapy; of course, there are instances when such barriers serve a beneficial purpose and should be allowed to remain until the client achieves his own resolution, but there are other times when their neurotic component serves no good and only delays therapy and causes the client more discomfort. The therapist must judge when action, through a behavior therapy technique, is warranted. Behavioral rehearsal, reciprocal inhibition including induced relaxation and systematic desensitization, verbal reinforcement (Woody, in press), clinical hypnosis (Sipprelle, 1964), and stimulated recall by means of video tape recordings (Woody, Krathwohl, Kagan, and Farquhar, 1965) have all been successfully integrated into insight psychotherapy for purposes of accelerating the therapeutic processes.

2. *Elimination of uncomfortable symptoms.* This use is based on the premise that there are times when it is clinically advisable to allow the client to enter into an insight-oriented psychotherapeutic relationship free from the irritation and restrictions produced by certain symptoms. This seems particularly beneficial for clients with psychosomatic problems, resistances to therapy, and crises in their daily lives (for example, acute depression). The one stipulation that should generally be made, especially when the therapist believes in the concept of an underlying neurotic conflict, is that the client must agree to continue in psychotherapy until such time as the therapist deems it advisable to return the power-to-terminate to him; in other words, clients should be told that behavioral techniques are being used to bring quick relief, that they may not eliminate the neurotic cause, and that they are therefore expected to remain in psychotherapy even though the presenting problem has been alleviated or eliminated.

3. *Treatment of therapeutically unresponsive clients.* Every therapist at some time or other encounters a client who will not respond to verbal psychotherapy. The possible reasons for this are legion. The point is that there are times when, even if the therapist staunchly denounces symptom removal, behavior therapy techniques can be used to help clients who have not noticeably benefited from insight psychotherapy. This seems to be especially useful for culturally deprived and mentally retarded clients, persons who may lack the verbal skills, logical reasoning, and introspective ability that are necessary for psychotherapy.

In each of the foregoing instances, which have been discussed in detail else-where (Woody, in press), the expertise of the clinician is the final criterion for determining when and how to integrate behavioral techniques into psycho-therapy. Perhaps the time will come when research will provide more clear-cut indications, but in the meantime the therapist must rely upon his professional skills and clinical judgment.

One final component of the psychobehavioral approach involves termina-tion of therapy. Some psychotherapists facetiously maintain that typically therapy has only two parts: striving for a definition of the relationship, and, once that is achieved, preparing for termination. The insightists do focus con-siderable attention on the importance of termination, but behaviorists do not consider this matter, except as concerns the overt behavioral problems; that is, no concern is directed at the feelings held by either the therapist or client toward the other. Clients treated primarily by behavior therapy feel a sense of unresolved frustration after their conditioning program is completed. Perhaps the situation is that behavior therapists strive so hard to keep their therapy impersonal that they refuse to feel for their client at the end of therapy, and perhaps it is only the clients who conjure up feelings for the real or non-existent (but desired) relationship. Nevertheless, there may be the aftereffects of transference phenomena—even in behavior therapy—which should be dealt with before termination if the therapy is to have optimal success.[6]

A certain amount of expertise is involved in determining a treatment program. For this purpose certain educators may obviously have fewer treatment resources to draw on than others; educators differ in the amount and types of relevant training that they have received. This adds impetus to the belief asserted throughout this book that services for the behavioral problem child necessitate cooperation between members of the school faculty. As will be apparent in later chapters, there are tech-niques that the classroom teacher can apply to help behavioral problem children, but there are other techniques that can be used only by someone with extensive training in psychology, and thus some techniques will be appropriate only for the school psychologist. Therefore, just as the staffs of mental health clinics typically have "staffing conferences" or "case con-ferences" to determine what is the best way to treat a particular client and who is the best member to undertake the treatment program, mem-bers of the school faculty should meet to determine jointly the psycho-educational services that are to be offered to a particular child.

In summary, it should be emphasized that all theories of counseling, psychotherapy, and behavior therapy have something to offer to certain types of persons, but none is universally applicable. Research evidence supports the view that counseling, psychotherapy, and behavior therapy

6 R. H. Woody, Toward a rationale for psychobehavioral study, *Archives of Gen-eral Psychiatry*, in press. Reproduced with permission of the Editor of the Journal of the American Medical Association and the Author.

are theoretically and technically related, and that they can be integrated. Psychobehavioral therapy, or integrative therapy, draws on all available theories and techniques, and any treatment program for a client would be determined on an individual basis. It is quite possible that a treatment program may have to be changed after it is started, if with increased knowledge of the client it becomes evident that other aspects are important. The primary guideline is: The preferred technique depends on the individual's needs. It may be that client-centered counseling would be offered initially, but if progress were not made or a therapeutic "block" occurred, the therapist might readily switch to an action-type technique; or, of course, the opposite could be true. Regardless of the pattern for the application of techniques, the following points are maintained: There is value in establishing a warm, understanding, congruent, empathic relationship with the client; behavior therapy techniques, based on principles of learning theory, appear to bring relatively quick changes in unpleasant and unacceptable behaviors; one of the objectives of treatment is to bring relief and happiness to the client, and this will usually necessitate observable changes in behavior; and the most comprehensive theoretical approach to effective treatment seems to be the integration of behavior therapy and the counseling-psychotherapy continuum.

REFERENCES

Albert, G. If counseling *is* psychotherapy—what then? *Personnel and Guidance Journal,* 1966, 45:124-129.

American Psychological Association, Committee on Definition, Division of Counseling Psychology. Counseling psychology as a specialty. *American Psychologist,* 1956, 11:282-285.

Arbuckle, D. S. *Counseling: philosophy, theory and practice.* Boston: Allyn and Bacon, 1965.

Axline, Virginia M. *Play therapy.* Boston: Houghton Mifflin, 1947.

Beech, H. R. Some theoretical and technical difficulties in the application of behaviour therapy. *Bulletin of the British Psychological Society,* 1963, 16:25-33.

Blocher, D. H. *Developmental counseling.* New York: Ronald Press, 1966.

Brammer, L. M., and Shostrom, E. L. *Therapeutic psychology: fundamentals of counseling and psychotherapy.* Englewood Cliffs, N.J.: Prentice-Hall, 1960.

Breger, L., and McGaugh, J. L. A critique and reformulation of "learning theory" approaches to psychotherapy and neurosis. *Psychological Bulletin,* 1965, 63:335-358.

Breger, L., and McGaugh, J. L. Learning theory and behavior therapy: a reply to Rachman and Eysenck. *Psychological Bulletin,* 1966, 65:170-173.

Cautela, J. R. Desensitization factors in the hypnotic treatment of phobias. *Journal of Psychology,* 1966, 64:277-288. (a)

Cautela, J. R. Hypnosis and behavior therapy. *Behaviour Research and Therapy,* 1966, 4:219-224. (b)

Clark, D. F. The treatment of hysterical spasm and agoraphobia by behaviour therapy. *Behaviour Research and Therapy,* 1963, 1:245-250.

Cooper, J. E. A study of behaviour therapy in thirty psychiatric patients. *Lancet,* 1963, 1:411-415.

Cooper, J. E., Gelder, M. G., and Marks, I. M. Results of behaviour therapy in 77 psychiatric patients. *British Medical Journal,* 1965, 1:1222-1225.

Eysenck, H. J. The effects of psychotherapy: an evaluation. *Journal of Consulting Psychology,* 1952, 16:319-324.

Eysenck, H. J. Learning theory and behaviour therapy. In H. J. Eysenck (Ed.), *Behaviour therapy and the neuroses.* New York: Pergamon Press, 1960, 4-21.

Eysenck, H. J. Learning theory and behaviour therapy. In G. Lindzey and C. S. Hall (Eds.), *Theories of personality: primary sources and research.* New York: John Wiley and Sons, 1965. (a)

Eysenck, H. J. The effects of psychotherapy. *International Journal of Psychiatry,* 1965, 1:99-142. (b)

Eysenck, H. J., and Rachman, S. *The causes and cures of neurosis.* San Diego: R. R. Knapp, 1965.

Fiedler, F. E. The concept of an ideal therapeutic relationship. *Journal of Consulting Psychology,* 1950, 14:239-245.

Ford, D. H., and Urban, H. B. *Systems of psychotherapy: a comparative study.* New York: John Wiley and Sons, 1963.

Geer, J. H. Phobia treated by reciprocal inhibition. *Journal of Abnormal and Social Psychology,* 1964, 69:642-645.

Geer, J. H., and Katkin, E. S. Treatment of insomnia using a variant of systematic desensitization: a case report. *Journal of Abnormal Psychology,* 1966, 71:161-164.

Gelder, M. G. Assessment of behaviour therapy. *Proceedings of the Royal Society of Medicine,* 1965, 58:525-529.

Ginott, H. G. *Group psychotherapy with children.* New York: McGraw-Hill, 1961.

Gustad, J. W. The definition of counseling. In R. F. Berdie (Ed.), *Roles and relationships in counseling.* Minneapolis: University of Minnesota Press, 1953, pp. 3-19.

Hammer, M., and Kaplan, A. M. (Eds.). *The practice of psychotherapy with children.* Homewood, Ill.: Dorsey Press, 1967.

Harper, R. A. *Psychoanalysis and psychotherapy: 36 systems.* Englewood Cliffs, N.J.: Prentice-Hall, 1959.

Hilgard, E. R. *Hypnotic susceptibility.* New York: Harcourt, Brace and World, 1965.

Katahn, M., Strenger, S., and Cherry, Nancy. Group counseling and behavior therapy with test-anxious college students. *Journal of Consulting Psychology,* 1966, 30:544-549.

Kessler, Jane W. *Psychopathology of childhood.* Englewood Cliffs, N.J.: Prentice-Hall, 1966.

Kiesler, D. J. Some myths of psychotherapy research and the search for a paradigm. *Psychological Bulletin,* 1966, 65:110-136.

Krasner, L., and Ullmann, L. P. (Eds.). *Research in behavior modification.* New York: Holt, Rinehart and Winston, 1965.

Krumboltz, J. D. Behavioral counseling: rationale and research. *Personnel and Guidance Journal,* 1965, 44:383-387.

Lazarus, A. A. Group therapy of phobic disorders by systematic desensitization. *Journal of Abnormal and Social Psychology,* 1961, 63:504-510.

Lazarus, A. A. The results of behaviour therapy in 126 cases of severe neurosis. *Behaviour Research and Therapy,* 1963, 1:69-79.

Lazarus, A. A. Behaviour therapy with identical twins. *Behaviour Research and Therapy,* 1964, 1:313-319.

Lazarus, A. A. Behaviour therapy, incomplete treatment, and symptom substitution. *Journal of Nervous and Mental Disease,* 1965, 140:80-86.

Lazarus, A. A. Behaviour rehearsal vs. non-directive therapy vs. advice in effecting behaviour change. *Behaviour Research and Therapy,* 1966, 4:209-212.

Lazarus, A. A., Davison, G. C., and Polefka, D. A. Classical and operant factors in the treatment of a school phobia. *Journal of Abnormal Psychology,* 1965, 70:225-229.

Lazarus, A. A., and Rachman, S. The use of systematic desensitization in psychotherapy. *South African Medical Journal,* 1957, 32:934-937.

Levitt, E. E. Psychotherapy with children: a further evaluation. *Behaviour Research and Therapy,* 1963, 1:45-51.

London, P. *The modes and morals of psychotherapy.* New York: Holt, Rinehart and Winston, 1964.

Mahrer, A. R. (Ed.). *The goals of psychotherapy.* New York: Appleton-Century-Crofts, 1967.

Marks, I. M., and Gelder, M. G. Common ground between behaviour therapy and psychodynamic methods. *British Journal of Medical Psychology,* 1966, 39:11-23.

McGowan, J. F., and Schmidt, L. D. (Eds.). *Counseling: readings in theory and practice.* New York: Holt, Rinehart and Winston, 1962.

Mowrer, O. H. The behavior therapies with special reference to modeling and imitation. *American Journal of Psychotherapy,* 1966, 20:439-461.

Nelson, R. C. Elementary school counseling with unstructured play media. *Personnel and Guidance Journal,* 1966, 45:24-27.

Patterson, C. H. The place of values in counseling and psychotherapy. *Journal of Counseling Psychology,* 1958, 5:216-223.

Patterson, C. H. Psychotherapy in the school. *Journal of School Psychology,* 1966, 4:15-29. (a)

Patterson, C. H. *Theories of counseling and psychotherapy.* New York: Harper and Row, 1966. (b)

Paul, G. L. *Insight vs. desensitization in psychotherapy: an experiment in anxiety reduction.* Stanford, Calif.: Stanford University Press, 1966.

Paul, G. L. Insight versus desensitization in psychotherapy two years after termination. *Journal of Consulting Psychology,* 1967, 31:333-348. (a)

Paul, G. L. Strategy of outcome research in psychotherapy. *Journal of Consulting Psychology,* 1967, 31:109-118. (b)

Paul, G. L., and Shannon, D. T. Treatment of anxiety through systematic desensitization in therapy groups. *Journal of Abnormal Psychology,* 1966, 71:124-135.

Peters, H. J., Shertzer, B., and Van Hoose, W. H. *Guidance in elementary schools.* Chicago: Rand McNally, 1965.

Rachman, S. The treatment of anxiety and phobic reactions by systematic desensitization theory. *Journal of Abnormal and Social Psychology,* 1959, 58:259-263.

Rachman, S. Introduction to behaviour therapy. *Behaviour Research and Therapy,* 1963, 1:3-15.

Rogers, C. R. *Client-centered therapy: its current practice, implications, and theory.* Boston: Houghton Mifflin, 1951.

Rogers, C. R. *On becoming a person.* Boston: Houghton Mifflin, 1961.

Ryan, T. Antoinette, and Krumboltz, J. D. Effects of planned reinforcement counseling on client decision-making behavior. *Journal of Counseling Psychology,* 1964, 11:315-323.

Sapolsky, A. Effect of interpersonal relationship upon verbal conditioning. *Journal of Abnormal and Social Psychology,* 1960, 60:241-246.

Schmidt, Elsa, Castell, D., and Brown, P. A retrospective study of 42 cases of behaviour therapy. *Behaviour Research and Therapy,* 1965, 3:9-19.

Sipprelle, C. N. Non-hypnotizability as resistance. *Psychotherapy: Theory, Research, and Practice,* 1964, 1:75-79.

Sipprelle, C. N. Induced anxiety. *Psychotherapy: Theory, Research, and Practice,* 1967, 4:36-40.

Smith, D. C. Counseling and psychotherapy in the school setting. In J. F. Magary (Ed.), *School psychological services in theory and practice: a handbook.* Englewood Cliffs, N.J.: Prentice-Hall, 1967, 142-170.

Strupp, H. H. Psychotherapeutic technique, professional affiliation, and experience level. *Journal of Consulting Psychology,* 1955, 19:97-102.

Super, D. E. Transition: from vocational guidance to counseling psychology. *Journal of Counseling Psychology,* 1955, 2:3-9.

Thorne, F. C. *Principles of personality counseling: an eclectic viewpoint.* Brandon, Vt.: Journal of Clinical Psychology, 1950.

Thorne, F. C. *Principles of psychological examining: a systematic textbook of applied integrative psychology.* Brandon, Vt.: Journal of Clinical Psychology, 1955.

Thorne, F. C. *Personality: a clinical eclectic viewpoint.* Brandon, Vt.: Journal of Clinical Psychology, 1961.

Truax, C. B., and Carkhuff, R. R. *Toward effective counseling and psychotherapy: training and practice.* Chicago: Aldine, 1967.

Winder, C. L. Psychotherapy. *Annual Review of Psychology,* 1957, 8:309-330.

Wolpe, J. *Psychotherapy by reciprocal inhibition.* Stanford, Calif.: Stanford University Press, 1958.

Wolpe, J. Reciprocal inhibition as the main basis of psychotherapeutic effects. In H. J. Eysenck (Ed.), *Behaviour therapy and the neuroses.* New York: Pergamon Press, 1960, 88-113.

Wolpe, J. Psychotherapy: the nonscientific heritage and the new science. *Behaviour Research and Therapy,* 1963, 1:23-28.

Wolpe, J. The comparative clinical status of conditioning therapies and psychoanalysis. In J. Wolpe, A. Salter, and L. J. Reyna (Eds.), *The conditioning therapies.* New York: Holt, Rinehart and Winston, 1964, 5-16.

Wolpe, J., and Lazarus, A. A. *Behavior therapy techniques.* Oxford, Eng.: Pergamon Press, 1966.

Woody, R. H. Behavior therapy and school psychology. *Journal of School Psychology,* 1966, 4:1-14.

Woody, R. H. Reactions of sexual deviants to integration of aversive therapy and psychotherapy. Unpublished manuscript, University of Maryland, College Park, 1967.

Woody, R. H. British behavioural counselling. *Educational Research,* 1968, 10:207-212. (a)

Woody, R. H. Integrating behavior therapy and psychotherapy. *British Journal of Medical Psychology* (in press).

Woody, R. H. Toward a rationale for psychobehavioral therapy. *Archives of General Psychiatry,* 1968, 19:197-204. (b)

Woody, R. H., and Herr, E. L. Psychologists and hypnosis: psychotherapeutic theories and practices. *American Journal of Clinical Hypnosis,* 1965, 8:80-88.

Woody, R. H., Krathwohl, D. R., Kagan, N., and Farquhar, W. W. Stimulated recall in psychotherapy using hypnosis and video tape. *American Journal of Clinical Hypnosis,* 1965, 7:234-241.

6

Types of Behavior Modification

The preceding chapter has provided an eclectic theoretical framework for changing the problem behaviors of children. This framework, which has been labeled *psychobehavioral* or *integrative,* allows the therapist to incorporate the warm, understanding, supportive, insight-oriented aspects of counseling and psychotherapy with the conditioning aspects of behavior therapy. Since counseling and psychotherapy have been discussed both in this text and extensively in other texts and have become relatively standard components of the training programs for psychoeducational personnel, the main emphasis in this book is, as has been stated previously, to clarify the theory, concepts, and techniques relevant to behavioral modification. Henceforth our attention will be focused primarily on the learning theory or conditioning aspects of behavioral modification, but the reader should always bear in mind that underlying the discussion will be the assumption that counseling and psychotherapy will also be made available to the children being treated. And there is also theoretical and clinical support for believing that behavior therapy and counseling and psychotherapy can be integrated (Woody, 1968, in press).

Techniques used in behavioral modification can be categorized, albeit in a general manner. Each type or category, although sharing the same broader underlying theoretical rationale with the other types or categories, is built upon a set of theoretical assumptions and sufficient research data to validate each of the assumptions.

When an attempt is made to categorize or type any group of items, regardless of their nature, controversy can result because of the individualized interpretations—that is, because of the selective perception of each rater or judge. The field of education has witnessed such rating or judgmental disagreements in a multitude of situations, one of which has already been discussed in detail: the question of what constitutes a behavior problem in the classroom. A similar conflict, resulting from the human aspects or individuality of perception, is readily discernible in the area of behavioral modification. While one psychologist might believe that categories A, B, and C are best for separating types of behavioral modification, another psychologist might prefer categories D, E, and F.

Some of the difference may be due solely to terminology; but the critical factor is that regardless of what set of categories is used, all of the general aspects of behavioral modification must be encompassed. It would be convenient if behavior modification research studies could be easily and consistently placed in *x* number of classifications or categories with neat, orderly boundaries. Regrettably perhaps, this is not the case. But to make a systematic presentation of the results of research, one must establish a set of categories.

The set of categories or types that will be used in this chapter are, like any other set, vulnerable, and are in a sense arbitrary. The flexibility and the scope of the many techniques employed in behavioral modification and the inclusion of various individualized approaches in many of the research studies make categorization difficult. Therefore, while specific types and aspects of behavioral modification, such as techniques, will be set forth in this and other chapters, the reader should recognize that certain studies may be cited that defy specific categorization; they may overlap in varied proportions or include aspects that are not specifically part of these general categories.

In discussing categories of conditioning, as based on the work of Skinner and Hull, Rachman (1963) states:

From the therapeutic point of view, the four most significant concepts are reinforcement, intermittent reinforcement, selective reinforcement and successive approximation. In operant conditioning, the strengthening of the response (reinforcement) is dependent on the response itself. Reinforcement cannot follow unless the response appears. It is the response which causes the reward to arrive and this reinforces (strengthens) the responses. This process is of course different from that described by Pavlov (classical conditioning). It will be noticed that the subject in the operant conditioning situation, plays an active role in the learning process whereas the subject's part in classical conditioning is a relatively passive one.[1]

It should be apparent that, of the four points deemed by Rachman to be most significant, reinforcement denotes the strengthening of the response, intermittent reinforcement denotes the scheduling of the factor that is given to strengthen the response, and selective reinforcement denotes the establishing of the specified characteristics of a response which will justify its being accorded the strengthening factor. Rachman (1963) defines the fourth point as follows:

"Successive approximation" refers to the gradual and graduated building up of a new response on the basis of the person's existing repertoire of responses. By careful planning it is possible to build up the person's simple responses

[1] From S. Rachman, "Introduction to Behavior Therapy," *Behavior Research and Therapy*, Vol. 1 (1963), p. 9. Reprinted by permission.

(such as pressing a lever) into complex patterns of socially co-operative behaviour.[2]

These four points related to operant conditioning are essentially based
on reinforcement. As we progress, it will be evident that there are different types of reinforcement, both positive and negative, that may be used
for modifying behaviors.

Two terms were introduced in the last paragraph which are important for defining the types of behavioral modification: *classical conditioning* and *operant conditioning*. One relevant explanation states:

Strategy in "behavior therapy" consists essentially of introducing reinforcement
contingencies that encourage the emergence of nondeviant response patterns.
This may be achieved by pairing the reinforcer with a *stimulus* (as is the case
in classical conditioning) and/or by making the reinforcer contingent upon a
response (as is the case in operant conditioning). (Lazarus, Davison, and Polefka,
1965, p. 225)

Kessler (1966) differentiates as follows:

. . . classical, Pavlovian conditioning, in which stimuli are associated with an
unconditioned response; and operant conditioning, in which the response itself
operates on the environment to produce certain results. (p. 13)

These two forms of conditioning constitute essentially the ways in which
new responses are learned. Both classical and operant conditioning procedures may be employed in behavioral modification.[3]

For our purposes, behavioral modification can be classified into three
categories (Schmidt, Castell, and Brown, 1965). The first category involves
techniques based on positive reinforcement contingencies: something
positive—that is, a reward—is given when a good or acceptable behavior
occurs but is withheld when a bad or unacceptable behavior occurs. The
second category includes the techniques that are based on negative reinforcement contingencies (this is generally called *aversive conditioning*):
something negative, that is, a punishment, is given when a bad or unacceptable behavior occurs. The third category includes the techniques or
treatment formats that use both positive and negative reinforcement con-

---

2 *Ibid.*

3 Inherent in both classical and operant conditioning procedures is the concept of
a stimulus-response (S-R) bond. When a stimulus occurs, a specific behavioral response
results, and the probability of the predicted response resulting is increased by the giving
of reinforcement. In the case of nocturnal enuresis, for example, a detector that can be
triggered off by urination to sound a bell or buzzer is placed under the child; each time
the child wets the bed, the alarm goes off and wakes him up. He soon builds up an
association (a conditioned bond) between a full bladder and the alarm going off. Consequently, he becomes conditioned to awaken before wetting the bed. Likewise, the
child could be rewarded for awaking before bed-wetting occurred.

tingencies: desirable behaviors or habits are encouraged by means of positive reinforcement, whereas undesirable ones are discouraged by means of negative reinforcement.

In later chapters these three categories will be applicable, in general, to the studies that are reviewed and the techniques cited for use with behavioral problem children in the schools; emphasis will, therefore, be placed on positive reinforcement, negative reinforcement, and reinforcement by a combination of positive and negative factors. Obviously, this is a somewhat gross categorization scheme; and subsumed under each will be subcategories, each of which will contain specific techniques that may be used for behavioral modification. After a more thorough analysis and discussion of each of these three categories or types of behavioral modification, attention can be given to relating research and the derived techniques to actual implementation by educational personnel.

POSITIVE REINFORCEMENT

One of the most frequently used approaches is positive reinforcement. From research, it seems safe to generalize that positive reinforcement, all things considered, is more effective in modifying behavior than negative reinforcement, such as punishment. Certainly it is more pleasant for the therapist, assuming he is mentally healthy, to administer positive stimuli than negative stimuli. For example, a number of behavior therapists who use negative or aversive conditioning, such as administering electric shocks when the client exhibits an unacceptable behavior (this will be discussed in greater detail shortly), have commented to me that they find this form of treatment as unpleasant as the client; that is, they do not feel comfortable within themselves when they punish the client. And when a research study is published that reveals a rather inhuman form of so-called "treatment" (such as a recent report that electric cattle prods were being used in one section of the United States to condition emotionally disturbed children), one cannot but stop and wonder at the inner motives of the investigator. Obviously, the thesis throughout this book is that conditioning techniques can be used to the advantage of the behavioral problem child, but *there is no reason why the treatment must be inhuman.*

Object and Social Recognition Rewards

Basically the idea of positive reinforcement in behavioral modification is as follows. When the behavioral problem child presents an unacceptable behavior, such as misbehavior in the classroom, the behavioral act is totally ignored. The fact that the person witnessing the act does not respond results in the act receiving no reinforcement. But when the child presents an act that is approved by the witness, such as the teacher, then a positive response is made that will thereby reinforce the acceptable behavioral act.

The positive reinforcement stimulus can take numerous forms. In particular, it can be either an *object reward* or a *social recognition reward*. An example of an object reward is the giving of a piece of candy, or it may be a coin or a token that can be redeemed for a privilege or desired gift. The object rewards are given, of course, only when the desirable behavior is acted out. Social recognition rewards might include a smile, a kind word of praise or encouragement, or literally a pat on the shoulder. Verbal responses constitute one of the most commonly used forms of positive reinforcement; for example, when a child behaves properly, the teacher commends him verbally. Incidentally, it is known that withdrawal of a social recognition reward, such as personal acknowledgment in a group setting, is perceived by the child as a punishment. Further clarification of each of the reinforcement forms will be made later.

There are several important factors in the use of reinforcement, whether it be positive or negative in nature. First, it is important that reinforcement be scheduled. That is, the reinforcing stimuli should be given on a prearranged schedule. In general, it is best to give the reinforcement stimulus as close in time as is possible to each behavioral act, a positive stimulus being given if the act is to be strengthened and a negative stimulus being given if the act is to be extinguished (eliminated). But after a bond has been built up between the act and the stimulus—that is, when the child performs the acceptable act more often than the unacceptable act because he knows it will be rewarded, the schedule can be gradually changed. The reward could be delayed in being given; or perhaps the preferred act could be rewarded every second time, then once out of every three times, and so on (this is called "partial reinforcement").[4] Eventually the act will persist whether it receives direct reinforcement or not. Likewise, the extent of the reward or punishment could be decreased after the bond is created. At this later stage, the reinforcement stimulus can be given randomly or at set intervals. Bijou and Baer (1961) discuss schedules of reinforcement in detail.

A second primary consideration, regardless of what format is followed, is: the reinforcement schedule must be consistent. This obviously means that the person providing the reinforcement, such as the teacher,

---

[4] Partial reinforcement—that is, reinforcing at set intervals (for example, three out of five trials)—is believed by many learning theorists to be superior to other conditioning schedules (Eysenck, 1957; Eysenck and Rachman, 1965; Hilgard and Marquis, 1961); it may promote behavioral changes that are most resistant to relapse.

must be personally capable of consistency. Although the unacceptable behaviors may become increasingly annoying and the teacher may be fatigued at times, if the behavioral modification is to be successful the reinforcer (the teacher) must maintain the schedule; his personal needs must not interfere with the behavioral modification procedures.

The use of object rewards and social recognition rewards should be relatively clear from the foregoing discussion. There are, however, two other positive reinforcement procedures that merit special attention at this time: reciprocal inhibition and verbal conditioning.

Reciprocal Inhibition

The principle of reciprocal inhibition is based largely on the work done by Joseph Wolpe (1958). The basic principle is described as follows:

. . . if a response inhibitory of anxiety can be made to occur in the presence of anxiety-evoking stimuli it will weaken the bond between these stimuli and the anxiety. (Wolpe, 1964, p. 10)

The term "reciprocal inhibition" is derived from the physiological phenomenon in which a set of nervous or muscular activities are functioning in a manner antagonistic to another set and this antagonism results in change, since both cannot occur simultaneously. Wolpe (1958, 1964) uses three types of anxiety-inhibiting responses: assertive, relaxation, and sexual.

In using *assertive responses,* the therapist encourages or instigates acting-out behavior, which is not necessarily aggressive, that will maneuver the client into behaving in a manner that is significantly different from the way he usually reacts as a result of his extreme anxiety. Let us take the example of a child who is afraid to defend his rights on the playground; perhaps the other boys will not let him take his turn on the swings. The therapist would train him to be assertive. He might ask him to imagine himself being assertive (perhaps by closing his eyes and pretending that he can picture himself on the playground, as if he were watching television). Or they might role-play different ways of being assertive (the therapist might pretend to be one of the bullies, and then switch roles, letting the child be a bully and thereby allowing him to feel what it is like to be assertive with someone). Through techniques like these, the child progressively overcomes his anxiety by means of the reciprocal inhibition principle; and he may also, through his practices, acquire an improved repertoire of responses—that is, he will have practiced different ways of reacting to anxiety-provoking situations and will know which is the most effective.

Relaxation responses are often used with a technique known as *systematic desensitization*. In this approach, a hierarchy of situations that are known to evoke anxiety in the child is developed. The child is systematically desensitized to the anxiety-provoking conditions by induced relaxation and experiencing, either actually or in his imagination, first a situation that provokes a small amount of anxiety; after repetition of the situation, it loses its ability to provoke anxiety. Then the child becomes desensitized in the same manner to a situation that used to provoke a bit more anxiety than did the first situation; and on up the hierarchy the child progresses, becoming desensitized to situations that originally provoked greater and greater amounts of anxiety. Moreover, for the anxious person, just learning to relax deeply serves as a means of overcoming anxiety; this anxiety could, of course, be the basis for certain behavioral problems.

The third type of reciprocal inhibition response, *sexual,* is used to inhibit anxiety responses connected with sexual situations. Since this type of response is of only limited relevance to this book, the explanation will be brief. Suffice it to say that the conditions of sexual situations are manipulated to allow the client to become progressively accustomed to the feelings, such as anxiety, that occur at each specific point in a sexual situation. Consequently, due to the reciprocal inhibition principle, the anxiety is progressively weakened. Such chronic anxiety response habits as impotence or premature ejaculation have been effectively treated by this technique in a very short time.

Verbal Conditioning

Another form of positive reinforcement is verbal conditioning. This will receive further discussion in Chapter 8, but its involvement in numerous techniques of behavioral modification necessitates a discussion of relevant points at this time.

Verbal conditioning has been used in a variety of settings and has proved to be very effective in facilitating behavioral modification. The basic assumption is that a social reinforcement, such as a verbal response from a significant person, if systematically given, influences the probability that the client, such as the behavioral problem child, will manifest a specifiable behavior. Most commonly this specifiable behavior is a type of verbal response. Verbal conditioning has frequently been used effectively in counseling and psychotherapy to increase a certain type of verbal response on the part of the client and thereby accelerate and increase the effectiveness of the counseling or therapeutic processes; in fact, Williams (1964), in a review of studies related to verbal conditioning, concludes that the majority of studies on verbal conditioning are most relevant to counseling and psychotherapy.

Experiments on verbal conditioning by Greenspoon (1951, 1955) attracted the attention of psychologists, and a great number of subsequent studies have confirmed the belief that *stimuli can be used to reinforce classes of verbal responses* (Binder, McConnell, and Sjoholm, 1957; Hildum and Brown, 1956; Sapolsky, 1960; Vogel-Sprott, 1964). Classes of verbal responses refer to such verbal units as emotional words, affect statements, comments about a particular content or subject area, and self-reference statements; and these can be reinforced by verbal conditioning (Krasner, 1965). More recently, a series of studies has successfully used verbal conditioning to reinforce information-seeking and decision responses in school counseling sessions with students in educational-vocational counseling (Krumboltz and Thoresen, 1964; Thoresen and Krumboltz, 1967). These efforts resulted in the counselees' engaging in educational-vocational information-seeking behavior outside of the counseling setting, thereby facilitating the over-all counseling processes.

Krasner and Ullmann and associates (Krasner, 1965) have investigated numerous response classes, reinforcers, and a number of variables that may be employed in verbal conditioning; they conclude that rather minimal social reinforcement can effectively influence a client's use of a specified class of verbal behavior, and that verbal conditioning of emotional words seems to be significantly associated with clinically meaningful changes in therapy. In summarizing the value of verbal conditioning, Krasner (1965) [5] states:

Verbal conditioning is an excellent technique for learning how human verbal behavior is systematically influenced by situational events; what are the conditions for effectively modifying such behavior; what other behaviors are associated with changes in verbal behavior; and what is the effect on verbal behavior of the interaction of subject-examiner variables.

There seems little doubt that verbal conditioning can facilitate many of the components deemed to be of value in counseling and psychotherapy, such as insight-oriented and self-reference responses, and that overt behavioral changes can result.

NEGATIVE REINFORCEMENT

The use of negative reinforcers for behavioral modification is also termed *aversive conditioning* or *aversive therapy*. As mentioned earlier, this approach involves administering a stimulus when an unacceptable behavior occurs; in all cases, the aversive stimulus should be unpleasant to the receiver. The receiver thus becomes conditioned to expect an unpleasant stimulus when he behaves in the unacceptable manner; and he consequently builds up a set against that behavioral act. The pain or discomfort caused by the aversive stimuli can be conceived of as negative reinforcement. Munn (1956) states:

Negative reinforcement is clearly present when negative conditioning occurs; that is, when the organism checks a response which has produced pain. (p. 201)

There seem to be two major types of stimuli employed in negative reinforcement behavioral modification: aversive stimuli and withdrawal of rewarding (positive) stimuli.

Aversive Stimuli

First, there is the use of stimuli (such as emetic drugs, electric shock, noise, fatigue, or any other factor) that can make the person feel uncomfortable or that are perceived as unpleasant. Aversive stimuli of this sort are applied in conjunction with the unacceptable behavior; the aversive stimuli create an unpleasant feeling for the person; since a relationship is created between the unpleasantness and the unacceptable behavior and since this relationship is certainly not enjoyable to the person, the frequency of the unacceptable behavior will be greatly reduced. If the aversive conditioning is continued long enough, the behavior will become extinguished; that is, it will not be used.

This form of aversive conditioning will be exemplified in Chapter 8, and especially the extent to which it is applicable to behavioral problem children. But let us consider just a few brief examples at this point. Emetic drugs make one vomit. For example, an alcoholic might be allowed to drink only if he agreed to take an emetic drug in connection with the act for which he is being treated, the drinking of alcohol; the drug might make him vomit and eventually he would not want to experience the discomfort involved in vomiting. Electric shock,[6] typically relatively mild (the intensity is determined according to the discomfort threshold of the particular individual being treated) has been used in various ways. The following case exemplifies the use of electric shock in behavior therapy: A young man had developed the sexual behavior of

6 The use of mild electric shocks in behavior therapy should not be confused with the electric shocks involved in electroconvulsive therapy (ECT) or electroshock therapy (EST), which constitute the "shock treatments" commonly used in psychiatric hospitals.

transvestism, that is, dressing in female clothing while he masturbated. This behavior had been pleasurable to him, and, in fact, just the process of dressing in female clothing was pleasurable; but his guilt about this behavior and his wish not to let his family find out about it brought him to the hospital for treatment. He was concurrently treated with insight-oriented psychotherapy by a psychologist and with aversive therapy by a psychiatrist. In brief, the aversive therapy process required him to start dressing in the female garments; at a given point (the interval was randomly determined) mild shocks were administered to him through electrodes attached to his wrists, and shocks continued until he had removed all of the female clothing. Thus the principle involved was that removing the female clothing resulted in the cessation of the aversive stimulus, the shock, and a more comfortable feeling was restored. Other techniques were used to improve his over-all psychological state, such as the short-term psychotherapy; but for the purpose of the example, it should be pointed out that a systematic use of aversive stimuli, by means of electric shock, resulted in his ceasing to be attracted to female clothing; and indeed he did not find it pleasant when he forced himself to cross-dress. This chronic sexual-behavioral problem was eliminated in only three weeks of inpatient treatment (outpatient psychotherapy continued and follow-ups after several months revealed that the aversive treatment remained effective). Regardless of what the aversive stimulus is—be it drugs, electric shock, or whatever—the principle is the same. Examples will later be cited of how this procedure has been applied to children.

As mentioned earlier, there are some drawbacks to this aversive approach. It certainly is not a pleasant experience for the client or for the therapist, and there are some philosophical reasons and, in some cases, institutional regulations (especially in the school systems) that would limit the use of this approach. Moreover, at this point research has not adequately determined that aversive conditioning is any more effective than other forms of behavioral modification; it may, therefore, be one of the less desirable approaches.

Withdrawing Rewards

The second major type of negative conditioning is the withdrawing of positive rewards. Obviously this, although in the same negative reinforcement vein as the discomfort-producing stimuli, is less severe, but in the long run it could be equally effective. This approach may be described as follows: If a person who is or is potentially a reinforcing agent for another person (such as a teacher for a behavioral problem child) will not give recognition or acceptance to a specific behavior (such as an unacceptable behavior in the classroom), then that behavior will not be positively reinforced, and its frequency of usage will decrease. In other words, if the teacher does not respond to the problem behavior, the child will tend not to behave in that manner as much; but if the teacher responds, even if it is with derision, the behavior has received positive reinforcement in the sense that at least the teacher responded. This is best likened to a similar situation in the home, where a child who cannot get enough love and affection from his mother may misbehave in order to get her to scold or punish him: even negative attention is better than none at all. Further, withdrawing a previously given reward, such as social recognition, is also perceived as punishment and has a negative effect on that behavior; this adds support for maintaining consistency of reinforcement, at least until the bond has been adequately developed. Giving a reward one time for a good behavior but failing to give a reward the next time for the same good behavior only serves to counteract the value of the first reward; but, as has been discussed, if the reinforcement schedule is consistently maintained until the behavior is firmly strengthened, then it will eventually be self-sustaining without as much reward and eventually without essentially any direct reward. Withdrawing a reward for punishment can contribute to behavioral modification, because if a positive reward given for good behavior is withdrawn when unacceptable behavior occurs, the child will want to restore the reward and will behave properly.

In summary of the use of negative reinforcement, it may be stated that the bond between the behavioral response and the aversive stimulus must provide the subject, such as the behavioral problem child, with a sense of displeasure or discomfort if the frequency of the act is to be decreased: if the act brings pleasure, even if it is in the form of a negative comment from the teacher but still is attention-getting, the frequency will increase.[7] Therefore, when negative reinforcement occurs, the child does not perceive the bond or the relationship as satisfying or pleasant; in fact, he finds it very unsatisfactory and unpleasant. The behavior that receives negative reinforcement will be avoided, and behavior that receives positive reinforcement will be preferred. In other words, if a punishment is consistently administered and bonded to a behavioral act that is unacceptable, that act will occur less and less.

[7] There could be an exception to this. If negative verbal comments are systematically used as punishment for an unacceptable behavior and positive verbal comments are used as rewards for an acceptable behavior (acceptable behavior relevant to the general pattern reflected in the punished behavior), then the negative comments could serve to facilitate extinction of the unacceptable behavior. The key point is that both positive and negative comments must be consistently made. If only negative comments are made, then the result will be an increase in the problem behavior because it is attention-getting.

COMBINED POSITIVE AND NEGATIVE REINFORCEMENT

In the format combining positive and negative reinforcement contingencies, techniques embodying any type of reinforcement contingency are feasible. In general, a review of the relevant research studies suggests that the primary use of negative reinforcement is in the previously described manner of withdrawing rewards. That is, if a child is to be rewarded with social acceptance and praise for an approved behavior in the classroom, when he performs an unacceptable behavior and the social acceptance and praise are not given, the unacceptable behavior receives negative reinforcement and will theoretically not be used as often as the acceptable behavior. But it is possible to use any of the positive reinforcement techniques in conjunction with any of the negative reinforcement techniques; for example, aversive stimuli, such as electric shock or an unpleasant noise, could be applied when an unacceptable behavior occurred, and positive stimuli, such as verbal praise or an object reward, could be awarded when an acceptable behavior occurred. The point is that behavioral modification can be promoted by using quite diverse techniques without necessarily contradicting the effects of each other. Although this may be a bit more laborious in some ways, many professionals feel that the combined use of negative and positive reinforcement contingencies is the most effective means for behavioral modification.

OTHER TYPES OF BEHAVIORAL MODIFICATION

As previously stated, the priority for these three major categories or types of behavioral modification may be questioned by some and supported by others. Admittedly, the boundaries are somewhat arbitrary, and certain aspects and studies inherent in the broad area of behavioral modification may overlap into more than one category or may not find accurate placement in one of the three types. But the boundaries are intended to be flexible.

Within this frame of reference, it will not come as a surprise if a new theoretical aspect emerges in a reviewed study. Since the field of learning theory is marked by diverse theoretical positions and consequently offers many differences in emphasis in the learning processes, no one theoretical approach to the use of learning theory principles in behavioral modification is totally without question.

In view of the arbitrary nature of the trichotomy of types, there are two other types of behavioral modification that merit separate consideration. These are *negative practice* and *clinical suggestion* or *hypnosis.*

Negative Practice

Negative practice could, presumably, be placed in the category of negative reinforcement. But in some ways it is incompatible with such a placement. The reinforcement position essentially holds that each occurrence of a response strengthens the probability that it will reoccur. In contradiction, the principle underlying negative practice is that continued repetition will satiate the reason for the response's occurrence, and eventually the response will be extinguished.

The procedure for negative practice is to have the person repeat an uncontrolled or involuntary response over and over. By repeating it long enough and under the control of the therapist, the behavior will eventually cease to bring satisfaction to the person, he will become fatigued and tired of doing the act, and since it is not pleasure-producing or satisfying, he will unlearn it—it will be extinguished from his repertoire of preferred behaviors.

The original idea of negative practice or behavioral satiation was set forth by Dunlap (1932), when he described the technique whereby his clients practiced actively and consciously the habit they wanted to lose. Dunlap recommended the use of this technique with stammering, tics, thumb-sucking, nail-biting, masturbation, and homosexuality. Lehner (1960) provides a review of relevant research and describes the considerations and techniques that constitute this form of treatment. It should be pointed out that the actual involuntary response that is to be extinguished may not be practiced *per se,* but rather a similar or approximation response may be used. The principle of generalization is applicable; that is, the response that is actually practiced may be only related to or appear similar to the response that is to be eliminated. For example, one behavior therapist explained the treatment for a case of his: a child who compulsively pulled out his hair was required to spend hours laboriously pulling strands from a large cotton bundle with a pair of tweezers.

Negative practice has been particularly successful with obsessive-compulsive disorders. For example, Humphrey and Rachman (Eysenck and Rachman, 1965) describe the treatment of a young boy who compulsively chewed, bit, and tore various materials. The boy was required to repeat these actions over and over again during his therapy sessions, despite the fact that he became fatigued with the act; within one week the compulsive behavior had declined and within three weeks it was totally gone. The psychomotor disorder of writer's cramp (Beech, 1960), hysterical aphonia or loss of voice (Walton and Black, 1960), various kinds of tics (Rafi, 1962; Yates, 1958), and numerous other problem behaviors (Case, 1960; Jones, 1956; Walton, 1960, 1961; Williams, 1959) have been treated by negative or massed practice. This technique has also been used to treat sexual fetishes and transvestism. With any disorder there seem to be two key factors: the person being treated must be motivated to lose the problem, and the behavior must be repeated well beyond the point where it ceases to be satisfying (to stop halfway would only serve to strengthen it).

In terms of research evidence, this approach scarcely provokes enthusiasm; this is one of the reasons why it is treated separately here. Although Lehner (1960) seems to suggest that it may be usefully employed with such problems as tics, stuttering, homosexuality, and learning difficulties, he also acknowledges that empirical data for this type of treatment are relatively meager, as compared with the data for other types of behavioral modification. The technique has received neither extensive clinical application nor experimentation. It may be effective with some problems, but even then only with certain individuals. In other words, while it might help Mark to quit stuttering, it might be completely ineffective (due to etiological differences?) in helping Richard eliminate a similar speech problem. There is not enough research to allow adequate evaluation of this approach, and there have been enough therapeutic failures with the approach to make it totally unwise to recommend it unconditionally as a clinical technique for use with behavioral problem children. It does, however, fit nicely into the framework of working with children; that is, children can perform the therapeutic tasks with little difficulty. If, therefore, future experimental evidence supports its value, negative practice may eventually become a promising technique for use with children.

Clinical Suggestion or Hypnosis

The second type of behavioral modification that merits special attention is *clinical suggestion*. Clinical suggestion refers to the concept and technique of inducing relaxation to achieve a heightened state of suggestibility, and then offering specific therapeutic suggestions that are designed to bring the client relief from his problems (Hilgard, 1965; Weitzenhoffer, 1953). And hypnosis might well be included in this frame of reference, because there seems to be a continuum between induced relaxation, such as is used with reciprocal inhibition techniques, and the so-called state of hypnosis. This approach will be dealt with in greater detail in Chapter 8.

Behavior therapists, in general, seem to prefer to believe that clinical suggestion is not part of their behavioral modification techniques. This is especially true of the techniques of systematic desensitization, which seem, at least on the surface, to be highly similar to, if not exactly the same as, those employed in the format of clinical suggestion or hypnosis (Cautela, 1966b). In their discussion of suggestion, Wolpe and Lazarus [8] (1966) state:

The classical forms of suggestion are designed to substitute desirable for undesirable behavior by direct verbal prescription. It now seems that when this works it is because the new response competes with the old, and, if it dominates, inhibits the latter. Whenever, either immediately or after repetition, this is followed by lasting diminution (or elimination) of the old response we have an instance of conditioning inhibition based on reciprocal inhibition. . . . Unfortunately it does not work very well.

Wolpe and Lazarus then go on to set forth their reciprocal inhibition approach for behavioral modification. In other words, they acknowledge that occasionally phenomena labeled "suggestion" result in behavioral change; but when this happens, they believe that it is really due to reciprocal inhibition, and that clinical suggestion in isolation is relatively ineffective.

The interesting point is that behavior therapists do employ procedures that cannot be distinguished on any count from those procedures employed by professionals providing clinical suggestion or hypnosis. Although some behavior therapists seem quite concerned about distinguishing the effects of clinical suggestion and hypnosis from those of their behavioral modification procedures, experimental research has actually given little consideration to this problem; and essentially it is safe to say that the degree of involvement of clinical suggestion and hypnosis in behavior therapy has not been determined. Behavior therapists do, however, endorse the use of hypnotic phenomena as an adjunct to their therapy. For example, Wolpe and Lazarus (1966) state that hypnotic techniques can be used independently or in conjunction with other behavior therapy techniques to modify behaviors. Hussain (1964) states unequivocally his belief that the use of hypnosis increases the effectiveness of behavior therapy techniques, and his results with hypnotic-behavior therapy are reported to be better than results obtained by other behavior therapists who do not use hypnosis. Although it is of no "objective" value,

8 From BEHAVIOR THERAPY TECHNIQUES, J. Wolpe and A. A. Lazarus, Pergamon Press, Oxford, 1967 (1966). P. 2.

numerous psychiatrists and psychologists, both in the United States and in Britain, have commented that they *usually* employ hypnotic procedures in their behavior therapy (and some have said that they *always* do!).

Admittedly, clinical suggestion or hypnosis, used in isolation, is of unpredictable efficacy for treating problems that are quite effectively treated by behavior therapy techniques (Cautela, 1966a), but there seems adequate evidence to believe two things: first, that the effects of clinical suggestion or hypnosis may be interwoven into the results of behavior therapy, particularly when the reciprocal inhibition principle is involved; and second, that clinical suggestion or hypnosis can be integrated with and indeed may increase the efficacy of behavioral modification procedures.

At this point we should be ready to move on to a discussion of actual techniques that can be used to help behavioral problem children in the schools. It is recognized that this chapter, although strictly dealing with types of behavioral modification, has already presented numerous techniques. Most of these will be exemplified further in Chapters 7 and 8. It must be stated emphatically at this time that the choice of techniques will depend upon the capabilities of the professional person attempting treatment and on the needs of the specific child being treated. In approaching the implementation of techniques, the reader must bear in mind that some educators can use some of the techniques that other educators will not be able or qualified to use. Thus the next three chapters will devote special attention to some of the factors that must go into the selection of behavioral modification techniques. The professional expertise of the user is obviously an important factor in the selection and implementation of behavioral modification procedures.

REFERENCES

Beech, H. R. The symptomatic treatment of writer's cramp. In H. J. Eysenck (Ed.), *Behaviour therapy and the neuroses*. New York: Pergamon Press, 1960, 349-372.

Bijou, S. W., and Baer, D. M. *Child development: I. A systematic and empirical theory*. New York: Appleton-Century-Crofts, 1961.

Binder, A., McConnell, D., and Sjoholm, Nancy A. Verbal conditioning as a function of experimenter characteristics. *Journal of Abnormal and Social Psychology*, 1957, 55:309-314.

Case, H. W. Therapeutic methods in stuttering and speech blocking. In H. J. Eysenck (Ed.), *Behaviour therapy and the neuroses*. New York: Pergamon Press, 1960, 207-220.

Cautela, J. R. Desensitization factors in the hypnotic treatment of phobias. *Journal of Psychology,* 1966, 64:277-288. (a)

Cautela, J. R. Hypnosis and behaviour therapy. *Behaviour Research and Therapy,* 1966, 4:219-224. (b)

Dunlap, K. *Habits, their making and unmaking.* New York: Liveright, 1932.

Eysenck, H. J. *The dynamics of anxiety and hysteria.* London, Eng.: Routledge, Kegan Paul, 1957.

Eysenck, H. J., and Rachman, S. *The causes and cures of neurosis.* San Diego, Calif.: R. R. Knapp, 1965.

Greenspoon, J. The effect of verbal and non-verbal stimuli on the frequency of members of two verbal response classes. Unpublished doctoral dissertation, Indiana University, 1951.

Greenspoon, J. The reinforcing effect of two spoken sounds on the frequency of two responses. *American Journal of Psychology,* 1955, 68:409-416.

Hildum, D. C., and Brown, R. W. Verbal reinforcement and interviewer bias. *Journal of Abnormal and Social Psychology,* 1956, 53:108-111.

Hilgard, E. R. *Hypnotic susceptibility.* New York: Harcourt, Brace and World, 1965.

Hilgard, E. R., and Marquis, D. C. *Conditioning and learning.* London, Eng.: Methuen, 1961.

Hussain, A. Behavior therapy using hypnosis. In J. Wolpe, A. Salter, and L. J. Reyna (Eds.), *The conditioning therapies.* New York: Holt, Rinehart and Winston, 1964, 54-61.

Jones, H. G. The application of conditioning and learning techniques to the treatment of a psychiatric patient. *Journal of Abnormal and Social Psychology,* 1956, 52:414-420.

Kessler, Jane W. *Psychopathology of childhood.* Englewood Cliffs, N.J.: Prentice-Hall, 1966.

Krasner, L. Verbal conditioning and psychotherapy. In L. Krasner and L. P. Ullmann (Eds.), *Research in behavior modification.* New York: Holt, Rinehart and Winston, 1965, 211-228.

Krumboltz, J. D., and Thoresen, C. E. The effect of behavioral counseling in group and individual settings on information-seeking behavior. *Journal of Counseling Psychology,* 1964, 11:324-333.

Lazarus, A. A., Davison, G. C., and Polefka, D. A. Classical and operant factors in the treatment of a school phobia. *Journal of Abnormal Psychology,* 1965, 70:225-229.

Lehner, G. F. J. Negative practice as a psychotherapeutic technique. In H. J. Eysenck (Ed.), *Behaviour therapy and the neuroses.* New York: Pergamon Press, 1960, 194-206.

Munn, N. L. *Psychology: the fundamentals of human adjustment* (3rd ed.). Boston: Houghton Mifflin, 1956.

Rachman, S. Introduction to behaviour therapy. *Behaviour Research and Therapy*, 1963, 1:3-15.

Rafi, A. A. Learning theory and the treatment of tics. *Journal of Psychosomatic Research*, 1962, 6:71-76.

Sapolsky, A. Effect of interpersonal relationships upon verbal conditioning. *Journal of Abnormal and Social Psychology*, 1960, 60:241-246.

Schmidt, Elsa, Castell, D., and Brown, P. A retrospective study of 42 cases of behaviour therapy. *Behaviour Research and Therapy*, 1965, 3:9-19.

Thoresen, C. E., and Krumboltz, J. D. Relationship of counselor reinforcement of selected responses to external behavior. *Journal of Counseling Psychology*, 1967, 14:140-144.

Vogel-Sprott, M. D. Response generalization under verbal conditioning in alcoholics, delinquents and students. *Behaviour Research and Therapy*, 1964, 2:135-141.

Walton, D. The relevance of learning theory to the treatment of an obsessive-compulsive state. In H. J. Eysenck (Ed.), *Behaviour therapy and the neuroses*. New York: Pergamon Press, 1960, 153-164.

Walton, D. Experimental psychology and the treatment of a ticqueur. *Journal of Child Psychology and Psychiatry*, 1961, 2:148-155.

Walton, D., and Black, D. A. The application of learning theory to the treatment of chronic hysterical aphonia. In H. J. Eysenck (Ed.), *Behaviour therapy and the neuroses*. New York: Pergamon Press, 1960, 259-271.

Weitzenhoffer, A. M. *Hypnotism: An objective study in suggestibility*. New York: John Wiley and Sons, 1953.

Williams, C. D. The elimination of tantrum behavior by extinction procedures. *Journal of Abnormal and Social Psychology*, 1959, 59:269-270.

Williams, Juanita H. Conditioning of verbalization: a review. *Psychological Bulletin*, 1964, 62:383-393.

Wolpe, J. *Psychotherapy by reciprocal inhibition*. Stanford, Calif.: Stanford University Press, 1958.

Wolpe, J. The comparative clinical status of conditioning therapies and psychoanalysis. In J. Wolpe, A. Salter, and L. J. Reyna (Eds.), *The conditioning therapies*. New York: Holt, Rinehart and Winston, 1964, 5-16.

Wolpe, J., and Lazarus, A. A. *Behavior therapy techniques*. Oxford, Eng.: Pergamon Press, 1966.

Woody, R. H. Integrating behavior therapy and psychotherapy. *British Journal of Medical Psychology* (in press).

Woody, R. H. Toward a rationale for psycho-behavioral therapy. *Archives of General Psychiatry*, 1968, 19:199-204.

Yates, A. The application of learning theory in the treatment of tics. *Journal of Abnormal and Social Psychology*, 1958, 56:175-182.

7

General Behavioral
Modification Techniques

In view of the fact that behavioral modification techniques differ in the degree of knowledge and skill they require of the therapist (and certainly educators differ greatly in personal and professional capabilities), the ensuing chapters pose a critical organizational problem. Should the technical materials be presented according to the type of professional who may use them (for example, a chapter for teachers, a chapter for school counselors, and a chapter for school psychologists)? Or should the presentation separate materials as to types of techniques (as discussed in Chapter 6)? To accept the former would mean failing to recognize that professionals holding similar positions differ in competency, and to accept the latter might result in a lack of clarity regarding the issue of who should use which technique. It seems unwise, therefore, to designate a set of techniques that is suitable for *all* classroom teachers or *all* school counselors or *all* school psychologists; and any attempt to categorize techniques will not be without a degree of uncertainty. To resolve this organizational conflict, a compromise seems most appropriate.

The question of who should use which techniques cannot be given an explicit answer. Undoubtedly, there are some professionals in each educational position who can use the techniques designated for their role, but likewise there are others in the same group who cannot use them all. And there are some professionals who are capable of crossing all boundaries created by position or role. Thus the best answer that can be given is that the personal characteristics and professional capabilities and perhaps other more practical factors, such as the administrative regulations that govern the psychoeducational services in a particular school system, must be used as the criteria for selecting the technique.

This chapter will, therefore, discuss the general behavioral modification techniques (and their research bases and exemplary studies) that seem applicable to most school personnel, including classroom teachers, school counselors, and school psychologists. Since a main objective of this book is a practical one, only limited attention will be given to research design and no attempt will be made to present an exhaustive review of published research. Attention will be focused instead upon how the results are usable in psychoeducational settings and particularly with behavioral problem children. The next chapter will present specialized techniques that are effective at modifying behaviors, but that require highly trained specialists to use them. In all probability the specialized techniques in Chapter 8 will be limited to school counselors and school psychologists, and even some of these may not be qualified to use all of them. Regardless of whether the specialized techniques are usable by each individual reader, it behooves all educators to be familiar, as far as is practical, with the techniques and procedures used by educators in roles other than their own. This organizational approach should provide the material for a well-developed understanding of the entire scope of behavioral modification techniques that are at least remotely suitable for use with behavioral problem children in the schools. This coverage provides an overview of the theoretical and technical considerations, which may perhaps be adequate for some professionals to implement a particular technique; but in general this should be supplemented with more formal training (to be discussed in Chapter 9).

POSITIVE REINFORCEMENT

In Chapter 6, there was presented an extensive discussion of positive reinforcement contingencies, with reciprocal inhibition, object and social recognition rewards, and verbal conditioning receiving special attention. This section will continue with these categories; but examples from research and practical situations will be used to illustrate technical procedures, and intermittently comments regarding means of implementing these techniques will be made.

Reciprocal Inhibition

The principle of reciprocal inhibition involves making a non-anxiety-provoking situation occur in the presence of an anxiety-provoking stimulus. There will be a reciprocal effect: the anxiety will be counteracted. Systematic desensitization occurs when the person is progressively helped through anxiety-provoking situations, staying at each degree or level of anxiety until the effects of reciprocal inhibition have successfully lowered the level of anxiety. Eventually the person will be able to experience with little or no anxiety situations that previously provoked extreme anxiety: he has then become *desensitized.*

Various forms of desensitization techniques, based on the reciprocal inhibition principle, have been used successfully to treat such diverse problems as pathological food avoidance or refusal to eat (Hallsten, 1965; White, 1957), school phobias (Lazarus, Davison, and Polefka, 1965), and essentially any type of behavior problem which has a component of anxiety within its structure. An analysis of the research suggests that there are basically three types of inhibitory responses that can be used in desensitization techniques; these are *affection, feeding,* and *social reassurance* (Eysenck and Rachman, 1965). The responsiveness of children to care and affection can be put to good therapeutic advantage. The actual techniques should vary with the particular situation, but the principle is that affection, comforting, or a security-giving stimulus (such as from the parent or from a teacher) can counteract anxiety. The therapeutic task is to begin using the stimulus with situations that provoke a relatively low amount of anxiety and progress upward, according to the systematic desensitization principle. Feeding responses have been widely used in experimental child psychology to counteract anxiety. One of the most famous examples was the case of Peter, who overcame a fear of a rabbit by being fed when the rabbit was in the room; the rabbit was placed some distance away from Peter and was gradually brought closer to him as the feeding of the child led to desensitization (Jones, 1924). Similarly, social reassurance from any significant person—parents, siblings, peers, or teachers—can be used to produce a reciprocal inhibition effect. These anxiety-inhibitory stimuli—affection, feeding, and social reassurance—have been used to modify a variety of anxiety-rooted behavior problems.

Much of the research on reciprocal inhibition has been with adults, but there are also some interesting studies involving children. And from these we can see many ways in which the reciprocal inhibition principle can be applied in educational settings. As has been cautioned repeatedly, the user of this and other behavioral modification techniques must be adequately trained to have a thorough understanding of the problem; but with an interprofessional approach that employs all of the available psychoeducational personnel in the diagnostic and planning procedures, this technique can readily be applied to a wide variety of educational problems typically encountered in the schools.

Relaxation, either alone or in conjunction with other behavioral modification techniques (such as desensitization procedures), can serve to lower anxiety that may be causing undesired behaviors. Relaxation was described initially by Jacobson (1938) and has since earned a prominent place in behavioral modification (Wolpe, 1958; Wolpe and Lazarus, 1966). Lomont and Edwards (1967) have demonstrated that the efficacy of systematic desensitization seems to be due to the muscular relaxation in the presence of the anxiety stimulus. This technique essentially involves the therapist's inducing physical and, in the process, mental relaxation for the child. The child is asked, for example, to sit comfortably and to visualize his feet and to realize how relaxed they can be if he concentrates on them. When relaxation is achieved in that part of his body, he is asked to visualize his legs and think how relaxed they can become. Gradually the child learns to relax his entire body and eventually can do this quite readily on his own, without the verbal instructions from the therapist. Wolpe and Lazarus (1966) describe in detail the verbal instructions for inducing relaxation. This technique serves to lower, in a manner compatible with the reciprocal inhibition principle, the amount of anxiety. It may also be used by some counselors and psychologists to induce the client to lower his resistances to other forms of treatment; and it may be used as an adjunct to other behavioral modification techniques. Relaxation techniques seem to be quite effective, especially when combined with other behavioral modification techniques, and they are certainly not difficult to perform; but a word of caution is in order. Although inducing relaxation is not dangerous in any manner, there is a strong degree of similarity between it and the set of phenomena that are generally labeled "hypnosis." Clinical hypnosis has a definite place in behavioral modification procedures, as will be discussed in Chapter 8, but its use requires special psychological training. Although relaxation techniques are not in themselves hypnosis and have no adverse effects in and of themselves, they are probably most appropriate for those professionals who are thoroughly trained in psychology. Thus it would be inappropriate to endorse this technique for classroom teachers; but it is quite possible that a school counselor or school psychologist could use induced relaxation in conjunction with a desensitization procedure that was being conducted by a classroom teacher.

Another technique based on the reciprocal inhibition principle is *emotive imagery*. Lazarus and Abramovitz (1962) have presented a detailed description of this reciprocal inhibition technique as it may be applied to behavioral problem children. The procedure is to determine the characteristics of the child's fears, such as the range, intensity, and circumstances associated with the fears. Then a graduated hierarchy of fears is drawn up. The therapist, such as a school psychologist or school counselor, would then have the child imagine selected events that are related to each of the items in the hierarchy. It is of paramount importance that the images that the child is asked to evoke begin with the least powerful anxiety-provoking imagined situations, and gradually progress to more powerful ones only as the child has become desensitized and able to cope with each step. The rationale for this therapeutic procedure is that the controlled imaginings introduce both the anxiety-provoking

and anxiety-inhibiting emotions into the imagery. The assumption, therefore, is that these induced emotions have autonomic effects that are incompatible with anxiety. Using the results of nine case studies with
phobic children, ages seven to fourteen, Lazarus and Abramovitz (1962)
assert that seven of the children "recovered" in only 3.3 sessions, and
follow-ups for up to one year did not reveal a relapse or symptom substitution.

To clarify what is necessary to use a behavioral modification technique, let us analyze the requirements for the use of a desensitization
technique such as emotive imagery. To begin with, the therapist must
build the hierarchy. The construction of the hierarchy is critical to the
eventual outcome of the treatment. Special care should, therefore, go into
the development of the list of anxiety-provoking situations. The hierarchy
is tailor-made to the psychological needs of each child. It might be noted,
however, that there is evidence that certain types of anxiety, such as
anxiety provoked by having to take a test, can be standardized; that is,
a standardized, as opposed to an individualized, hierarchy might feasibly
be used with a number of children experiencing the same type of anxiety
(Emery and Krumboltz, 1967). This approach is still relatively uninvesti-
gated, so the best guideline at this point is to construct each hierarchy
with great care on an individual basis.

Building the hierarchy requires more than asking the child, "What
are you afraid of?" Rather the therapist must probe into the child's psychological structure and follow up clinical cues. To be able to do this,
the user must have a knowledge of personality theory and clinical interviewing techniques. To be realistic, one must say that this desensitization technique, in its current form, can best be used by school psychologists and school counselors. But position title, as has been said before,
does not alone distinguish who should use a technique. The following
true incident illustrates the need for proper knowledge of desensitization
procedures: A school counselor with limited training, just beginning in
the profession, attempted to apply "emotive imagery." He proceeded to
ask the student to imagine a specific anxiety-provoking situation; he had
not, however, developed a hierarchy of fear-provoking situations, and
the situation that he asked the student to imagine was relatively high in
anxiety-provoking power. Consequently, the imagery was so vivid and
so anxiety-provoking that the student, to the dismay of the would-be
therapist, became very distraught. Had he developed a hierarchy and
understood the requirement of a graduated presentation of anxiety-provoking stimuli, he would have realized that the particular situation that
he asked the student to imagine was one that was much too anxiety-
provoking to start with. In other words, the distance between what the
student could cope with successfully and the induced imagined situation
was too great to allow an inhibitory influence on the anxiety without a

rather severe reaction. The idea behind the hierarchy is to build up gradually to the more advanced levels of anxiety-provoking situations. Citing of this example is not meant to suggest that the use of reciprocal inhibition is unwise because it carries risks. It carries risks only if the therapist is not adequately trained to use it, but then one acknowledges that any activity, even (or especially) driving an automobile, carries a risk if the person is not trained. Reciprocal inhibition techniques offer the trained professional—whether he be classroom teacher, school counselor, or school psychologist—an excellent means to behavioral modification.

An extremely pertinent example of the use of reciprocal inhibition or desensitization techniques with a school-related problem is found in the work that has been done to help children overcome their fear of going to school or of the teacher—in other words, a school phobia. Although we might well delve into the possible etiological reasons for this problem behavior (research suggests that it may be related to an over-dependence on the mother), let us focus primarily on ways to treat this problem; this will also serve to exemplify the general bases for other desensitization techniques.

School-phobic children may be treated by behavioral modification procedures in numerous ways. Lazarus, Davison, and Polefka (1965) provide one example of how several conditioning procedures can be employed. But let us just consider the generalities. Obviously the basic goal is to detach the child from his unrealistic haven, the home, and the stimuli therein that tend to draw him away from the school (which may or may not be related to his feelings about his mother or insecurity) and begin moving him toward the school and regular attendance and participation in class activities. With this objective and following the desensitization model, the procedure would be to establish a relationship with the child that would facilitate communication and acceptance (in fact, this might best be termed a "counseling" relationship), develop a series of anxiety-provoking situations related to his school phobia (this hierarchy would result from discussion, questioning, and probing between the therapist and the child), and finally begin the actual desensitization therapy.

The process of desensitization therapy, whether for a school phobia or some other problem that is to be treated with this technique, is to maintain the child's acceptance of the therapist, thereby giving the child a supportive and understanding, helping relationship, and to gradually progress through the various anxiety-provoking situations. The "progressing through" could be done by having the child actually experience the situations (called *in vivo* desensitization) or by vicarious (simulated) means.

Taking the example of a school phobia, let us assume that the hierarchy of fear-provoking situations included the following ten steps (in a real situation it is quite probable, and indeed usually preferable, that more than ten steps be used; some therapists believe that approximately twenty steps are necessary for most fears of children):

1. Watching children pass his house on their way to school
2. Walking out of his house with schoolbooks
3. Walking the route to school
4. Seeing the school in the distance
5. Standing in front of the school
6. Standing alone on the playground
7. Standing on the playground with other children
8. Standing at the doorway of the school
9. Standing in the hallway of the school
10. Standing in the classroom

The first step, No. 1, would be the least anxiety-provoking, and the steps increase in anxiety-provoking power on to No. 10. If the mode of treatment was *in vivo* or actual experiencing, the therapist would stand with the child at his front window and watch the children pass on their way to school; he and the child could discuss how the child was feeling (counseling). And when the child felt comfortable watching the children, the therapist might accompany the child, carrying books, out of the house; this could be repeated (as could each step) and discussed until the child no longer felt anxiety or became upset when he walked out of the house as though going to school; then perhaps the therapist would ask the child to do it alone while he waited inside the house and watched him through the window. Step No. 3 might include a gradual walk toward the school; that is, several trials might be limited to walking one block from the child's house and then returning to the security of the home, but when the child's condition would allow, the walk would be increased until the child finally reached Step No. 4 without experiencing anxiety. And so the treatment would continue until the child could actually enter the school, first with the therapist and then alone, and eventually remain in the classroom (possibly for short periods at first but increasing the length of time gradually).

The child could also experience these same steps vicariously, and in many cases it is advisable to do this before trying to have the child experience the actual situations. Vicarious experiencing could be done by having the child visualize himself in each of the respective situations; as soon as he began to experience anxiety as the result of the visualization, he should be told to forget about the anxiety-provoking situation, think of something pleasant, and relax; and when he was comfortable, he would be requested to visualize again the same anxiety-provoking situation, until it no longer provoked anxiety. Another technique of vicarious experiencing is to use photographs; in the case of the school phobia, the child would view photographs of another child (a social behavioral model) doing the same steps. Or the anxiety-provoking stimuli could be written on cards and the child could read them or look at them until anxiety started, and then he would be told to relax; or objects related to the phobia (such as a model school) could be used for desensitization. The type of stimulus used—words, pictures, imagination, or actual experiencing—will depend upon how much anxiety is provoked by the given stimulus.

To summarize this desensitization process, it is usually preferable that the child be taught to relax, and then helped to experience progressively, actually or vicariously, the anxiety-provoking situations. After repeated experiencing of any situation, it will eventually lose its power to provoke anxiety, and the next step in the hierarchy can be treated. Each experience should be stopped at the point where the child becomes uncomfortable from the anxiety; and relaxation or a pleasant feeling should be invoked and support from the therapist given. It is also possible to use object rewards with this technique; for example, when the child makes progress, he could be given candy or a toy or just simple praise from the therapist, but the reward would not be given unless he did do well.

Desensitization techniques have proved repeatedly to be effective with children. They have been used successfully to treat a wide variety of childhood problems, such as fears of height, separation from mother and family, death, school, teachers, other children, animals, and doctors. The potential of desensitization techniques is great, and they seem especially valuable for use with children. The amount of required professional skill on the part of the technician, assuming that there are consulting services regarding the child's over-all psychological condition, is not great. It is quite feasible for the desensitization procedures to be performed by any educator, and possibly even by the parents of the child, but in these instances it is critical that professional supervision be available.

Assertive practice is a technique frequently used to promote the occurrence of improved assertive responses. As with other desensitization techniques, assertive behavior can be modified by imagined or actual experiences. Another technique to be discussed shortly, *behavior rehearsal,* offers an intermediate step. Since imagined and real experiencing have been discussed in relation to other desensitization procedures, let us limit this section to consideration of assertive responses and how the intermediate step of behavior rehearsal can be used.

Many behavioral problem children lack the ability to assert themselves in social and learning activities. The shy, withdrawn child is one example, but many other problem behaviors, such as lack of motivation for learning in the social group-centered setting of the classroom, result from less obvious influences of restricted assertive ability. It has been found that persons can progressively become more assertive, in a constructive manner, and that behavioral modification will result (due to the principle of reciprocal inhibition).

The techniques used for developing assertive behavior are quite logical; they follow the principles of systematic desensitization, with a gradual learning of progressively more assertive behaviors. The assertive practice technique has been described as follows:

While being trained in assertive behavior, patients are told to keep careful notes of all their significant interpersonal encounters and to discuss them in detail with the therapist. It is necessary to know the circumstances of the encounter, the patient's feelings at the time, the manner in which he reacted, how he felt immediately after, and his own subsequent appraisal of the situation.[1]

From the last sentence of the quotation, it is apparent that the therapist must have some degree of clinical knowledge of feelings and behaviors to use this technique; this may limit its applicability for some psychoeducational personnel.

After the program for assertive behavior has been developed (and, of course, it can always be modified at a later point if new evidence becomes apparent), such regular desensitization techniques as imagining assertive behaviors or actually trying out more assertive behaviors in real-life situations can be initiated. *It is usually best to provide the person with some sort of antianxiety insurance during these procedures.* For example, in imagined assertive behaviors, each trial could be preceded and followed by a brief period of relaxation or imagining of a pleasant, non-anxiety-provoking situation; this period might last only a few seconds, but it should be long enough for the person to restore his equilibrium in regard to the briefly experienced anxiety-provoking imagined situation. Or in the case of actually trying out new, more assertive behaviors, the clinical suggestion might be given during the therapy sessions that when anxiety is experienced in these real-life trials, the person will become increasingly able to cope with it, and since this is to be expected, the anxiety will not be overwhelming. Another antianxiety technique is to help the person become conditioned to relax on a given cue, such as by saying a word like "calm" or "relax"; in other words, if during the therapy sessions the person can learn to relax quickly whenever he utters or thinks the word "calm" or a similar antianxiety word, he will eventually be able to carry this antianxiety insurance word with him when he begins to experience actual situations that at one time would have been very anxiety-provoking.

[1] From BEHAVIOR THERAPY TECHNIQUES, J. Wolpe and A. A. Lazarus, Pergamon Press, Oxford, 1967 (1966). P. 46.

Behavior rehearsal provides another technique that can be used to facilitate assertive behavior. With this technique, the therapist uses the identified anxiety-provoking situations as the basis for role-playing or play-acting situations during the therapy sessions. For example, the therapist and the child would act out the parts of persons who might be involved in an anxiety-provoking situation. The child who is afraid of "fighting for his rights" (verbally, of course) could role-play this behavior, with the therapist role-playing the part of the more dominant classmate. And then the roles could be reversed, thereby enabling the child to experience what it is like to be the more assertive person being challenged.

It seems quite likely, although behaviorists frequently do not acknowledge it, that this type of play-acting not only teaches the child new, more assertive behaviors and counteracts the anxiety-producing power of the situations (according to the reciprocal inhibition principle), but also gives the child insight into his own needs and motives and insight into those of other children. This technique contains many of the same insight-oriented components of psychodrama or sociodrama, techniques used for years by counselors and psychotherapists; thus this does not seem to be solely a behavioral technique, because it undeniably also promotes insight. In fact, the technique of behavior rehearsal has also been called "behavioristic psychodrama" (Sturm, 1965; Wolpe, 1958). This technique, whatever its name and its theoretical explanation, has produced excellent results and does indeed seem to be an effective means of modifying problem behaviors (Lazarus, 1966).

Object and Recognition Rewards

Object and recognition rewards constitute another set of behavioral modification techniques based on positive reinforcement contingencies. This approach employs the giving of rewards to reinforce appropriate or acceptable behavior.

Several research studies have used *object rewards* for school-related problems. Miller (1964) used food to reinforce the study behavior of a normal seventeen-year-old high school girl. The reward (food) was given in conjunction with the use of flash cards. The girl was given enough food at breakfast to provide her with strength to attend school, but all other food during the day had to be earned by means of her study behavior. During the semester prior to the experiment, the girl had a D average; in the semester of the experiment she earned a B— average; and during the two semesters following the experiment her grades regressed to the original D average. It appeared, therefore, that the food-reward schedule successfully modified the student's study behavior. There seems to be good reason, however, to be concerned about the girl's feelings after the experiment, when she began encountering failure and experiencing personal defeats that she had successfully avoided during the experiment. Her regression in study behavior, incidentally, would be explained on the basis that the conditioning had not lasted long enough for her to unlearn permanently her unadaptive habits and to recognize adequately the benefits or rewards attained from increased study. Obviously, it is not recommended that food be withheld from the child who will not study, but this experiment does provide an excellent example of how object rewards can be used, if programed systematically, to modify educationally related behaviors. The principles inherent in a study like this could be used to develop similar (but less severe and more comprehensive) designs for modifying behaviors based on an object reward technique.

It should be pointed out that behavioral modification techniques are, in general, effective with behaviors resulting from both emotional and neurological factors. Patterson, Jones, Whittier, and Wright (1965) provide a good example of how behavior problems resulting from a neurological basis can be modified: A ten-year-old hyperactive brain-injured boy was conditioned to more acceptable classroom behavior. An auditory stimulus (such as a buzzer or a bell) was paired with rewards of candy and pennies. The boy was fitted with an earphone that could be activated by a radio device during his classroom activities. Poor behavior, such as wiggling around in his chair or leaving his seat, received no reward. But when the boy successfully controlled his behavior, such as by sitting still in his chair for a certain length of time, the radio device would transmit the auditory stimulus indicating that the boy had earned a reward for his behavior, and he would later receive the reward. The data from this study seem to suggest that even hyperactive behavior, possibly due to neurological damage, can be modified and controlled through conditioning or behavioral modification techniques.

This example, with the underlying principles apparently being generalizable, seems suited for use in any type of classroom, assuming that the therapist, who may be the classroom teacher, has the training, the willingness, and the ingenuity to create the circumstances necessary for the behavioral modification. Ingenuity is an extremely important asset for the would-be behavioral modification therapist. Any of the techniques cited can be of little value unless the therapist has the ingenuity to adapt the relevant principles to the particular situation with which he is going to work.

Apparatus can be developed to aid in the conditioning procedure. McKerracher (1967) provides one example: An eleven-year-old boy with low educational achievement, poor reading ability, stammering, and occasional enuresis failed to respond to three months of remedial teaching and supportive therapy in a child guidance clinic; thus it was decided to use behavioral modification techniques. An apparatus with lights was set up; the lights would go on progressively with successful samplings of reading. When a predetermined level of success was achieved, which was marked by lights, the boy received an object reward of candy. Similarly, a buzzer would sound when the boy mispronounced words. McKerracher found that this operant reinforcement procedure helped the boy make significant progress in reading.

There have been similar object reward studies with mentally retarded children. Although the intellectual deficit may add numerous special factors to the conditioning process and, moreover, to the factors underlying the occurrence of problem behaviors, it has been proved that behavioral modification procedures are, in fact, effective with the mentally retarded. Ellis (1963) has presented a comprehensive coverage of the use of conditioning with mentally retarded persons. Since a thorough analysis of research relevant solely to mentally retarded persons is beyond the scope of this book, a few examples of applications will suffice. Birnbrauer, Wolf, Kidder, and Tague (1965) worked with mentally retarded children in an experimental classroom; emphasis was on studying the effects on the child of verbal approval (praise from the teacher), knowledge of results (being told how well he has performed), and tokens as rewards. Special attention was focused on the necessity of keeping the token rewards as part of the reinforcement schedule (this format obviously involves several types of positive reinforcement). Numerous forms of behavioral problems have been successfully modified for mental retardates. For example, Hundziak, Maurer, and Watson (1965) used an operant conditioning format to toilet-train severely mentally retarded boys in a residential institution. A reinforcement device issued an object reward of candy for each successful defecation and urination; elimination habits were rapidly improved and the results transferred to the subjects' living arrangements outside of the experimental conditions. Even this example, although not in a school setting, may have something to offer the classroom teacher. It seems safe to say that almost every elementary classroom teacher has at some time had to cope with the problem of helping a student develop proper toilet habits. Perhaps the time has come for teachers not only to allow but also to encourage the eating of candy in the elementary classroom—but on a reward schedule, of course.

As a final note on the subject of mental retardation, it should be mentioned that therapists of all descriptions have long believed that mentally retarded persons benefited little, if at all, from counseling and psychotherapy. Therapeutic efforts with the mentally retarded have been of questionable success, but with the advancement and improvement of counseling and psychotherapy, there are indications that this negative view must be reappraised. Indeed, there is evidence that mentally retarded persons can benefit from traditional approaches to counseling and psychotherapy, and it appears that learning principles can be used in these insight-oriented approaches (Stacey and DeMartino, 1957; Woody, 1966; Woody and Billy, 1966). Moreover, the efficacy of behavioral modification seems to suggest that these techniques can fulfill a much-needed role in therapeutic services for the mentally retarded.

The second type of reward used in positive reinforcement is *social recognition.* Zimmerman and Zimmerman (1962) modified unproductive classroom behavior for two emotionally disturbed boys by structuring the situations in such a manner that unacceptable or poor behavior had no social consequences. For example, the classroom teacher totally ignored a student's attempt to get a reaction from her for a misspelled word. The teacher would not make any response until a correct spelling or, to be more general, an acceptable behavioral response was performed; and the teacher would then give positive reinforcement in the form of a commendation (that is, reinforcement of the acceptable response), and only then allow progress to the next step of the lesson. It was found that the number of inappropriate or unreinforced responses decreased with each successive spelling word. Brown and Elliott (1965) investigated means of controlling aggressive responses of twenty-seven nursery school boys (three and four years of age). To modify the behaviors of the children, the teacher systematically ignored aggressive responses and attended only to responses that were incompatible with aggression. After a relatively brief conditioning period, it was found that physical, verbal, and over-all aggressive responses had been successfully modified. Brison (1966) reports how a kindergarten teacher used social reinforcement, via attention and approval, to condition a nontalking boy to interact. Both verbal and nonverbal communication factors were reinforced, and within four weeks, after a year of not talking in school (tape recordings of his speech at home revealed at least average development), the boy began to talk. Barclay (1967) found that such action strategies as social reinforcement from the teacher, as well as combining insight techniques (for example, classroom sociodrama) with social reinforcement, could result in more favorable attitudes on the part of elementary school children.

Obviously, behavioral modification by ignoring unacceptable behaviors and reinforcing, by means of social recognition, only acceptable behaviors is applicable to the classroom setting; but, admittedly, it may be difficult to perform and maintain systematically. There is no reason to believe that the requirements of this type of behavioral modification technique exceed the training of any classroom teacher; the main requirements seem to be patience, fortitude, and ability to recognize the type of behavior and to consistently maintain the reinforcement program. None of these factors need be academic in nature. In fact, Davison (1964) found that even nonprofessionals can be trained in conditioning procedures to modify the behavior of emotionally disturbed children; the use of nonprofessionals as reinforcers will be discussed in detail shortly. This form of behavioral modification technique, therefore, is very appropriate for the regular classroom and for any educator.

Because of the long acceptance of established practices and procedures in our classroom, it may be a bit difficult to initiate this form of behavioral modification. Not only does the behavioral problem child have to be conditioned, but every person in the group—that is, all of the children in the classroom—must accept the behavioral boundaries; the reinforcement should apply to all of the students. Moreover, the other teachers and the administrators in the school must be helped to realize that this conditioning approach becomes increasingly effective. It might result in a rather disrupting situation initially, but as consistency is maintained, acceptable and more productive behaviors will result. This approach to behavioral modification seems especially useful in special education classrooms or in specially developed small groups.

As one might infer, a combination of object and recognition rewards can be used to modify behavior. In an interesting study designed to modify the unacceptable behavior of delinquents, Schwitzgebel and Kolb (1964) divided the boys (mean age 17.8, age range 15-21 years) into experimental and control groups. The experimental subjects were hired to "make a fast buck" (an object reward) by coming to the psychological laboratory and talking into an audio tape recorder about anything they wished (this act may well have promoted counseling and psychotherapeutic effects). The experimenters reinforced the boys' participation and efforts with giving of money, including unexpected bonuses, sharing of an orange, giving unexpected privileges, and verbal praises for "good work" (note that these procedures involve object, verbal, and recognition rewards). Bonuses were given when the subject discussed his feelings and experiences in detail and with affect; in other words, components compatible with insight-oriented counseling and psychotherapy were promoted via reinforcement. The length of "employment" with the project was from nine to ten months. A follow-up of the subjects three years after the end of the experiment revealed that the experimental subjects had a significant reduction in arrests and amount of time in jail as compared to the control subjects who had received no reinforcements. The number of subjects returning to jail was not significantly different between the two groups. Schwitzgebel and Kolb concluded that it seemed that the experimental reinforcement procedures, involving both object and social recognition rewards, successfully reduced but did not totally eliminate the delinquent behaviors.

An example of combining recognition and object rewards and play therapy is found in a study of school phobias by Patterson (1965). The school phobia, according to Patterson, develops because the separation of the child from the parents serves as an eliciting stimulus, which leads to an anxiety reaction, which evolves to escape and avoidance behaviors that are then manifested in a phobia for school; this explanation is quite compatible with the previous comments on school phobia in the section on reciprocal inhibition. Following a procedure similar to the Wolpe-type hierarchy of fear-provoking situations, Patterson presented the eliciting stimulus in a graduated series of doll play activities, designed to accommodate initially a low-intensity escape and anxiety reaction; in other words, the dolls were engaged in anxiety-producing activities, with the effects being generalized to the child's actual condition (a desensitization process). Recognition and object rewards were also given. A total of twenty-three twenty-minute sessions of desensitization-type conditioning doll play with the school-phobic child, plus twenty bags of chocolates used for object rewards, and structured ten-minute interviews with parents (counseling integrated with behavior therapy) resulted in significant behavioral changes.

Browning (1967) also combined positive reinforcement procedures, namely tokens, relaxation, and social reinforcers; these were used with a speech problem, the stuttering of a nine-year-old schizophrenic boy. The combined procedures successfully lowered the percentage of stuttering in the boy's speech samples from 22 percent (pretreatment) to 2 percent in reading and 4 percent in conversation (posttreatment). Risley and Wolf (1967) summarize the use of numerous behavioral modification techniques with speech problems.

Although several of the foregoing research studies were conducted in clinic settings, the fact that they involved children makes essentially all the principles transferable to a school setting. In other words, in the case of a behavior problem that can be programmed for social or object rewards, one would assume that educational personnel can use the clinical and/or laboratory findings as the basis for practical techniques in the schools.

Reinforcing Agents

Research has shown that not only educators but also the parents and even the peers of children can be agents of reinforcement procedures. Since these nonprofessionals will have little or no technical knowledge, the primary task of determining the reinforcement schedule—the way in which reinforcement is to be implemented—will probably rest with the teacher and other educational personnel; but with an educator serving as consultant, parents and peers can act as auxiliary reinforcing agents and thus reduce the amount of time required of the educator.

Successful use of parents as positive reinforcers for behavioral modification of problem children has been reported in several research studies (Bijou, 1965; Russo, 1964; Straughan, 1964; Wahler, Winkel, Peterson, and Morrison, 1965). To cite just a few in some detail: O'Leary, O'Leary, and Becker (1967) worked with two brothers (three and six years old) who were frequently engaged in assaultive, destructive, and disruptive behaviors. A professional therapist, using candy and verbal praise concurrently, established the conditioning schedule, but eventually transferred the therapeutic reinforcement role to the boys' mother (the therapist and the mother used a set of hand signals to help her learn when to reinforce and when not to). The treatment was successful; behavior reinforced during therapy did generalize to other times and situations, and the mother was able to carry out her reinforcing skills in the home. Although one of the boys had been diagnosed as brain-damaged, even he made marked improvement. Gardner (1967) held three weekly counseling sessions with the parents of a ten-year-old Negro girl who was having psychogenic seizures. In these three sessions, he trained the parents to reinforce appropriate behaviors but not inappropriate behaviors (for example, seizures). There was rapid and complete cessation of the seizure behavior.

The procedure is to provide the parents with training in behavioral modification techniques. This training is, of course, limited to the aspects with which the parents will actually be involved; but it could and should also include a general orientation to behavioral modification to insure the parents' understanding and cooperation. Most frequently the parents are trained in the use of verbal and social recognition reinforcement. Initially, the therapist, such as a member of the psychoeducational staff, would be part of the therapeutic relationship; in other words, the therapeutic relationship would involve the professional therapist (such as the school counselor or school psychologist), the parent or parents, and the behavioral problem child. Thus the parents and child are placed in a relationship that can be supervised by the professional educator-therapist and that can be consistently and directly continued by both parents and child when they leave the treatment setting and return home. This should alleviate the complaint expressed by many parents of behavioral problem children who have received counseling: that they, the parents, are capable of increased understanding while with the counselor or therapist, but are unable to carry this over into the daily activities with their children at home, a setting that has carried a previously established emotional tone and behavioral norms for essentially all of the child's life. This therapeutic combination of therapist, parents, and child has as one of its objectives the modifying of the child's behaviors in the home, and it is possible that when the child's behaviors change, there will be an influence strong enough to modify the behaviors of all the members of the family. Furthermore, it seems highly important to the over-all success of child therapy, regardless of setting, to involve parents in changing psychologically with their children. This is one reason why many child guidance clinics will not treat a child unless the parents are willing to be involved in the therapy.

The format for involving parents in the behavioral modification of their children might be as follows: The child would start therapy in a conventional manner, such as by starting counseling or engaging in play therapy with the school counselor or school psychologist. During the first few sessions of the therapy with the child, the parents or parent (usually the mother) would receive an orientation to the therapeutic procedures from another counselor or psychologist (this also has the advantage of fostering intrastaff involvement, such as the counselor and psychologist working together). The mother might be trained to react to certain of the child's acts in a manner entirely different from the way she would typically react at home. For example, if the child misbehaves—that is, breaks the rules for acceptable behavior—the mother must not react; but when he behaves properly, she must consistently react with positive reinforcement of the behavior. In this manner, the mother is reinforcing the socially approved or acceptable behavior by the giving of social recognition, affection, attention, and approval; and she punishes by withholding these positive reinforcement stimuli when the appropriate behaviors do not occur. And in some cases object rewards, such as toys or candy or money, can also be used. In this format, as the parent receives training, the therapist is available to help her overcome the emotional responses that she has relied upon for years; indeed, the parent is also, in a sense, conditioned.

It is highly essential to the success of the therapy that the parental reinforcing role be maintained in the home. It is not enough to have the parents follow the reinforcement schedule while in the school psychologist's office; they must also carry it into their everyday lives. It is logical, therefore, that the most desirable format would be to have both parents, and possibly siblings, involved in the behavioral modification program. And the rules for "acceptable" and "unacceptable" behaviors that are applied to the child being treated, the behavioral problem child, must be applicable to his brothers and sisters as well; there can be no double standards or favoritism. This principle is equally applicable to the manner in which a classroom teacher responds to his students—the same standards must be applied to all of the students in the classroom; otherwise any attempt to change the behaviors of a problem child will be nullified.

Assessment of parental involvement in the modification of behavioral problem children has revealed that the feelings, emotions, and behavioral controls change with the primary subject, the child, and that the experience helps the parents also to become more emotionally relaxed

(Russo, 1964); thus, the behavioral modification procedures may influence both parents and child. It is quite possible that this exposure to behavioral modification can serve as an impetus for some parents, who may reflect as many behavioral difficulties as their children, to seek professional help in changing their own social roles. In fact, if the processes for reinforcing acceptable behaviors and not reinforcing unacceptable behaviors are fully and consistently practiced within the home, it would theoretically hold that the entire family structure would progressively be modified.

In summary, the involvement of parents and their role as reinforcing agents definitely seem advantageous to behavioral modification attempts. Obviously some parents may be emotionally or intellectually incapable of this participation; and it is therefore necessary that some impression of their ability to fulfill this role be gained by the therapist before actually involving them. It could become a secondary goal of behavioral modification to bring the parents to the point where they can be involved. Not only is parental participation helpful for improving the efficacy of the therapy, but it also provides an excellent means of implementing behavioral modification techniques in an educational setting. That is, if the parents are taking part in and favor the procedures, many of the unnecessary obstacles, such as stereotypes of what procedures the psycho-educational staff should be allowed to use, can be overcome with relative ease.

As will be evident from further studies to be cited in later sections, other nonprofessional adults can be involved as reinforcers. Moreover, they can actually conduct certain behavioral modification activities. Their work is typically done in conjunction with a professional who serves as a supervising cotherapist or as a consultant. Suffice it to say at this point that there is strong support for using such nonprofessionals as "teacher-moms" or "teacher-aids" or other types of adult volunteers.

Peers may also be instrumental in the changing of the problem behaviors of their classmates, but they vary in effectiveness. In a study of nursery school children (four and five years old), it was found that the peers could be effective verbal reinforcing agents. The peers said "good" and "fine" as the experimental child performed a task; but it was revealed that this verbal reinforcement influenced the child's performance in such a manner that the assigned task was better maintained when the reinforcing agent was a disliked rather than a liked peer (Hartup, 1964). Similarly, a subsequent study found that a significant increase in performance on an assigned activity occurred when reinforcement was made by an unpopular peer within a group of elementary school children; the performance did not change when the reinforcing person was an isolate (was not known by the experimental child); and it tended to decrease when the peer was a popular acquaintance (Tiktin and Hartup, 1965). These experimental studies seem to indicate that peers can reinforce specific behaviors of their classmates but that they vary in effectiveness; apparently children are challenged by peers who are other than close friends and who are, in fact, perceived somewhat negatively. More discussion on peers as reinforcing agents will be presented in the next section on the topic of social modeling and shaping of behaviors.

Social Modeling and Shaping Behaviors

A significant amount of research has confirmed that people are influenced by social models—that is, people whom they observe performing particular behaviors. Most notable perhaps is the research provided by Bandura and colleagues (Bandura, 1965; Bandura and Walters, 1963). The basic assumption is that behavior can be shaped by exposing the individual, such as the behavioral problem child, to the behaviors of a social model, such as a well-behaved child; this is, of course, a positive reinforcement process.

Exposure to the modeled behaviors can be done in numerous ways, such as seeing films or video tapes, or observing a live demonstration, or reading about the specific behaviors of someone else. Problem behavior is shaped into a desired alternative (nonproblem) behavior by exposing the subject (the behavioral problem child) to a hierarchic progression of modeling experiences. The procedure is quite similar to the desensitization approach: the child observes a modeled behavior that is slightly different from that which he currently acts out, and this leads him to change his behavior toward that of the model; and then he is exposed to another modeled behavior that is even more different from his initial behavior, and so on. In other words, the social model demonstrates behaviors that the behavioral problem child (the observer) has not yet learned to perform, and through this observational vicarious experiencing, the behavioral problem child reproduces the demonstrated behaviors in almost identical form; this is the modeling effect.

In experiments, models have successfully provoked a wide variety of behaviors, such as aggressive responses and inhibitory responses. And, as will be noted in the next chapter, these principles have also been introduced into counseling, with counselees modeling their own counseling behaviors after those of filmed counseling models. The key influence in this vicarious experiencing is the way in which the model is reinforced; that is, if a film model is punished, it is unlikely that the observer will choose that behavior, especially if another film model receives a positive reward for a more acceptable behavior.

The influence of identification with a peer model may be found in a study by Walters and Parke (1964). In this study, eighty-four boys (mean age five years and eleven months) were randomly assigned to one of the four subgroups: film model rewarded for deviation, film model punished for deviation, no consequence to film model for deviation, and no film. It was found that the children who had viewed the film in which the child actor, the subjects' model for peer identification, had been rewarded for the behavioral deviation and also the children who viewed the film in which there was no consequence for deviation tended readily to deviate during their own play sessions in the same manner as the child in the film. But the children who saw the film of the child being punished for his deviation or who did not see any film deviated very little from previous play patterns. It seems, therefore, that children are influenced by viewing a film of the behavior of a model peer; and the consequences experienced by the model peer for a specific behavior influence the behavior of the viewer, such as a behavioral problem child. Other results complementary to this study have been reported by Bandura (1965).[2]

Modeling techniques can be used separately or in conjunction with other treatment methods, and there is evidence that they serve to accelerate the therapeutic processes. On this basis, it would seem that the use of films or video tapes of acceptable behavior might be employed in the modification of problem behavior. The content of the film should be carefully controlled and applied within a predetermined approach to treatment; a spasmodic use of unselected films or video tapes of peer behavior would probably have little effect. The models should represent situations and behaviors that are meaningful to the selected behaviors of the problem child or children who are to view the scenes of modeled behaviors. And the use of films or video tapes should be consistent and should be incorporated into a comprehensive approach to coping with the unacceptable behavior. Finally, the behaviors depicted should also be reinforced during the daily activities in the classroom by the teacher's own behavior.

Modeling can also result from watching persons actually performing tasks. Here again, the tasks, in order to shape the observer's behavior, should be progressive. Lovaas, Freitas, Nelson, and Whalen (1967) have developed a training program for schizophrenic children based on imitative behavior—that is, successive approximation of adult's behavior. The program involves sixty nonverbal tasks ranging from easy to complex. Initially, prompting and food (a sweet cereal) were used to reinforce cor-

2 In view of the results of the social modeling research studies, one cannot help but wonder how much of a child's behavior is shaped by the models he views on television and in the commercial movies. While the cries of certain critics that scenes of violence and crime on television and in the movies increase juvenile delinquency may be exaggerated and reactionary to a degree, there seems little doubt that these media could well serve as behavioral influences. The primary consideration for assessing this possibility would be, according to the research, the type of reaction the television or movie actor's behavior provokes: is the character rewarded for his violence and crime, or does he meet with totally negative results?

rect behavior. The effects of the program could presumably be extended to therapeutic usefulness and day-to-day functioning. This type of program exemplifies how graduated tasks, performed by someone like a teacher, can shape the child's behavior.

The principles intrinsic to modeling techniques, used either in isolation or in conjunction with other behavioral modification techniques, can be adapted to numerous situations encountered in schools. One good example of how modeling can be used in the classroom would be to place a behavioral problem child, perhaps a boy who acts out to get attention, in a group of well-behaved children. The well-behaved members would both put peer group pressure on him to behave (that is, to conform to the group's behavioral norms) and provide him with appropriate behavioral models. And it should be noted that modeling is effective with mentally retarded children (Kliebhan, 1967) as well as with children of normal intelligence. Over all, modeling procedures are especially suited for use with children in educational settings and by educational personnel.

POSITIVE REINFORCEMENT COMBINED WITH PUNISHMENT

The term "punishment" in this section has a meaning slightly different from that of the term "aversive stimuli." Aversive stimuli are used to produce discomfort and perhaps even pain in relation to an unacceptable form of behavior, whereas punishment, when considered in the frame of reference of positive reinforcement theory, is the withdrawal or withholding of a positive reinforcement stimulus that the client (the behavioral problem child) has previously experienced. For example, when a child has been conditioned with positive reinforcement, such as the giving of an object or recognition reward for an acceptable behavior, the process of taking away the reinforcement stimulus (the object or recognition reward) actually assumes the properties of punishment.

There are a number of experimental studies that measure the effects of withdrawing reinforcement. Let us consider some examples. Baer (1961), in a study of ten six-year-olds, found that the withdrawal of a positive reinforcement reward (allowing the children to view a cartoon film) was perceived as punishment by the children; withdrawal of the reward served to depress a previously strengthened reinforced behavioral response (the initial reinforced behavioral response was the children's performance of a manual task for which they received an object reward, a peanut). In a follow-up study,[3] Baer (1962) found further support for the proposition that the withdrawal of positive reinforcement actually serves as a punishment. In this second study, nursery school children with an unusually high rate of thumb-sucking were conditioned out of their behavior by giving them positive reinforcement, again the viewing of a cartoon film, and by withdrawing the positive reinforcement as punishment, this time programming interruptions of the films, when they sucked their thumbs.

An example of combining positive reinforcement with punishment (the latter term meaning the withdrawal of social recognition rewards) is found in a case study presented by Wolf, Risley, and Mees (1964). A preschool boy, three and a half years old at the beginning of the study, had severe behavioral and physical handicaps: he had tantrums, sleeping problems, and cataracts in both eyes; he did not eat properly, lacked normal social and verbal repertoires, and had such self-destructive behaviors as head-banging, face-slapping, hair-pulling, and face-scratching. Specialists had offered a number of diagnoses, including mental retardation, brain damage, and psychosis; and each of these three major categories had received a number of conflicting diagnostic subcategories. Mild punishment and extinction comprised the initial conditioning procedure. That is, when a tantrum occurred, the boy was isolated in a room until the tantrum ended and no social contact was given during his isolation; social contact (or social recognition) would have served to reinforce the tantrum, even if it had been an admonishment. At bedtime, the boy was cuddled and the door was left open (affection and social recognition reinforcements); if, however, a temper tantrum occurred, the door was shut and he was left alone until it ended (punishment by withdrawal of positive reinforcement). This conditioning procedure was first performed in the hospital setting but was eventually transferred, gradually, to the child's parents and into his home. Other problems, such as the resistance to wearing glasses, his limited verbal repertoire, and poor eating habits, were also improved by conditioning. Verbal reinforcement, such as praise, was used to develop the verbal behavior and to improve the eating habits. The boy remained in the hospital for 180 days. Six months after his discharge and his return to his home, his mother reported that he was still wearing his glasses, was not having tantrums, had no sleeping problems, and was becoming increasingly verbal. This boy was followed up three years after the initial

[3] One problem frequently encountered in behavioral science is that follow-up studies are not conducted. If a study is conducted and interesting results are found, they are all too commonly accepted without question, when actually they need replication (repeating the same study with another sample of subjects) and follow-up studies whose design is closely related to, but slightly different from, that of the first study. This would accommodate validity checks on all inherent components of the results and would lead to greater validity for subsequent studies.

treatment (Wolf, Risley, Johnston, Harris, and Allen, 1967). Behavioral modification procedures had continually been applied, being altered according to the condition of given behaviors, and being conducted by persons outside the clinic setting—the parents, among others. After three years, the boy had progressed from "hopeless" to the point where he was able to be enrolled in a public school special education program.

The combination of positive and negative reinforcers seems effective for modifying unacceptable behaviors of various types of exceptional children. Although most of the cases cited in this section are those of children who were brain-damaged or who had a social-emotional disturbance, the same procedures could be used with mentally retarded children. Wiesen and Watson (1967) used aversive consequences (for example, the attendant-counselors made negative comments) when unacceptable behavior occurred and positive object rewards (such as candy) for desired, acceptable behaviors with a six-year-old retarded boy. This schedule led to a rapid decrease in the amount of unacceptable attention-seeking behavior, and within five days the boy's behavior had been successfully modified. McConnell (1967) also reports success in using behavioral modification techniques, namely social reinforcement, with mentally retarded persons.

One of the basic principles of combining positive reinforcement with punishment is to make sure that the withdrawal is complete—in other words, that the child does not receive reinforcement in some other manner. In a case study by Burchard and Tyler (1965), a thirteen-year-old delinquent boy was perfunctorily placed in an isolation room when he displayed an unacceptable behavior. To avoid positive reinforcement from outside sources during his punishment (confinement) period, a radio played during the waking hours to eliminate the possibility of his communicating with other boys in neighboring isolation rooms. The isolation room was kept free of nonessential objects, and the staff members were instructed not to pay unnecessary attention to the boy—that is, not to give him a social recognition reward during his punishment period. Finally, for each period that he maintained good behavior while in isolation, he received tokens as rewards, and he was subsequently allowed to purchase with the tokens material things such as cigarettes, and nonmaterial things such as recreation privileges. A steady, gradual decline in the frequency of unacceptable behavior was achieved; for example, a 33 percent decline in the number of times that the boy was placed in isolation was measured between the first and fifth months of the conditioning processes.

Wetzel (1966) presents a case that combines positive and negative reinforcement and also demonstrates how the professional can serve as a consultant to nonprofessionals who conduct the actual behavioral modification program. The nonprofessionals were trained in the observation, recording, and modification of behavior. The subject was a ten-year-old boy with a history of compulsive stealing who lived in a home for mildly disturbed children. Previous attempts at punishment by scolding and disapproval had only served to strengthen the stealing behavior; now social acceptance was withdrawn whenever the boy stole. Thus all attention-getting value was eliminated, and withdrawing a positive stimulus, social acceptance (in this case, companionship with a favorite cook), was used. Within three and a half months, the stealing had been eliminated. For further comment on this study see Lang (1966). These studies indicate that the school should take advantage of such nonprofessional help as teacher aids or volunteers; they can be of service in helping to deal with behavioral problem children.

These procedures for combining positive reinforcement with punishment can readily be applied in an educational setting. Perhaps one of the most common examples is the practice of sending a child out of the classroom when he misbehaves. Typically the child is told to stand in the hall or in the corner of the classroom or in another unused room. If the excluded student is allowed or is able to talk to other students passing in the hallway or if his position in the corner leaves him free to see, hear, or speak with his peers, or if his placement in an unused room allows him to view his peers (such as a room that overlooks the playground), the punishment will certainly be less effective than if he is totally removed from potentially rewarding external stimuli. In other words, in being able to see or be seen, or talk with or observe others, the student is receiving in varying degrees reinforcement for his behavior during exclusion; and this counteracts the desired effects. Thus the ideal procedure for sending a child out of the classroom for unacceptable behavior would be to consistently and immediately make the exclusion as soon as and whenever the specific behavior occurred and to place the child in a room that denies him visual, verbal, and auditory contact with others.

Tyler and Brown (1967) used immediate and total isolation with fifteen teen-age delinquent boys. Whenever a boy demonstrated a misbehavior, he was promptly placed for fifteen minutes in a "time-out room." The results of the research revealed decreasing rates of misbehavior during the periods when the confinement procedure was being used. Tyler and Brown conclude that swift, brief confinement is a useful behavioral control device.

Further, if the child's behavior is acceptable during his period of exclusion, positive reinforcement could be added; for example, if he behaved properly during his period of punishment, he might be allowed to spend part of the punishment period in the school library, or perhaps be given something to play with or to read for the remainder of the period, or be allowed some privilege like spending a few minutes on the playground. The use of rewards in situations like this must be carefully controlled; that is, care must be exercised to assure that the rewards are bonded to the good behavior (during the punishment period) and do not attain properties that would serve to motivate the student to behave improperly in the classroom in order to receive a postpunishment reward. The reward-punishment procedure can be applied to many different problem behaviors that are frequently encountered in the schools. This form of behavioral modification should be suitable for essentially any educator.

AVERSIVE CONDITIONING

Another type of technique set forth in Chapter 6 was aversive conditioning: techniques that are based on negative reinforcement contingencies. The use of aversive stimuli, such as unpleasant noise and electric shock, seems to involve factors that limit it to exceptional situations. It is, therefore, considered to be beyond the scope of "general" techniques, and will receive special attention in the next chapter.

Before leaving the idea of aversive treatment, however, it would be wise to consider the possibility of a slightly different form of negative reinforcement—the use of paddlings and disciplinary actions that are typically called "punishments" (the word now being used in a manner different from that of the previous section, where punishment meant the withdrawing of a positive reward).

The idea of "punishing" a child (which is nothing other than using negative reinforcement) when he misbehaves is certainly not new. The old adage of "spare the rod and spoil the child" has been an accepted part of American education for many years. During the past few decades, child psychologists have increasingly taken the position that these negative, punishing techniques are not necessarily the best to use for behavioral modification; in fact, it may be said that positive reinforcement is usually more effective than negative reinforcement. Of course, many educators maintain that this type of belief may be fine for the theorists, but in real life situations there is a time and place for disciplining a child by the use of punishment, such as by paddling. And more than one teacher has remarked to the effect that "if those psychologists would leave their 'ivory towers' and try teaching my students for just one day, they would have to throw away all their theories." But this type of comment, although colorful, is hardly valid.

To abbreviate what could be an extensive discussion, suffice it to say that there is evidence that negative reinforcement or punishment may indeed have effects that are counter to what is desired. A previously cited example indicated that many children would rather be punished, thereby getting some attention, than totally neglected. And this possibility is not incompatible with psychological research. There is also the possibility that if a child is punished for an unacceptable act, such as talking without permission in the classroom, the fear of the punishment could result in the developing of extreme anxiety in conjunction with the general form of behavior that was punished; and even the desirable behaviors, such as fluent social talking at appropriate times, might be adversely affected. And if a desirable habit is inhibited because the related undesirable habit was punished, the desirable behavior cannot occur, cannot be rewarded, and cannot therefore become the preferred behavioral pattern (Bandura, 1961). In general, it is believed by psychologists that negative reinforcement or punishment (with the connotation used in this section) is not especially valuable in behavioral modification, and may even be futile. This form of negative reinforcement is, however, quite different from the aversive behavioral modification techniques that will be discussed in the next chapter; the latter is a special, controlled therapeutic procedure that is not synonymous with "punishment" in the ordinary classroom, which often includes manifestations of the teacher's emotions.

To summarize, negative reinforcement, such as by paddling or verbal condemnation, may be effective in some cases; but in general it is less desirable as an approach to behavioral modification than is the use of positive reinforcement. When negative reinforcement is used, it should be in conjunction with positive reinforcement. It then conforms to the original definition of the word: the child feels punished when positive reinforcement is withheld.

REFERENCES

Baer, D. M. Effect of withdrawal of positive reinforcement on an extinguishing response in young children. *Child Development*, 1961, 32: 67-74.

Baer, D. M. Laboratory control of thumbsucking by withdrawal and re-presentation of reinforcement. *Journal of Experimental Analysis of Behavior*, 1962, 5:525-528.

Bandura, A. Psychotherapy as a learning process. *Psychological Bulletin*, 1961, 58:143-159.

Bandura, A. Behavioral modification through modeling procedures. In

L. Krasner and L. P. Ullmann (Eds.), *Research in behavior modification*. New York: Holt, Rinehart and Winston, 1965, 310-340.

Bandura, A., and Walters, R. H. *Social learning and personality development*. New York: Holt, Rinehart and Winston, 1963.

Barclay, J. R. Effecting behavior change in the elementary classroom: an exploratory study. *Journal of Counseling Psychology*, 1967, 14:240-247.

Bijou, S. W. Experimental studies of child behavior, normal and deviant. In L. Krasner and L. P. Ullmann (Eds.), *Research in behavior modification*. New York: Holt, Rinehart and Winston, 1965, 56-81.

Birnbrauer, J. S., Wolf, M. M., Kidder, J. D., and Tague, Cecilia E. Classroom behavior of retarded pupils with token reinforcement. *Journal of Experimental Child Psychology*, 1965, 2:219-235.

Brison, D. W. A non-talking child in kindergarten: an application of behavior therapy. *Journal of School Psychology*, 1966, 4:65-69.

Brown, P., and Elliott, R. Control of aggression in a nursery school class. *Journal of Experimental Child Psychology*, 1965, 2:103-107.

Browning, R. M. Behavior therapy for stuttering in a schizophrenic child. *Behaviour Research and Therapy*, 1967, 5:27-35.

Burchard, J., and Tyler, V., Jr. The modification of delinquent behaviour through operant conditioning. *Behaviour Research and Therapy*, 1965, 2:245-250.

Davison, G. C. A social learning therapy programme with an autistic child. *Behaviour Research and Therapy*, 1964, 2:149-159.

Ellis, N. R. (Ed.). *Handbook of mental deficiency*. New York: McGraw-Hill, 1963.

Emery, J. R., and Krumboltz, J. D. Standard versus individualized hierarchies in desensitization to reduce test anxiety. *Journal of Counseling Psychology*, 1967, 14:204-209.

Eysenck, H. J., and Rachman, S. *The causes and cures of neurosis*. San Diego: R. R. Knapp, 1965.

Gardner, J. E. Behavior therapy treatment approach to a psychogenic seizure case. *Journal of Consulting Psychology*, 1967, 31:209-212.

Hallsten, E. A., Jr. Adolescent anorexia nervosa treated by desensitization. *Behaviour Research and Therapy*, 1965, 3:87-91.

Hartup, W. W. Friendship status and the effectiveness of peers as reinforcing agents. *Journal of Experimental Child Psychology*, 1964, 1:154-162.

Hundziak, M., Maurer, Ruth A., and Watson, L. S., Jr. Operant conditioning in toilet training of severely mentally retarded boys. *American Journal of Mental Deficiency*, 1965, 70:120-124.

Jacobson, E. *Progressive relaxation*. Chicago: University of Chicago Press, 1938.

Jones, Mary C. A laboratory study of fear: the case of Peter. *Journal of Genetic Psychology*, 1924, 31:308-315.

Kliebhan, Joanne Marie. Effects of goal-setting and modeling on job performance of retarded adolescents. *American Journal of Mental Deficiency,* 1967, 72:220-226.

Lang, P. J. The transfer of treatment. *Journal of Consulting Psychology,* 1966, 30:375-378.

Lazarus, A. A. Behaviour rehearsal vs. non-directive therapy vs. advice in effecting behaviour change. *Behaviour Research and Therapy,* 1966, 4:209-212.

Lazarus, A. A., and Abramovitz, A. The use of "emotive imagery" in the treatment of children's phobias. *Journal of Mental Science,* 1962, 108: 191-195.

Lazarus, A. A., Davison, G. C., and Polefka, D. A. Classical and operant factors in the treatment of a school phobia. *Journal of Abnormal Psychology,* 1965, 70:225-229.

Lomont, J. F., and Edwards, J. E. The role of relaxation in systematic desensitization. *Behaviour Research and Therapy,* 1967, 5:11-25.

Lovaas, O. I., Freitas, Lorraine, Nelson, Karen, and Whalen, Carol. The establishment of imitation and its use for the development of complex behavior in schizophrenic children. *Behaviour Research and Therapy,* 1967, 5:171-181.

McConnell, O. L. Personality correlates of responsiveness to social reinforcement in mental retardates. *American Journal of Mental Deficiency,* 1967, 72:45-49.

McKerracher, D. W. Alleviation of reading difficulties by a simple operant conditioning technique. *Journal of Child Psychology and Psychiatry,* 1967, 8:51-56.

Miller, L. K. A note on the control of study behavior. *Journal of Experimental Child Psychology,* 1964, 1:108-110.

O'Leary, K. D., O'Leary, Susan, and Becker, W. C. Modification of a deviant sibling interaction pattern in the home. *Behaviour Research and Therapy,* 1967, 5:113-120.

Patterson, G. R. A learning theory approach to the treatment of the school phobic child. In L. P. Ullmann and L. Krasner (Eds.), *Case studies in behavior modification.* New York: Holt, Rinehart and Winston, 1965, 279-285.

Patterson, G. R., Jones, R., Whittier, J., and Wright, Mary A. A behaviour modification technique for the hyperactive child. *Behaviour Research and Therapy,* 1965, 2:217-226.

Risley, T., and Wolf, M. Establishing functional speech in echolalic children. *Behaviour Research and Therapy,* 1967, 5:73-88.

Russo, S. Adaptations in behavioural therapy with children. *Behaviour Research and Therapy,* 1964, 2:43-47.

Schwitzgebel, R., and Kolb, D. A. Inducing behaviour change in adolescent delinquents. *Behaviour Research and Therapy,* 1964, 1:297-304.

Stacey, C. L., and DeMartino, M. F. (Eds.). *Counseling and psychotherapy with the mentally retarded.* Glencoe, Ill.: Glencoe Free Press, 1957.

Straughan, J. H. Treatment with child and mother in the playroom. *Behaviour Research and Therapy,* 1964, 2:37-41.

Sturm, I. E. The behavioristic aspect of psychodrama. *Group Psychotherapy,* 1965, 18:50-64.

Tiktin, Susan, and Hartup, W. W. Sociometric status and the reinforcing effectiveness of children's peers. *Journal of Experimental Child Psychology,* 1965, 2:306-315.

Tyler, V. O., Jr., and Brown, G. D. The use of swift, brief isolation as a group control device for institutionalized delinquents. *Behaviour Research and Therapy,* 1967, 5:1-9.

Wahler, R. G., Winkel, G. H., Peterson, R. F., and Morrison, D. C. Mothers as behaviour therapists for their own children. *Behaviour Research and Therapy,* 1965, 3:113-124.

Walters, R. H., and Parke, R. D. Influence of response consequences to a social model on resistance to deviation. *Journal of Experimental Child Psychology,* 1964, 1:269-280.

Wiesen, A. E., and Watson, Edith. Elimination of attention seeking behavior in a retarded child. *American Journal of Mental Deficiency,* 1967, 72:50-52.

Wetzel, R. Use of behavioral techniques in a case of compulsive stealing. *Journal of Consulting Psychology,* 1966, 30:367-374.

White, J. G. The use of learning theory in the psychological treatment of children. *Journal of Clinical Psychology,* 1957, 15:227-229.

Wolf, M., Risley, T., Johnston, Margaret, Harris, Florence, and Allen, Eileen. Application of operant conditioning procedures to the behaviour problems of an autistic child: a follow-up and extension. *Behaviour Research and Therapy,* 1967, 5:103-111.

Wolf, M., Risley, T., and Mees, H. Application of operant conditioning procedures to the behaviour problems of an autistic child. *Behaviour Research and Therapy,* 1964, 1:305-312.

Wolpe, J. *Psychotherapy by reciprocal inhibition.* Stanford, Calif.: Stanford University Press, 1958.

Wolpe, J., and Lazarus, A. A. *Behavior therapy techniques.* Oxford, Eng.: Pergamon Press, 1966.

Woody, R. H. Counselling the mentally subnormal: an American model. *Journal of Mental Subnormality,* 1966, 12:73-79.

Woody, R. H., and Billy, J. J. Counseling and psychotherapy for the mentally retarded: a survey of opinions and practices. *Mental Retardation,* 1966, 4:20-23.

Zimmerman, Elaine H., and Zimmerman, J. The alteration of behavior in a special classroom situation. *Journal of Experimental Analysis of Behavior,* 1962, 5:59-60.

8

Specialized Behavioral
Modification Techniques

The techniques in this chapter are set apart from those in the previous chapter because there seem to be factors related to expertise and training that limit their usage. It is highly unlikely that these specialized techniques, with the exception perhaps of certain verbal conditioning principles, could be used by any classroom teacher or school administrator; they require psychological training that is not part of the preparation of these persons. School counselors and school psychologists may, however, be qualified to use most of these techniques; but again some techniques require training that would probably not be part of subdoctoral training programs; and thus some of these procedures may be restricted to doctoral-level counseling, school, and clinical psychologists.

It should be obvious that these advanced specialists, including subdoctoral school counselors and school psychologists, are generally capable of working with problem behaviors too severe to be treated by classroom teachers. Many of the techniques in Chapter 6, therefore, are "general" techniques and may be used by essentially any educator, but school counselors and school psychologists should be able to carry them on to work with cases of behavioral problem children that are more severe. Of course, there may also be cases of behavioral problem children that will require referral to even more highly trained specialists, who may in turn apply essentially the same behavioral modification techniques, at least in principle, but will do so at a more advanced level. For example, positive reinforcement techniques may be used by most educators to some degree to modify behaviors of emotionally disturbed children, but when the child reaches a state of disturbance that would be labeled childhood autism or schizophrenia it is necessary that his primary therapist be a highly trained specialist (a classroom teacher could perhaps serve as an adjunct therapist to the primary specialist-therapist by applying certain therapeutic procedures in the classroom setting).

The specialized techniques in this chapter will not be categorized according to the three types used in Chapters 6 and 7. The basic category to which they belong will, however, be noted during the respective discussions. There seem to be three major sets of techniques that should be considered "specialized"; these include behavioral counseling, aversive conditioning, and clinical suggestion and hypnosis.

BEHAVIORAL COUNSELING

Behavioral counseling, at this point in its evolution, is essentially the use of verbal conditioning in the counseling setting. But it is quite probable that, as research on behavioral modification techniques accumulates, behavioral counseling will employ not only verbal conditioning but also other techniques derived from learning theory.

Verbal conditioning, as was explained in Chapter 6, is based on the use of verbal and nonverbal stimuli to positively reinforce behaviors. The reinforcing stimuli are typically designed to show praise or approval, and the behaviors that are reinforced are commonly certain types of verbal responses made by the counselee.

Most contemporary counseling practices are aligned with the insight position; that is, counselors believe that their function is to facilitate the client's gaining of insight and understanding of ideas, thoughts, motives, feelings, and behavior. In view of this alignment, it is not surprising that many counselors are hesitant or resistant to taking such direct action as modifying observable behaviors.

It seems, however, that the counselor does have the responsibility of carrying through with the client until the problems that brought the client to him have been resolved—primarily to the satisfaction of the client, and secondarily to the satisfaction of the counselor. Although a previously cited dichotomy suggested that actionists want the removal or alleviation of the symptoms or problems as their major goal of therapy and that the insightists essentially disregard the presence of the symptoms or problems and are interested primarily in helping the client understand or gain insight into their behaviors (London, 1964), it seems likely that even those counselors who identify with an insight approach to counseling must also be concerned with the client's perceiving a solution to or resolution of the problems that led him to enter counseling. Schmidt (1965) provides three types of concerns regarding the activities and behavior of counselors—legal, professional, and ethical; and under the section on professional factors, Schmidt focuses attention on the counselor's responsibility to the counselee:

Once a counselor agrees to counsel with a client he must also accept the obligation of seeing this person through at least some initial or contributing solution to his difficulty, no matter how unpleasant or stressful the situation may become. This often entails the responsibility of making professional judgments that may have far-reaching consequences both for the client and for the counselor. (p. 379)

The processes involved in "the responsibility of making professional judgments" may easily be aligned with behavioral counseling; that is, the counselor uses his professional capabilities to fulfill his responsibilities to the client by determining, recommending, and programming an approach, which is primarily based upon principles of learning theory, that will help the client find satisfaction for his motives for coming to the counselor. If, therefore, the counselee preferred that his problem behaviors be alleviated or eliminated, the counselor's responsibility would be to reckon with this preference.

Behavioral counseling, as compared with counseling in general, unequivocally places emphasis on the modification of behaviors. The involvement of the counselor, as interpreted from the behavioral point of view, is clarified by Krumboltz (1965):

The central purpose of counseling, then, is to help the client resolve those problems for which he requests help. If a client terminates his contact with a counselor and is still bothered by the same problem that brought him to the counselor in the first place, that counselor has failed. If, on the other hand, the client has either solved the problem he brought to the counselor or planned a course of action that will eventually lead to a resolution of his problem, then the counselor has succeeded. Within limits, it is each client's wishes that dictate the criteria of success for that client.[1]

But in regard to the latter part of this statement, Krumboltz clearly indicates that the client's wishes directly influence the end results but not the means to these ends; he believes that the professional counselor must determine the treatment format, such as the techniques that will be used. He then sets forth the following definition of counseling:

Counseling consists of whatever ethical activities a counselor undertakes in an effort to help the client engage in those types of behavior which will lead to a resolution of the client's problems.[2]

The activities engaged in by the client-centered (insight) counselor and those used by the behavioral (action) counselor can be related to this definition: both select the activities that will facilitate what they theoretically consider to be the "resolution" of the client's problems. The difference, however, is that those endorsing the insight approaches do

1 From J. D. Krumboltz, Behavioral Counseling: Rationale and Research, *Personnel and Guidance Journal*, Vol. 44 (1965), p. 384.
2 *Ibid*.

not define the problems in terms of overt behavioral problems, no matter
how much discomfort they may cause the client, but rather emphasize
that resolution of the problems results from understanding why the problem behaviors occur.

As previously discussed in Chapter 5, it is possible for aspects from
the counseling-psychotherapy continuum to be integrated with behavioral
modification techniques, and elsewhere clinical examples of this integration have been presented (Woody, in press). Therefore, in this section
on behavioral counseling, emphasis will be placed on the behavioral factors (since that is the primary theme of this book), although the reader
should remember that there is evidence that both insight and behavioral
counseling can be used by the same counselor and with the same counselee. And as will be discussed shortly, there is evidence that even client-
centered counseling has components of behavioral counseling—for example, verbal reinforcement, within its current theoretical and practical
structure (Truax, 1966a).

To return now to the counselor's responsibility of dealing directly
with the requests of each individual client, one should note that there
are limits to the client's prerogative for determining the counseling goals.
There may well be some types of requests that the counselor should not
attempt to serve. Krumboltz (1965) sets forth three types of limitations
to which counselors should adhere: the counseling interests of the counselor, the competency limits of the counselor, and the ethical standards
of the counselor. So despite the fact that clients are justified in stating
the preferred goals for their counseling, the counselor is equally justified
in refusing to accept these requests; but this refusal should be open and
explained to the client, the explanation possibly being based on one or
more of the three above-mentioned criteria. Thus some clients may present problems in their requests for counseling that are not within the
interest boundaries or professional competency limits of the counselor,
and the counselor may decide that the client could receive greater benefit
from seeking counseling from another counselor, one who is interested in
or capable of working with those specific difficulties. And ethically the
counselor must be able to cope with the problems presented by the client;
for example, the counselor, faced with a request from a client to help
him modify his behavior in order that he may be able to engage in some
other behavior that is perhaps contradictory to social values, morals, or
ethics, must be able to reason whether such a request can be and, moreover, should be accommodated by counseling services.

Several examples of how the counselor's ethical standards enter into
the determination of therapeutic goals should underscore the significance
of this matter. In one case, an eighteen-year-old, single, female student
requested help in becoming more affectionate with her boy friend. They
had attempted sexual intercourse several times, and on each occasion

she could not respond but became anxious; in fact, although she professed to want very much to have sexual relations with the young man, she could not even feel comfortable when they embraced and caressed. Matters were complicated by the fact that her parents did not know that she was requesting treatment. And here we have the difficulty: the counselor could quite easily treat this type of anxiety reaction problem by the use of behavioral modification techniques, namely desensitization for the anxiety-provoking situations; but he also had to consider the facts that she was a teen-ager, unmarried (her request being contradictory to social mores for sexual behavior in certain cultures), and that her parents did not know of her request for treatment. The counselor's own ethical standards obviously had to come into play. Had this been a counselor affiliated with a religious institution, such as a minister-psychologist, his religious views might have been of paramount significance; to answer this girl's request might have meant violating his personal ethical and moral standards. Although the outcome is certainly debatable, the psychologist involved (who, incidentally, was female) did accept the girl's request and treated her accordingly; but this was that particular psychologist's decision. It is not being suggested in any manner that this therapist used the correct means of dealing with this type of request from a client; another psychologist might have justly refused.

A second case involved a young married man who was experiencing all sorts of anxiety in conjunction with sexual problems; rather than go into a detailed clinical case history, the point can be made by noting that the psychologist recommended that the young man masturbate more frequently. Again we have a decision, made by a well-trained psychologist, that could conceivably be contrary to one that would be made by another psychologist whose ethical standards were different; this psychologist felt, however, that this action was justified and that it would prove to be therapeutically beneficial to his client. Similarly, certain therapists have deemed it "entirely proper" to encourage a husband who is experiencing sexual difficulties to find a woman other than his wife (assuming that his wife will not cooperate and all other "reasonable efforts" have failed) who will be sexually responsive to him (Wolpe and Lazarus, 1966); again the ethical and moral implications are apparent. The main point is that there is no right answer to these decision-making situations; we can only hope that the professional is well trained—and this includes possession of a strong set of ethical guidelines that he has evidence for believing are justified.

It is not only clients who may request services that are in conflict with professional ethics. That such requests may even come from other professionals is evidenced in the following true situation. A local counselors' association made a request for a psychologist to demonstrate "probing" techniques with children. As it turned out, the children were not already in counseling but were to be brought in solely for this demonstration, there were no arrangements to follow up on them after the demonstration, and the psychologist would be unavailable to assume continuing therapeutic responsibility for them. He pointed out to the representatives of the association that he felt it would be unethical for him to demonstrate means to "open a child up" since it would not be of service to the child and especially since there was no way of helping the children to achieve any kind of closure or resolution to problems or conflicts that might emerge during the demonstration. This situation clearly exemplifies how professionals might interpret ethics differently. Value judgments definitely play a part in determining responsibility.

When this problem of ethics is considered in the educational context (and some of the foregoing examples are admittedly a bit more clinical in nature than most school counselors and school psychologists will typically encounter), it becomes clear that the behavioral counselor must assess each facet of each request for counseling. If the request is suited to his personal, professional, and ethical characteristics, he then assumes the responsibility for seeking relief, alleviation, elimination, or resoluton of the difficulties for the client. In assuming this responsibility, the counselor essentially takes over full responsibility for determining the means to the end—that is, the counseling or therapeutic procedures to be used to achieve the counseling goals. The counselor is a professional and is professionally equipped to make judgments, supposedly based on scientific knowledge, that will more effectively achieve the counseling goals than if the decisions or judgments regarding direction were made by the client. Perhaps one of the best analogies, which may be a bit trite, is that just as the medical physician uses his professional skills to diagnose and prescribe medication (the means) to cure his patient (achieve the goals), the counselor or psychologist uses his professional skills to diagnose (but not necessarily in a psychometric framework) and prescribe the approach to counseling—that is, the counseling or therapeutic techniques (the means)—that will cure his client (achieve the goals).

There is one obvious difficulty here. Counselors, particularly in educational settings, have not heretofore been accorded the same professional status as the medical physician. In fact, even the medical physicians in the United States have less awe-inspiring professional status than those in other countries; for example, Erickson (1966) indicates that medical physicians using clinical hypnosis to treat psychosomatic disorders in some other countries—but not in the United States—find that "the prestige of the professional man is sufficient to effect both ready trance induction and remarkably effective immediate responses to hypnotic suggestion" (p. 173). It is certainly apparent that counselors and psychologists seldom, if ever, have any hypnotic effect and perhaps, at least philosophically, need never strive to attain this type of status. But this should not keep them, the counselors and psychologists, from assuming responsibility for the services that they provide.

What is needed is a professional and public awareness that counselors and psychologists are sufficiently trained to make ethical judgments as to what are the most appropriate counseling role and techniques to use. As yet, it is certainly questionable whether even the most highly trained counselor or psychologist is truly free from unjustified restrictions, from both professional and lay sources, to select and practice the procedures he deems to be the most suitable for the particular client. It could, of course, be argued justifiably that such "checks and balances" serve to protect both the client and the professional in the long run, and indeed this is probably true. But there are situations where professionals are unreasonably restricted, at least according to some standards, by stereotyped ideas or regulations.

One of the goals for psychoeducational professionals should be the overcoming of unjustified restrictions. This will necessitate concentrated efforts by applied counselors and psychologists and by the university programs that train personnel for the schools; and these training programs should encompass not only the obvious ones in counseling and psychology, but those in other areas of education as well, particularly in educational administration.

Having established the theoretical rationale, definition, and possible concerns necessary for the use of behavioral counseling techniques, we can now turn to a detailed discussion of verbal conditioning, the underlying basis for behavioral counseling. This should prepare us for a review of several of the research studies that are especially relevant to the use of behavioral modification techniques in counseling.

Verbal Conditioning

Verbal conditioning is one of the primary means of behavioral counseling. Simply stated: the behavioral counselor reinforces verbal behaviors. As is the case with other forms of conditioning that involve reinforcement, the reinforcing aspects in behavioral counseling may be object rewards, such as the giving of objects or privileges for specific verbal behaviors; or recognition rewards, such as the counselor's acknowledging in some manner a specific type of response that he wishes to reinforce. Most commonly the counselor's reinforcing response involves two types of stimuli: a physical gesture that denotes acceptance or a positive verbal comment. And, of course, these two categories of counselor responses can be combined.

Positive reinforcement may be given by *physical gestures* denoting acceptance of a response from the counselee. These gestures might in-

clude a smile, a nod, leaning closer toward the client, relaxing the position of the body, uncrossing the arms, unclenching a fist, uncrossing the
legs, or any type of bodily, nonverbal action that could be perceived
either consciously or unconsciously by the counselee as acceptance of the
response by the counselor. In many cases, clients viewing video tapes of
their counseling sessions commented that actions, such as those just
listed, by the counselor did make them feel a certain way when the
actions occurred during the session, but that they, the counselees, were
not conscious of the feeling aroused until they experienced the stimulated recall of the session by viewing the video tape (Kagan, Krathwohl,
and Farquhar, 1965). Thus these nonverbal, physical gestures do reinforce
a client's behavior, and the most effective counseling would capitalize on
this fact and control the reinforcements so that they might serve a constructive purpose—that is, use them systematically.

Verbal comments by the counselor have also proved to have powerful reinforcement effects, and it is this type of stimulus that is accorded
an integral part in behavioral counseling research. The procedure is as
follows: When the counselor responds to a comment made by the client
by saying "Good," or "Yes," or "I agree," or something similar, the
client will tend to favor the use of that type of response more than a type
which the counselor does not respond to at all or which he responds to
with a comment like "I don't agree," or "That is silly," or "No." A good
example of this practice in everyday life is that a person tends to talk
about the same subjects with acquaintances, subjects that have made the
relationship comfortable during previous interactions: there are some
persons whom one always asks about their family, while with others
personal matters like the family are not mentioned, but impersonal
topics like work activities or sports events are expected; topics have been
reinforced by their acceptance or rejection in previous discussions.
Everyone does respond to verbal reinforcement to some degree, and thus
it is logical that planned, systematic usage of it in a counseling relationship could produce desired effects.

In addition to obvious positive reinforcing responses from the
counselor like "Good," it is also believed that even ambiguous verbal
responses, depending upon the relationship between the counselor and
client, will be interpreted by the client to be either accepting or rejecting. For example, in a series of experiments with college students, Sapolsky (1960) found that the quality of the interpersonal relationship between the subject and the experimenter, whether it was positive or negative, was reflected in the subject's performance in a verbal conditioning
format. That is, when the two persons were compatible "the reinforcing
value of 'mm-hmm' was enhanced," and when the two persons were incompatible (the attraction was low) "no significant increase in the use of
the reinforced pronouns occurred . . ." (p. 245).

The use of an ambiguous verbal response and a clear-cut nonverbal reinforcing response is exemplified in a study by Rogers (1960). Using thirty-six male college students, Rogers provided a series of interviews in which he reinforced all self-reference verbalizations with a simultaneous "mm-hmm" and a nod of his head; one group was conditioned for positive self-references and the other group was conditioned for negative self-references. Each subject received only six ten-minute interviews. Rogers concludes:

Operant conditioning of verbal behavior in a quasi-therapy situation was demonstrated. . . . It was found that negative self-references could be increased by interpolating simple reinforcing stimuli and that such conditioning could be accomplished without the S's awareness. It was further shown . . . that whereas positive self-references without reinforcement tended to extinguish themselves in quasi-therapy, with reinforcement their extinction could be arrested, this too without the S's awareness. (Rogers, 1960, p. 252)

Neither the initial level of anxiety nor the emotional adjustment of the subject was related to conditionability.

It should be noted that verbal conditioning seems effective with children of all intellectual levels. Research evidence indicates that verbal conditioning can even potentially alter the behaviors of mentally retarded persons (Doubros, 1967).

Selective Responding in Counseling

Studies like the two just discussed have provided the empirical basis for the assertion made by behavior therapists that many insight-oriented counselors and therapists are in fact conditioning their clients in much the same manner as would the behavior therapist using verbal conditioning techniques. One of the most frequently cited examples is that of the client-centered counselor. The client-centered counselor relies on reflection of feelings, and uses such verbal responses as "mm-hmm" or "I see" or "you feel that . . ." and such nonverbal responses as nods of the head. It might seem, therefore, that the client-centered counselor selects, admittedly on a much more unconscious level perhaps than the behavior therapist's planned selections, responses from the client to reinforce by a counselor-response. Thus there is the possibility that the client-centered counselor actually *directs* the verbal behaviors and consequently the overt behaviors of the client. Truax (1966a) has made an analysis of recordings of psychotherapy sessions conducted by Carl R. Rogers, one of the foremost exponents of client-centered theory. He concludes:

The therapist significantly tended to respond selectively with differential levels of empathy, warmth or directiveness to high and low levels of five of the nine classes of patient behavior. He did not significantly vary his level of empathy, etc., with four classes of patient behavior. Thus, a clear and significant pattern of selective responding was indicated.[3]

Further, as one might expect from the body of research on verbal reinforcement, of the five types of patient behavior that were selectively reinforced, four revealed significant changes in frequency of occurrence over the duration of therapy in the expected direction; of the four classes of patient behavior that were not selectively reinforced, three did not show an increase or a decrease over the duration of therapy. Similarly, it has been found that even psychologists who identified themselves as client-centered in orientation used, on occasion, very directive and manipulative techniques (Woody and Herr, 1965).

It should be noted that Roberts and Renzaglia (1965) have found that counselors are less client-centered when they know that their interviews are being tape-recorded and will, therefore, possibly be subjected to analysis. It seems that to determine and assess what a counselor's behavior *actually* is in the day-to-day, unmonitored counseling situations may be difficult, or perhaps even impossible.

In view of the available research, particularly that furnished by Truax (1966a, 1966b), there appears a strong likelihood that counselors may have been practicing selective responding or verbal reinforcement unconsciously or at least unadmittedly. It is probable that some proponents of behavior therapy would seize on this point to assert that behaviorists may be the most ethical therapists after all, because they (such as behavioral counselors) are aware of and freely admit the intention of their functions in the counseling or therapy sessions: the behavioral counselor is an active agent in the modification of his counselee's behaviors. And facetiously it might be added that psychoanalytically oriented counselors and psychologists would probably feel justified in pointing their "reaction formation" fingers at the insight-oriented professionals who decry their behaviorally oriented counterparts.

Counterconditioning in Counseling

As may be recalled from previous discussions, the principle of reciprocal inhibition holds that if an anxiety-inhibiting response occurs in the presence of anxiety-evoking stimuli, the bond between the stimuli and the anxiety will be weakened (Wolpe, 1964); and a person becomes desensitized to the anxiety-evoking stimuli by progressively experiencing a hierarchy of situations. As the person becomes desensitized to a par-

[3] From C. B. Truax, Some implications of behavior therapy for psychotherapy, *Journal of Counseling Psychology*, Vol. 13 (1966), p. 167. Reprinted by permission.

ticular anxiety-provoking situation, he can move to a more advanced
level of anxiety-provoking situations. In addition to the belief that
counselors, even those who are client-centered in orientation, may actually be reinforcing certain client behaviors, there is also evidence that
the counseling processes may be aligned with the principle of reciprocal
inhibition. As Truax (1966b) states:

Using the model of systematic desensitization the traditional therapist would
aim at empathic responses which would move to the patient's self-exploration
of anxiety-laden material *gradually,* along an ascending hierarchy of anxiety
cues at a pace which would allow for desensitization of cues *before* moving on
to new material (or more anxiety-arousing cues). *The traditional therapist
would be using the human "relationship" as the source for countercondi-
tioning.*[4]

If this assertion is applied to counseling, it would suggest that counseling
involves a series of encounters which actually results in systematic
desensitization; the counseling would be permissive early in the relationship and would gradually become more intimate and would deal
with more anxiety-provoking or affective material related to the counselee's situation. In other words, the more intimate the counseling relationship, the greater the desensitization.

Research on Behavioral Counseling

In view of the recent development of behavioral counseling, it is
not surprising that most relevant experimental research comes from
allied areas, such as verbal conditioning studies. There are, however,
several well-designed research studies that are directly related to the use
of these reinforcement tchniques in a counseling setting.

In a study of sixty male college students, Ryan and Krumboltz
(1964) found that when counselors verbally reinforced (by using such
verbal responses as "Good," "Fine," and "That's a good idea") *deliberation responses* made by the clients during the counseling sessions, there
was an increase in the frequency of deliberation-type responses; and this
type of response decreased when the reinforcement was withdrawn (the
reader will recall that the withdrawal of a positive reinforcing response
tends to serve as a punishment). It was also found that *decision responses*
increased in the same manner when the counselor reinforced them verbally, and decreased in frequency when the verbal reinforcement was
withdrawn. It is interesting to note that the counselors varied in reinforcing effectiveness; the differential factors related to the reinforcement

---

[4] *Ibid.,* p. 165.

effectiveness of counselors constitute an area that merits further research.

Perhaps the most significant point about this study is that the counselors' reinforcements effectively changed the frequency of deliberation and decision responses; that is, the counselees tended to make these types of responses more frequently because of the verbal reinforcement. And both of these types of responses are generally believed to contribute beneficially to the counseling processes. Even insight-oriented counselors believe that when the client engages in deliberation and eventually assumes the responsibility for making a decision the counseling has progressed.

A similar study has been conducted with high school students. Krumboltz and Thoresen (1964) studied 192 high school students who received individual and group counseling. The students, according to their initial grouping of individual and group counseling, were assigned to one of four types of treatment: reinforcement (from the counselor) of verbal information-seeking behavior, presentation of a tape-recorded model counseling interview followed by reinforcement counseling, presentation of a film or filmstrip with a discussion period for a control group (but no reinforcement counseling), and an inactive control group. Thus, the first two types of treatment involved behavioral counseling, with the counselor verbally reinforcing *information-seeking responses* or behaviors. As in the study by Ryan and Krumboltz (1964), the reinforcing stimuli were verbal expressions that indicated that the counselor approved of the type of verbal expression used by the counselee. It was found that both the model-reinforcement counseling (treatment number two) and the reinforcement counseling without a model (treatment number one) produced more information-seeking behavior outside of the counseling sessions than did the control procedures. Group and individual settings seemed to be equally effective. Thoresen and Krumboltz (1967) similarly reinforced the information-seeking responses of eleventh-grade students in counseling and found that the reinforced responses did correlate with actual information-seeking behaviors outside of counseling; as an aside, the clients' ratings of the helpfulness of the counseling were not significantly associated with their information-seeking behaviors. Dicken and Fordham (1967) compared students receiving reinforcement counseling (where positive self-references and statements of positive affect were reinforced by the counselor) with students receiving client-centered counseling and students receiving no interviews. The reinforced group showed the greatest change on the personal functioning measure (the California Psychological Inventory) and had a greater, but not significant, amount of talk (presumably a greater number of verbal responses would be a desired outcome, since verbal material and/or interactions could possibly relate to achieving insight).

These studies support that critical response classes, such as information-seeking behavior, can be influenced by reinforcement from the counselor. The importance of this fact to school counseling is readily apparent: it is often necessary for a student with the goal of selecting a college or vocation to engage in information-seeking behavior—for example, looking through occupational information or college catalogs in the library; and innumerable problems encountered in counseling require self-references and affective responses if resolution is to be achieved. It would appear that the total counseling process, including factors relevant to insight, could be facilitated by behavioral counseling.

In regard to the use of models, a technique described in the section on social modeling and shaping behaviors in Chapter 7, the Krumboltz and Thoresen (1964) study found that when a male model was used on the tape recording, model-reinforcement counseling achieved greater success for the males, but not for the females, than did reinforcement counseling. And Varenhorst (1964) found that a video tape recording of a model female counseling client was effective with female clients. In a study of 168 eleventh-grade girls who had requested educational or vocational counseling, Krumboltz, Varenhorst, and Thoresen (1967) found evidence that viewing a video tape recording of a model counseling session served to increase information-seeking behavior more than control procedures (there were female social models in the taped interviews); and they conclude that data from this and previous studies give strong support for the belief that an appropriate social model is an effective means for increasing information-seeking for both males and females. These studies and others (Thoresen, Krumboltz, and Varenhorst, 1967) might be interpreted as suggesting that the use of tape recordings, either video or audio, or films of a model counseling client facilitates the reinforcement-type behavioral counseling processes when the model and the observer-client are of the same sex.

The use of behavioral counseling for promoting career planning for high school students was further explored by Krumboltz and Schroeder (1965). From a total of fifty-four high school students seeking educational and vocational counseling, the subjects were randomly assigned to one of three types of groups: reinforcement counseling, where information-seeking responses were reinforced; model-reinforcement counseling, where a tape recording of a model male counselee was played to each client before the reinforcement counseling; and control. The counselor's verbal responses furnished positive reinforcement (such as using praise, encouragement, and agreement) for a client's information-seeking responses; and the counselor used nonverbal reinforcing behaviors (such as smiling, gesturing, and giving approving nods of the head). It was found that, after two counseling sessions one week apart, the students who received reinforcement counseling, both with and without the tape-recorded model of a counseling session, engaged in more information-seeking behavior outside the interview than did the control subjects. The experimental female subjects who received reinforcement counseling without the tape recording of a model client displayed more external information-seeking behavior than the female controls, but this was not true for the males. Conversely, with the model-reinforcement counseling group, the males were significantly greater in information-seeking behavior than the controls but the females were not. It was also found that the ratio of information-seeking responses to other types of responses in the counseling session was positively correlated with information-seeking behavior outside of counseling.

These research studies should exemplify adequately the techniques used in behavioral counseling. They have obviously been successfully applied in schools. Further, Thoresen (1966) provides a basic example of behavioral counseling techniques within an educational setting.

The practical use of behavioral counseling is illustrated in the following case. During a counseling intern's initial interview with a young mother who had sought counseling-advisement about how to handle her behavioral problem child, the mother's own personality factors greatly restricted interpersonal communication with the counselor. She found it very difficult to look at her counselor and to communicate verbally. The mother was being seen for psychotherapy for her own problems by another psychologist who had asked the counselor to teach the mother some of the basic principles of conditioning childhood behavior in the home. The counselor recognized these communication difficulties and interpreted and discussed them with the young woman. He then directly told her that, in order to teach her the principles for use with her son, he would use their counseling relationship as a model. The procedure was as follows: After telling her that he was aware of her strong motivation for learning how to cope with and help her son (which may well have served as a clinical suggestion), he would respond to her only when she communicated openly with him; that is, when she looked at him and talked freely, the counselor would look at her and respond freely with information about child rearing and discuss the situations that she described; but when she avoided eye-contact and verbally blocked (and it was known from her own psychotherapy that this was not a typical condition for her), he would say nothing, give no facial expression, and might even turn his chair slightly and look out of the window until she was ready to continue talking. During the next psychotherapy session with her regular psychologist, the mother laughingly told of the experience and how "within ten minutes I found I had to look at him and talk or he wouldn't even acknowledge that I existed." And she was very pleased over the initial success of the same techniques when she applied them to her child at home. This mother of a behavioral problem child had learned quickly about conditioning or behavioral modification techniques by experiencing them herself.

One final research study on behavioral counseling may be found in a project conducted with elementary school children (Johnson, 1964). It was found that when their counselor gave them positive reinforcement (such as warmth, praise, and support) for verbal participation, their verbal participation increased both in their counseling sessions and in their classrooms. In this type of situation, the classroom teacher could provide a consistent continuation of the reinforcement in relation to verbal conditioning; for example, the shy, withdrawn, nontalkative child might receive behavioral counseling from the school counselor and the classroom teacher would continue to reinforce the verbal participation when the child returned to the classroom.

The research studies discussed above give strong support for the belief that behavioral counseling, based on verbal conditioning, can be used for varied school-related problems (Woody, 1968). Assuming that the school counselor has the general training that is necessary for a school counseling position, there is no reason why he could not learn to apply these behavioral counseling techniques to facilitate his regular counseling encounters. Perhaps the most pertinent use would be with students who want vocational and educational counseling. Instead of spending an extended period of time progressing through the stages of letting the counselee determine the goals and what means should be used to fulfill them, the counselor would accept the client's initial problem—the request for counseling to help gain an understanding of vocational and educational goals—and would then reinforce information-seeking behavior. Or in the case of counseling for personal or social problems, verbal reinforcement could promote self-reference, affect, probing, deliberation, and decision responses. The use of behavioral counseling would in no way mean that the relationship could not continue after the initial goal had been reached. For example, perhaps the student wanting vocational counseling also wanted personal-social counseling; it is quite likely that a successful behavioral counseling relationship for the vocational goal would enhance rather than restrict the probability of the counselee's continuing on to what might seem like the primary and underlying reason for coming to counseling, the wish to receive help with personal-social difficulties.

Stimulated Recall in Counseling

Before leaving the topic of behavioral counseling, brief attention should be given to *stimulated recall* techniques. Because these procedures are directed at rather critical psychological mechanisms, they are probably closer to therapy than to counseling, but it seems that some of the procedures can be used by counselors as well as by psychotherapists or behavior therapists. Some professionals would deny that these techniques should be included in behavioral modification materials; that is, some proponents of stimulated recall techniques maintain that the procedures are insight-oriented rather than action-oriented. It appears, however, that there are components of both insight and action in these methods.

Basically, stimulated recall involves the counselor's use of a technique that will prompt his client to remember, recall vividly, re-experience, or relive a clinically significant event. It is generally believed that the act of recalling facilitates understanding of or insight into the psychological components underlying the situation, and psychoanalytically oriented professionals believe that cathartic release (the alleviation of affiliated anxiety) also occurs.

Stimulated recall techniques can take numerous forms. Verbally ventilating (*catharsis*) was one of the early aspects of Freudian psychoanalysis (Ford and Urban, 1963; Harper, 1959); the analysant (the client) was encouraged to think back into his earlier life and recall experiences and talk about them with the psychoanalyst. This practice evolved to hypnotic *revivification* and *age regression,* which are still quite frequently used in psychotherapy (Hilgard, 1965; Kroger, 1963; Rubenstein and Newman, 1954). Clinical hypnosis is used with each of these techniques. In revivification, the client relives, in his mind, earlier actual events that he has experienced. In age regression, the client role-plays or acts out previous events in the context of the present.

A related technique is *free imagery* (Reyher, 1963). In many ways free imagery is similar to emotive imagery, described in Chapter 7. The use of emotive imagery requires that the client imagine anxiety-producing situations that may be real or fantasy (both of which would typically rely on recall of actual, feasible, or symbolic circumstances), but free imagery may or may not involve recall. It requires that the person, in a relaxed state produce images and experience the affect connected with them; the image-production and affect-experiencing are facilitated by therapeutic (insight-oriented) handling. Procedures like therapeutic catharsis, revivification, age regression, and emotive imagery require the therapist to have a high degree of clinical competency; thus these procedures are limited preferably to doctoral-level clinical, counseling, and school psychologists.

These techniques, all of which involve stimulated recall and experiencing, are closely related to another procedure that is somewhat less demanding and seems to be applicable to a broader range of counselors and psychologists. This procedure produces *stimulated recall via audio and video tape recordings.* The early uses of stimulated recall via recordings employed audio tapes for the purpose of analyzing covert behavior in classroom situations (Bloom, 1954; Gaier, 1952). Later Nielsen (1962) therapeutically used films of stress-provoking situations when he had his clients view the situations and experience "self-confrontations." With the advent of video tape facilities, both audio and video stimuli were available for immediate use; thus it was not necessary to delay the stimulated recall sessions until the films had been processed.

One of the most useful examples of research in the area of stimulated recall via tape recordings may be found in the published studies emanating from the Interpersonal Process Recall Project at Michigan State University (Kagan, Krathwohl, and Farquhar, 1965). The general procedure for stimulated recall via either audio or video tape recordings is as follows: A regular counseling session is conducted and recorded; immediately following this, another counselor or "interrogator" (in the nonpunitive sense of the word) replaces the original counselor and replays the tape recording with the client; as the second counselor and the client view and/or listen to the recording, they periodically stop (at the discretion of either of them) and discuss what was going on in the original sessions; thus the client is stimulated into recalling what were his original feelings, thoughts, and behaviors, and giving his interpretation of verbal comments, facial expressions, body movements, or gestures. The techniques for conducting this type of stimulated recall counseling are described in detail elsewhere (Kagan, Krathwohl, and Miller, 1963; Woody, Krathwohl, Kagan, and Farquhar, 1965). Incidentally, it is possible that both the initial counseling and "interrogation" (the stimulated recall session) could be conducted by the same counselor or psychologist. Although research is continuing on this procedure, it appears that stimulated recall counseling (or the Interpersonal Process Recall procedure) can increase the client's sensitivity to cues; improve his verbalizations about his perceptions of underlying feelings, attitudes, thoughts, and emotions; and accelerate in general the counseling processes (Boyd and Sisney, 1967; Kagan, Krathwohl, and Farquhar, 1965; Kagan, Krathwohl, and Miller, 1963; Woody, 1965; Woody, Krathwohl, Kagan, and Farquhar, 1965).

The use of stimulated recall procedures, such as those by means of video and audio tape recordings, can be extended from the therapy or counseling room to the classroom. As one example, Thoresen (1966) demonstrated how seven college history instructors were helped to change their classroom behaviors after a counselor replayed for them video tapes of their discussion classes. Specifically, the technique seemed capable of improving the teachers' awareness of verbal and nonverbal cues that potentially influence students' behaviors; the playbacks seemed equally effective whether done individually or in groups.

As mentioned earlier, many endorsers of stimulated recall techniques identify them as insight-oriented rather than action-oriented. But the following facts are clearly evident: the counselor or therapist determines what technique will be used (action); he is at liberty to stop or proceed to another recall situation at any point he chooses in the session (action); and quite likely he practices selective reinforcement in the process (action). Each of these three points is definitely in accord with the principles of behavioral modification. Admittedly, the goal of the counseling relationship is to promote increased understanding or insight for the client, and any decision to change overt behavior is left to the client; that is, the counseling could be termed successful without the alleviation or elimination of the problems that brought the client into counseling. All things considered, it appears that stimulated recall by means of recording tapes within the counseling format represents an eclectic composite, one that is compatible with the theoretical guidelines set forth in Chapter 5 for a psychobehavioral, or integrative, approach. Similarly, the other stimulated recall techniques—revivification, age regression, and free imagery—involve more direct therapist action than would be appropriate for a pure insight approach; and thus these may also fit the integrative format.

AVERSIVE CONDITIONING

Another set of specialized behavioral modification techniques is grouped under the heading of aversive conditioning; these procedures are based on negative reinforcement contingencies. In behavioral modification, this may involve the use of emetic drugs, electric shock, noises, fatigue, or any other condition or stimulus that will make the person feel uncomfortable or that will be perceived as unpleasant. The general procedure is as follows: When an unacceptable behavior occurs an unpleasant (aversive) stimulus is administered to the subject; eventually there develops a conditioned bond between the unacceptable behavior and the unpleasant result, the aversive stimulus. For example, he may come to expect that every time he starts to suck his thumb he will receive a mild electric shock. Thus the unacceptable behavior will tend not to occur because the subject does not wish to experience the unpleasant aftereffects that he has been conditioned to anticipate.

It should be pointed out that the aversive stimuli are usually relatively mild, with the intensity of the stimuli being determined by the given individual's threshold for discomfort. For example, aversive sound would only be as loud and shrill as was necessary to be unpleasant (the sound is presented through headphones so that the therapist does not hear it and does not, therefore, also become conditioned), and electric shock is mild, usually being produced by means of dry-cell batteries.[5] The intensity of the aversive stimuli may, however, have to be altered as the conditioning program progresses, because a person could adapt to a given intensity, and it would then cease to be aversive. Emetic drugs present a slightly different situation; they are used to produce physical discomfort. For example, when the subject acts in an unacceptable manner, the drug is administered to induce nausea or vomiting. This is a rather severe treatment, and it is obvious that the use of emetic drugs requires close medical attention; although the severity of this treatment might alone make it questionable for use with children (or with anyone!), the need for medical supervision further restricts its use in an educational setting.

It is apparent that aversive conditioning techniques are manipulative, punitive, and sometimes severe in their effects. It is not surprising that the use of aversive stimuli has been limited, especially with children. With adults, however, aversive stimuli have been successfully applied to various behavioral disorders (Grossberg, 1964). They have been used successfully to modify such chronic behavioral habits as alcoholism, smoking, transvestism, sexual fetishes, masochistic practices, and numerous forms of compulsive behavior.

Although the use of aversive conditioning is more common with adults than with children, there are several relevant studies. Aversive conditioning, particularly involving electric shock, has been used with autistic children. Ferster (1961) provides a good description of the autistic child:

Infantile autism . . . is a very severe psychotic disturbance occurring in children as young as 2 years. At least outwardly, this childhood schizophrenia is a model of adult schizophrenia. Speech and control by the social environment are limited or absent; tantrums and atavistic behaviors are frequent and of high intensity; and most activities are of a simple sort, such as smearing, lying about, rubbing a surface, playing with a finger, and so forth. Infantile autism is a relatively rare form of schizophrenia and is not important from an epidemiological point of view. The analysis of the autistic child may be of theoretical use, however, since his psychosis may be a prototype of the adult's; but the causal factors could not be so complicated, because of the briefer environmental history.[6]

And from Ferster's total presentation it is apparent that, theoretically, childhood schizophrenia or autism may be influenced therapeutically

[5] A description of the apparatus used for aversive conditioning by means of electric shock may be found in an article by McGuire and Vallance (1964).

[6] From C. B. Ferster, Positive reinforcement and behavioral deficits of autistic children, *Child Development*, Vol. 32 (1961), pp. 437-456. Reprinted by permission of The Society for Research in Child Development, Inc.

by conditioning procedures. Lovaas, Schaeffer, and Simmons (1965) found that painful electric shock could successfully modify the behavior of five-year-old identical twins who had been diagnosed as childhood schizophrenics. Certain pathological behaviors, such as self-stimulation and temper tantrums, were eliminated. After developing an association between socialization with adults and shock reduction (that is, the children learned that they could reduce the occurrence of shocks if they would associate with adults), the children approached adults and their affectionate and other social behaviors in relation to adults increased. The increase in affectionate and social behaviors might well have also been reinforced by the social recognition rewards, as well as by the elimination of the shocks, that they received from the adults. Breger (1965), in a published reaction to the foregoing study, admits that the results demonstrate the possibility of simple shock avoidance learning in schizophrenic children, but questions that there is evidence that transfer of this behavior is indicated; and he believes that extension of these findings to other children would be a dubious procedure without additional research.

Aversive conditioning need not, of course, involve just electric shocks, a form of stimulus that seems to carry a negative connotation for many professionals. The use of unpleasant noise stimuli, for example, does not produce as extreme discomfort for the subject and may be quite effective for modifying certain behaviors. As is the case with other aversive stimuli, the use of aversive noise has not been subjected to enough research yet to allow for a statement regarding specific behaviors that it can modify. To illustrate how it might be useful, however, let us consider one clinical case study.

A teen-age boy had become increasingly withdrawn and would not communicate verbally with either peers, teachers, or parents; consequently, he had to be removed from school and placed in a residential program for the emotionally disturbed. Then the diagnostic procedures started. Psychiatric examinations failed to reveal conclusive evidence, primarily because the boy would not talk with the psychiatrist; neurological and electroencephalographic examinations failed to produce any significant evidence, the boy appearing to be neurologically normal; and the clinical psychologist could not get the lad to respond to any type of psychometric instruments (in fact, the boy would answer questions only occasionally, frequently pausing for a long time before making a response, if he made any at all). Thus therapeutic procedures were necessarily deferred. Some experimental use of medication was tried, but counseling and psychotherapy could obviously not be given, his education was completely disrupted, and little progress was being made in determining a reasonably valid and reliable diagnosis. Finally a psychologist suggested trying a form of aversive conditioning. In a few experimental trials of presenting questions to the boy, it was noted that he seemed to block more on personal questions than on impersonal ones. On this basis, the following procedure was used: Unpleasant (aversive) noise was presented through headphones to the boy at times when he blocked; that is, a question was asked, and after a few seconds of silence that would allow him to respond and thereby avoid the aversive stimulus (the noise), the noise was turned on and continued until the boy responded verbally. It should be noted that the questions were initially impersonal, but as the conditioning progressed, they were gradually changed to more personal ones; this was done to condition the boy to talk freely about personal subjects, a much needed ability if he were to engage in productive counseling or psychotherapy. Verbal and social recognition rewards were also given: The therapist would smile and give praise when the lad responded well to questions. Other factors compatible with learning theory principles were controlled: A relaxation period of one minute was allowed after each trial (from the end of one of his responses to the start of the next question); the intensity of the stimulus was adjusted periodically; and he was informed that a set number of trials would be given at each of the twice-daily sessions or a specific amount of talking time (whichever came first) and that he could avoid having to move on to another trial (and the inevitable aversive stimulus) if he continued to discuss the topic question with the therapist. This example illustrates how a rather mildly unpleasant but nonpainful aversive conditioning procedure can be used to prepare the client for other types of services—in this case, the improvement of the boy's verbal skills to facilitate both diagnostic and therapeutic procedures.

It seems at present that great enthusiasm for aversive conditioning is not warranted, especially when children are involved. There is impressive evidence, however, that aversive conditioning can effectively modify relatively severe and chronic problem behaviors. These techniques have been especially effective with adults and, in more limited instances, with children. The academic and technical knowledge necessary to use these techniques is not great; it is quite likely that most school psychologists could use them. If they are used, it would seem advisable that medical or preferably psychiatric consultation be available. But it seems highly unlikely that these aversive techniques, except in rare instances, could be used in the school setting. The regulations imposed by society and professional educators on psychoeducational personnel make it improbable that even the most highly trained school psychologist could have unlimited freedom to use these procedures. And it appears still premature, in terms of available research evidence, to believe that aversive conditioning has enough advantages to counteract its disadvantages or that it is preferable to another form of behavioral modification. For example, the long-term effects of aversive therapy have yet to be evaluated. It is possible that aversive conditioning can be used in certain childhood cases, but this will most likely be in a clinical setting, such as a child guidance clinic. It is also possible, however, that future research will provide stronger justification for the use of aversive therapy techniques with children.

CLINICAL SUGGESTION AND HYPNOSIS

The usefulness of suggestion and hypnosis in clinical services has been amply documented (Hilgard, 1965; Kroger, 1963; Shor and Orne, 1965; Weitzenhoffer, 1953). No attempt will be made in this section to teach principles of clinical suggestion and hypnosis; there are far too many complicating factors. And it should be noted that while the stereo-typed "dangers" of these procedures are much overdone, there are legal, professional, and academic considerations that restrict their use to only the more highly trained psychologists, medical physicians, and in some cases dentists. In addition to legal statutes in many states that restrict the use of any hypnotic procedure, it is professionally recommended that users should hold a doctorate in psychology or its equivalent. For example, membership for psychologists in both the Society for Clinical and Experimental Hypnosis and the American Society for Clinical Hypnosis, the two primary professional organizations, is limited to persons holding a doctoral degree, membership in the American Psychological Association, and specialized training. The psychological processes dealt with by these techniques are complex and require the user to be a well-trained clinician. This section, therefore, is designed to acquaint the reader with the possibilities of these techniques, *not to teach their use.*

There seems to be evidence to support the belief that relaxation, as used in behavior therapy, presents a continuum that runs from self-induced slightly conscious relaxation to the therapist-induced deep relaxation that has the concomitants of the so-called *hypnotic phenomena,* which might even include amnesia for what occurs during the state of relaxation. The characteristics of the hypnotic state, which varies with the individual and which may set in at a very slight degree of relaxation, seem to include the following: The subject relinquishes the "planning function" to the therapist, seemingly being unable to carry through his own plans; the subject's attention is selective, redistributed, or refocused from his normal "waking" state; [7] the subject has available stronger

[7] The term "waking" should not be interpreted as meaning that persons experiencing induced relaxation or hypnosis are asleep in the usual sense of the word. Experiments have revealed that the conditions of hypnotic relaxation are quite distinct from those of normal sleep.

visual memories and an improved ability for the production of fantasies; reality testing (such as looking around and scratching) is more limited; the person is more suggestible; the person willingly adopts a suggested role; and amnesia for the events may occur (Hilgard, 1965).

The term "clinical suggestion" designates one specific technique that is closely related to clinical hypnosis, both being limited to use as clinical or therapeutic procedures (the popular stage hypnotists and their commercial activities have no place in this discussion). Clinical suggestion refers to the therapist's giving the client a suggestion that is intended to be therapeutically beneficial; and clinical hypnosis refers to other therapeutic phenomena and techniques, such as hypnotic revivification and age regression.

In clinical suggestion and hypnosis, one of three procedures is typically followed while the client is in an induced state of relaxation. Direct suggestions are given; psychoanalytic principles are applied (this is commonly called *hypnoanalysis*); or clinically relevant scenes are visualized, possibly to promote insight or to facilitate desensitization (Cautela, 1966a). A survey of doctoral-level psychologists known to be trained in and to endorse clinical suggestion and hypnosis indicates that the following areas are appropriate for modification by these techniques: motivation for learning, study skills, concentration and attention, reading improvement, control of unacceptable social behavior, symptom removal, and alleviation of resistances to counseling and psychotherapy (Woody and Herr, 1965). Perusal of professional journals, such as the *American Journal of Clinical Hypnosis* and the *International Journal of Clinical and Experimental Hypnosis,* readily reveals a host of specialized techniques that have been used with varying degrees of success for a wide variety of problem behaviors. One brief example of clinical suggestion in an educational setting is Krippner's (1966) report of using hypnotic suggestion with elementary and secondary school children in a summer reading program. Hypnotic suggestions were given regarding tension, motivation, concentration, and spelling problems. By the end of the summer school session, those children receiving hypnotic suggestion as part of their reading improvement programs made greater progress than those children who received only the conventional (nonhypnotic) reading improvement services.

Although some behavior therapists question the applicability of clinical suggestion and hypnosis to behavioral modification techniques (Cautela, 1966b), Wolpe and Lazarus (1966) state the clinical opinion:

Hypnosis, regarded here as trance behavior based on *verbal conditioning,* may be employed in its own right (direct suggestion, posthypnotic suggestion, training in autohypnosis, the use of time distortion, etc.) or as a therapeutic adjunct, e.g., in systematic desensitization so as to enable certain patients to achieve more vivid and realistic images, and/or deeper and more satisfactory levels of relaxation. It is desirable for the behavior therapist to be proficient at several hypnotic induction techniques and to be well informed about the established phenomena of hypnosis.[8]

There is conflicting evidence as to how much Wolpe uses hypnosis. In one article it is stated that he uses hypnotic procedures in one out of four cases when desensitization procedures are used (Cautela, 1966b); but elsewhere Wolpe and Lazarus (1966) state that one-third of their cases are performed under hypnosis. Moreover, Wolpe and Lazarus state that those who cannot be hypnotized are told to relax and close their eyes according to instructions, and many theorists believe that persons who cannot initially respond to the hypnotic induction procedure eventually develop a trance state in almost a spontaneous manner; thus it may well be that more behavior therapy patients are in fact hypnotized than is acknowledged in the research literature.

An extremely controversial technique employing clinical hypnosis and behavioral modification principles is "emotional flooding," as described by Wolpe and Lazarus (1966). This procedure involves the inducing of an abreaction (that is, the re-experiencing) of traumatic situations or fear-producing situations or stimuli while the client is under hypnosis. This supposedly allows the patient to become deconditioned to the stimuli. Abreactions have also been used therapeutically in psychoanalytic forms of psychotherapy. But it must be emphasized that the validity of this technique has not been proved, and even Wolpe and Lazarus question its general value. There may well be reason to believe that this technique can potentially do more harm than good, and any professional should exercise caution with its use, regardless of level of training.

It should be noted that some behavior therapists believe that their behavioral modification techniques are enhanced by clinical suggestion and hypnosis. One British psychiatrist stated that he always induces hypnosis when doing behavior therapy because it gives him clearer indications of how relaxed his patients are than if he just instructs them to relax. In this situation it is also possible, therefore, that the effects are due not only to the behavior therapy, such as desensitization techniques, but also, at least in part, to clinical suggestions given to the patients when they are in a heightened state of suggestibility. Hussain (1964) treated 105 psychiatric outpatients with desensitization combined with hypnosis. It is his belief that conditioning is facilitated by hypnosis. With this approach, following a desensitization-hierarchy format, he obtained a 92.5 per cent over-all recovery rate, with no signs of underlying neurotic conflict afterward (based on psychiatric opinion); and

[8] From BEHAVIOR THERAPY TECHNIQUES, J. Wolpe and A. A. Lazarus, Pergamon Press, Oxford, 1967 (1966). P. 135.

follow-ups from six months to two years later failed to reveal a single case of symptom substitution.

While there are strong research data to support the use of clinical suggestion and hypnosis with behavioral problem children, there is also reason to caution against its use in an educational setting. That is, despite the fact that clinical suggestion and hypnosis seem to be effective in modifying behaviors and problems that are typically encountered by school psychologists (Woody and Herr, 1965), there seem to be social and philosophical reasons for not using these techniques. In a survey of doctoral-level psychologists known to be trained in and endorsers of clinical suggestion and hypnosis, it was found that although they attributed value to the techniques for dealing with problems commonly found in educational settings, they were uncertain about using these techniques in the elementary and secondary schools (Woody and Herr, 1966); they were, however, more confident about using them in a university or college counseling center. Obviously if these highly trained psychologists were dubious about using the clinical suggestion and hypnotic techniques because of the "contemporary philosophies and practices in education," it is logical that full-time school personnel, even the doctoral-level school counselor or school psychologist, would be subjected to as much or more of a feeling of restriction. This does not mean that the qualified professional should not work toward gaining acceptance of any clinical technique which he is qualified to use, including clinical suggestion and hypnosis and even aversive conditioning, but it seems prudent to plan to implement such clinical usage only after the professional and lay persons concerned have been adequately oriented. In any case, with the possible exception of systematic use of clinical suggestion (nonhypnotic) in behavioral counseling by verbal reinforcement, the use of any technique that is labeled "hypnotic" in any sense of the word should be restricted to doctoral-level psychologists. It does seem appropriate, however, to include clinical suggestions in behavioral counseling, because consistent, subtle, and systematic use of them in selected instances might well contribute to the behavioral modification processes.

Three groups of specialized techniques have been presented in this chapter: behavioral counseling with emphasis on verbal reinforcement conditioning and stimulated recall techniques; aversive conditioning employing unpleasant stimuli, such as electric shock and shrill noise; and clinical suggestion and hypnotic techniques that may involve direct suggestions, hypnoanalytic procedures, or scene visualizations as an independent or adjunctive behavioral modification approach. There is research evidence to support the belief that all of these procedures are potentially valuable for behavioral modification and, moreover, applicable (in varying degrees) to behavioral problem children. The primary point that must be emphasized is that these techniques involve factors which call for a high level of psychological training; in most cases their use will be limited to experienced school counselors and school psychologists, and even then there are some professionals and some techniques that will be ethically incompatible. Even the doctoral-level counselor or psychologist must have special training in these advanced behavioral modification techniques; aspects of training for all educators will be discussed in the next chapter. As some of these specialized techniques are controversial, even more so than the general techniques presented in Chapter 7, it will, therefore, be necessary to implement them judiciously.

REFERENCES

Bloom, B. S. The thought process of students in discussion. In S. French (Ed.), *Accent on teaching*. New York: Harper, 1954, 23-46.

Boyd, H. S., and Sisney, V. V. Immediate self-image confrontation and changes in self-concept. *Journal of Consulting Psychology,* 1967, 31:291-294.

Breger, L. Comments on "Building social behavior in autistic children by use of electric shock." *Journal of Experimental Research in Personality,* 1965, 1:110-113.

Cautela, J. R. Desensitization factors in the hypnotic treatment of phobias. *Journal of Psychology,* 1966, 64:277-288. (a)

Cautela, J. R. Hypnosis and behaviour therapy. *Behaviour Research and Therapy,* 1966, 4:219-224. (b)

Dicken, C., and Fordham, M. Effects of reinforcement of self-references in quasi-therapeutic interviews. *Journal of Counseling Psychology,* 1967, 14:145-152.

Doubros, S. G. An investigation of verbal conditioning in level II adolescent retardates. *American Journal of Mental Deficiency,* 1967, 71:806-810.

Erickson, M. H. Editor's comment. *American Journal of Clinical Hypnosis,* 1966, 8:173.

Ferster, C. B. Positive reinforcement and behavioral deficits of autistic children. *Child Development,* 1961, 32:437-456.

Ford, D. H., and Urban, H. B. *Systems of psychotherapy: a comparative study.* New York: John Wiley and Sons, 1963.

Gaier, E. L. Selected personality variables and the learning process. *Psychological Monographs,* 1952, 66:1-28.

Grossberg, J. M. Behavior therapy: a review. *Psychological Bulletin*, 1964, 62:73-88.

Harper, R. A. *Psychoanalysis and psychotherapy: 36 systems*. Englewood Cliffs, N.J.: Prentice-Hall, 1959.

Hilgard, E. R. *Hypnotic susceptibility*. New York: Harcourt, Brace & World, 1965.

Hussain, A. Behavior therapy using hypnosis. In J. Wolpe, A. Salter, and L. J. Reyna (Eds.), *The conditioning therapies*. New York: Holt, Rinehart and Winston, 1964, 54-61.

Johnson, C. L., Jr. The transfer effect of treatment group composition on pupil's classroom participation. Unpublished doctoral dissertation, Stanford University, 1964.

Kagan, N., Krathwohl, D. R., and Farquhar, W. W. *IPR—Interpersonal process recall: stimulated recall by videotape in exploratory studies of counseling and teaching-learning*. Educational Research Series, No. 24. East Lansing, Mich.: Michigan State University, 1965.

Kagan, N., Krathwohl, D. R., and Miller, R. Stimulated recall in therapy using video tape—a case study. *Journal of Counseling Psychology*, 1963, 10:237-243.

Krippner, S. The use of hypnosis with elementary and secondary school children in a summer reading clinic. *American Journal of Clinical Hypnosis*, 1966, 8:261-266.

Kroger, W. S. *Clinical and experimental hypnosis*. Philadelphia: J. B. Lippincott, 1963.

Krumboltz, J. D. Behavioral counseling: rationale and research. *Personnel and Guidance Journal*, 1965, 44:383-387.

Krumboltz, J. D., and Schroeder, W. W. Promoting career planning through reinforcement. *Personnel and Guidance Journal*, 1965, 44:19-26.

Krumboltz, J. D., and Thoresen, C. E. The effect of behavioral counseling in group and individual settings on information-seeking behavior. *Journal of Counseling Psychology*, 1964, 11:324-333.

Krumboltz, J. D., Varenhorst, Barbara B., and Thoresen, C. E. Nonverbal factors in the effectiveness of models in counseling. *Journal of Counseling Psychology*, 1967, 14:412-418.

London, P. *The modes and morals of psychotherapy*. New York: Holt, Rinehart and Winston, 1964.

Lovaas, O. I., Schaeffer, B., and Simmons, J. Q. Building social behavior in autistic children by use of electric shock. *Journal of Experimental Research in Personality*, 1965, 1:99-109.

McGuire, R. J., and Vallance, M. Aversion therapy by electric shock: a simple technique. *British Medical Journal*, 1964, 1:151-152.

Nielsen, G. *Studies in self confrontations*. Copenhagen, Denmark: Munksgaard, 1962.

Reyher, J. Free imagery: an uncovering procedure. *Journal of Clinical Psychology,* 1963, 19:454-459.

Roberts, R. R., Jr., and Renzaglia, G. A. The influence of tape recording on counseling. *Journal of Counseling Psychology,* 1965, 12:10-16.

Rogers, J. M. Operant conditioning in a quasi-therapy setting. *Journal of Abnormal and Social Psychology,* 1960, 60:247-252.

Rubenstein, R., and Newman, R. The living out of "future experiences" under hypnosis. *Science,* 1954, 119:472-473.

Ryan, T. Antoinette, and Krumboltz, J. D. Effect of planned reinforcement counseling on client decision-making behavior. *Journal of Counseling Psychology,* 1964, 11:315-323.

Sapolsky, A. Effect of interpersonal relationships upon verbal conditioning. *Journal of Abnormal and Social Psychology,* 1960, 60:241-246.

Schmidt, L. D. Some ethical, professional, and legal considerations for school counselors. *Personnel and Guidance Journal,* 1965, 44:376-382.

Shor, R. E., and Orne, M. T. (Eds.). *The nature of hypnosis: selected basic readings.* New York: Holt, Rinehart and Winston, 1965.

Thoresen, C. E. Behavioral counseling: an introduction. *School Counselor,* 1966, 14:13-21. (a)

Thoresen, C. E. Video in the college classroom: an exploratory study. *Personnel and Guidance Journal,* 1966, 45:144-149. (b)

Thoresen, C. E., and Krumboltz, J. D. Relationship of counselor reinforcement of selected responses to external behavior. *Journal of Counseling Psychology,* 1967, 14:140-144.

Thoresen, C. E., Krumboltz, J. D., and Varenhorst, Barbara. Sex of counselors and models: effect on client career exploration. *Journal of Counseling Psychology,* 1967, 14:503-508.

Truax, C. B. Reinforcement and nonreinforcement in Rogerian psychotherapy. *Journal of Abnormal Psychology,* 1966, 71:1-9. (a)

Truax, C. B. Some implications of behavior therapy for psychotherapy. *Journal of Counseling Psychology,* 1966, 13:160-170. (b)

Varenhorst, Barbara B. An experimental comparison of non-verbal factors determining reinforcement effectiveness of model-reinforced counseling. Unpublished doctoral dissertation, Stanford University, 1964.

Weitzenhoffer, A. M. *Hypnotism: an objective study in suggestibility.* New York: John Wiley and Sons, 1953.

Wolpe, J. The comparative clinical status of conditioning therapies and psychoanalysis. In J. Wolpe, A. Salter, and L. J. Reyna (Eds.), *The conditioning therapies.* New York: Holt, Rinehart and Winston, 1964.

Wolpe, J., and Lazarus, A. A. *Behavior therapy techniques.* Oxford, Eng.: Pergamon Press, 1966, 5-20.

Woody, R. H. Stimulated recall in psychotherapy using hypnosis and video tapes: a case follow-up. *American Journal of Clinical Hypnosis,* 1965, 8:69-71.

Woody, R. H. Integrating behavior therapy and psychotherapy. *British Journal of Medical Psychology,* in press.

Woody, R. H. Reinforcement in school counseling. *School Counselor,* 1968, 15:253-258.

Woody, R. H., and Herr, E. L. Psychologists and hypnosis: psychotherapeutic theories and practices. *American Journal of Clinical Hypnosis,* 1965, 8:80-88.

Woody, R. H., and Herr, E. L. Psychologists and hypnosis: II. Use in educational settings. *American Journal of Clinical Hypnosis,* 1966, 8:254-256.

Woody, R. H., Krathwohl, D. R., Kagan, N., and Farquhar, W. W. Stimulated recall in psychotherapy using hypnosis and video tape. *American Journal of Clinical Hypnosis,* 1965, 7:234-241.

9

Implementing Behavioral
Modification in the Schools

Acquiring knowledge of the proc-
esses of recognition, diagnosis, and behavioral modification in relation
to behavioral problem children is basic to the goal of helping these children; but more than pure knowledge is needed. This leads us to one of
the most crucial steps in this entire quest: *implementation*.

The first chapter emphasized that schools no longer have a singular
responsibility—the provision of academic knowledge—but must now cope
with a complex set of responsibilities, which include academic, social, psychological, and physical factors related to the total development of the
student. As would be the case in any institution (and the school is certainly no exception), change can foster concerns, conflicts, and misper-
ceptions unless each relevant person is involved in the step-by-step planning and initiation of the procedures for change. Acceptance and efficacy
are facilitated if every person is well oriented and contributory to some
degree to the processes of change. Gaining the acceptance of others
involves, of course, debate, discussion, critical analyses, and compro-
mises before the decision is reached to move to the next phase of change.

The crux of the matter is that the persons forming the institution—
the faculty, the administrators, the students, the allied professionals, and
the lay community—must be prepared for changes in responsibility and
actions. This requirement, preparing the persons involved, is of primary
concern if behavioral modification practices in the schools are to be
implemented effectively; and such preparation will also increase the
willingness of all educators, regardless of position, to feel responsibility
for helping behavioral problem children—a responsibility that rests
squarely on the shoulders of any educator who wants to help these children. Classroom teachers, school counselors, school psychologists, other
psychoeducational personnel (such as speech and hearing therapists,
school social workers, and special consultants), and school administrators
—all have the responsibility of helping in the preparation of the rest of
the community.

Preparing relevant persons is especially critical to the use of behavioral modification techniques. It would be hiding our heads in the sand if we did not acknowledge that some aspects of behavioral modification are controversial. But we are armed with the knowledge that behavioral modification procedures have been subjected to rigorous experimental and clinical investigations, that they have been applied successfully in a variety of school-related situations, and that their efficacy appears to be as great (and greater in some cases) as that of any other single approach for dealing with behavioral problem children. If our concern for behavioral problem children is to be manifested in constructive, beneficial services, we must be prepared to cope with any controversy, justified or unjustified, that may arise. A thorough understanding of the scientific bases and practical uses of behavioral modification procedures (which has been the goal of this book) and a realistic personal frame of reference (which will be discussed shortly) should more than adequately prepare the endorser of behavioral modification procedures to begin to fulfill the requirement of preparing relevant persons.

The assumption of responsibility for modifying behavioral problem children demands both *professional* and *personal commitment.* Professionally, the educator who wishes to help the behavioral problem child must accept the basic responsibility of becoming trained and qualified to provide direct services to the child. Although printed materials, such as are in this book, foster professional knowledge, it is undeniably evident that "do-it-yourself" methods cannot insure adequate training; and in an area such as behavioral modification, which can have far-reaching influence on the lives of the children and their families, it is crucial that adequate professional preparation be relatively guaranteed. We will therefore focus considerable attention on factors related to the training of professional educators to deal with behavioral problem children by means of behavioral modification procedures.

In regard to personal commitment, because of the intricate involvement of personality and social values in behavioral modification, the best-trained professional must be concerned with developing the personal characteristics and qualifications that will accommodate the assumption of direct responsibility toward the child. This is not an easy thing to accomplish; what one thinks is understanding of self may actually be an unrealistic and highly subjective appraisal.

It has long been the practice in training programs for counseling and clinical psychologists, psychiatrists, and psychoanalysts to recommend or require that the trainees, the would-be therapists, undergo therapy themselves to assure some degree of realistic self-understanding. Although this practice is open to dispute among professionals, there seems to be ample reason for endorsing the view that the professional who is striving to become an astute practitioner of behavioral modification should consider or engage in a planned, systematic means of understanding his own personal characteristics and how they could hinder, facilitate, or affect in general his attempts at modification of behavior. This does not mean that everyone who uses behavioral modification techniques needs to undergo insight counseling or psychotherapy. On the contrary, it is likely that the majority of persons to whom this book has been directed—that is, educational personnel—will be dealing with a type of problem or degree of behavioral difficulty that can be handled without their own personal characteristics being of major significance. But for those who want to work with more severe cases of behavioral problem children, for instance those who progress to the stage in which they use some of the more specialized behavioral modification procedures (as presented in Chapter 8), realistic self-understanding seems requisite. For example, as intimated earlier, the professional who uses aversive conditioning, where unpleasant stimuli are applied to the client, should certainly have an understanding of what this treatment-behavior means to himself psychologically. Does he psychologically enjoy inflicting discomfort on his clients, in a sadistic sense of the word? Or does it psychologically bother him so much that it causes him to experience anxiety at having to treat a client in that manner? Several behavior therapists have commented that they feel very uncomfortable psychologically when they use aversive conditioning techniques, and in fact some have said that they believe this is why they conduct research on aversive conditioning: they hope that they can disprove the value of the aversive procedures in order to eliminate their use. Regardless of the extent of use of behavioral modification procedures, self-understanding can only serve to improve the educator's potential for helping others, even in a teaching capacity.

The suggestion that self-understanding or insight can be beneficial to those using behavioral modification procedures is not contradictory to the theoretical premises of psychobehavioral or integrative therapy. Admittedly it is contradictory to positions maintained by some pure behavior therapists; but these behaviorists also do not acknowledge that insight procedures can be and, in many cases, are part of behavioral modification. While it is questionable that insight-oriented factors alone can produce the extensive change in problem behavioral habits that is needed when dealing therapeutically with behavioral problem children, there is justification for the belief that understanding and insight are of great value to the professional person. That is, both insight and action are needed.

From the foregoing discussion it should be evident that both professional-academic factors and personal factors are involved in the implementation stage. It seems that the implementation of behavioral modification in the schools necessitates consideration of four major areas: educational philosophy, involvement of colleagues and other allied professionals, orienting the lay community, and professional training. As will be evident, there are distinct interrelationships between these areas, and the success of the implementation depends to a large degree on the satisfactory accomplishment of each.

EDUCATIONAL PHILOSOPHY

Although the school, as an institution, has assumed increasing responsibility for the total development of the student and both lay and professional communities have, in fact, demanded that this responsibility be accepted, numerous restrictions are still placed on the institutional functions. These restrictions are safeguards against detrimental actions that could potentially occur within the school. But occasionally some of these restrictions are so distorted that they become constrictions.

There are situations in which the educational philosophy, justifiably dictated by the opinions of lay and professional sources, has been contradictory. On the one hand, the school is expected to develop the student into an acceptable, contributing member of the society, while on the other hand, the school is expected not to inject strict controls on behavioral development. Philosophically it is believed that self-developed controls will emerge if self-responsibility is the basis for education. And indeed this seems sound. But the contradiction occurs when educators allow the child to be self-determining, to strive for an emergence of a social and productive self-concept, and yet the very processes inherent in this development result, as would be expected, in certain behaviors that are not apparently constructive. Then, often, the public reaction is one of indignation, and educators are decried as being unable to "teach our children to be good citizens—they let them run wild." In other words, there is the demand that educators must not be human cyberneticians, manipulative programers of human behavior; yet they must also be responsible for assuring that the students will display acceptable behavior at all times.

Moreover, the techniques that the educator uses to fulfill this philosophical mandate will also be subjected, justifiably, to public scrutiny and criticism. A familiar example is the controversial practice of spanking school children, an issue that receives endless publicity. From the materials set forth in this book we know that such punitive action is of dubious value in effecting behavioral change unless positive reinforcement is also given to acceptable behaviors; but the point is that the teacher must cope with the problem behavior, yet the means of coping may be censured by the public.

Several years ago an appropriate but unfortunate example occurred. A high school student literally locked his science teacher in a large kiln in the science laboratory. The teacher, incidentally, was academically well qualified but believed in allowing the students to develop self-determined behavioral controls. The student was not punished; in fact, the board of education later dismissed the teacher because he could not maintain discipline. It would be safe to say, however, that if the teacher had maintained discipline, for example, by subjecting the student to the same types of anxiety that he, the teacher, had to suffer (such as being locked in the furnace for punishment), the board of education would still have dismissed him. Ironically, during the same academic year, the same board of education dismissed one of the chief administrators for being a strict disciplinarian and for enforcing behavioral controls.

A study relevant to this point which was cited early in this book merits repetition. Eaton, Weathers, and Phillips (1957) found that the inability to cope with behavioral problem children influenced many teachers, particularly beginning teachers and teachers on the secondary level, to leave the teaching field; added to this difficulty was the teachers' feeling that not enough administrative assistance in handling behavior problems was given. It seems, therefore, that an "occupational hazard" of education is that behavioral problem children can wreak havoc on the teacher's personal and professional life; but the teacher is not allowed to react without restrictions, even to the point that the professional techniques that are used may be restricted.

This discussion is not presented to condemn the influence of lay and professional opinions on the philosophical issues that permeate educational institutions; these opinions are undoubtedly much needed and well justified in our democratic society. But it must be acknowledged that these influences do exist, that there are philosophical contradictions, and that the educator must, as part of his professional role, attempt to cope with and to work toward the resolution of the philosophical conflicts.

Educational philosophy will undoubtedly directly affect learned attempts at behavioral modification. Although there seems to be adequate scientific justification for the use of behavioral modification procedures and there is an undeniable need for improved services for behavioral problem children, the educator must be prepared to consider the educational philosophy under which he must function. The optimum goal is that each person involved with the educational system—and this definitely includes the parents of the students and the lay and professional communities in general—must become accepting of and active in the services for behavioral problem children. It is only when a general acceptance of responsibility for these children has been created that the means of accomplishing the behavioral changes, in a manner compatible with our contemporary educational philosophy, can be implemented.

INVOLVEMENT OF COLLEAGUES
AND OTHER ALLIED PROFESSIONALS

At various points in this book, emphasis has been placed on the necessity of intrastaff and interdisciplinary cooperation; this obviously includes professionals both within and outside of the school system. This cooperation was demonstrated to be important to servicing behavioral problem children at the recognition, diagnosis, and behavioral modification stages. And, as has just been discussed, there is reason why this cooperation, which encompasses understanding and acceptance of the services for behavioral problem children, must also include the members of the lay community. It is, therefore, without dispute that implementation necessitates involvement.

At this implementation stage, the classroom teachers, school counselors, and school psychologists—the persons who will most likely be applying behavioral modification procedures—must provide their colleagues in the school and professionals in allied disciplines outside the school with an orientation to behavioral modification services for behavioral problem children. Not only should these other professionals be provided with opportunities to learn about the theoretical rationale, related research, procedures, and techniques of behavioral modification; they should also be accorded the right and the responsibility to be involved in the planning for the implementation. If a lesson can be borrowed from communication theory and group dynamics, it should be recognized that involvement of each person, no matter how peripheral to the actual use of behavioral modification procedures, will facilitate more understanding and greater acceptance. Consequently, the user of behavioral modification procedures will have more professional freedom. He will be free from the stereotypes and misconceptions of the uninformed and will be able to use to the full his behavioral modification capabilities.

In view of the almost universal concern within education for the problems created by unacceptable behaviors in the schools, it is unlikely that any one group of educators, such as teachers or administrators in general, will be resistant to the implementation of behavioral modification procedures. Those individuals who do object or resist might be in either (or both) of two categories: those who do not understand or do not appreciate the procedures on academic grounds; and those who will not accept the procedures because of their own personalities.

Educators who do not accept behavioral modification procedures because of not understanding them academically or do not approve of the educational philosophy involved are unquestionably justified. To minimize and resolve conflicts, the endorser of the techniques must be prepared to discuss extensively the rationale, research, and practical uses with all faculty and administrative personnel. The measure of success of this orientation task might well be gauged by the number of professionals who reject the procedures on academic grounds. It seems, however, that academic justification of behavioral modification is strong enough to win converts. Perhaps the key point will be to make sure that it is recognized that behavioral modification procedures can get rather immediate, observable, and permanent behavioral results, that they do not condition the child into being a controlled automaton, and that they can and should encompass components of counseling—warmth, understanding, support, and insight—as well as principles of learning theory.

There will undoubtedly be educators who object to behavioral modification procedures because of their own personality factors. There are professionals in all educational positions, including the areas of school counseling and school psychology (unfortunately), who possess such a degree of personal insecurity that any action, regardless of subject or area, will be so threatening to them that they may avoid involvement, or refuse to cooperate, or even try to hinder the efforts of others for fear that others' actions will reflect on them. This type of neurotic person is not, of course, confined to educators, but there is evidence that some educators do suffer from unrecognized mental problems that would inevitably influence their professional lives (Kaplan, 1959). For these persons, the implementation of behavioral modification procedures will have to proceed as best it can. It would probably be unwise to take direct action against these individuals, because the majority will possess other assets that can contribute beneficially to the over-all educational program and their personality problems will likely be too deep-seated to be amenable to change by a colleague's actions. The wisest approach seems to be one of convincing the majority of the values of behavioral modification, and then gradually focusing convincing evidence on the minority opposition. There is no reason to expect immediate and total support for behavioral modification procedures.

It is extremely important that school administrators receive special attention during the orientation processes, preparatory to the implementation stage. Although educational administrators, such as principals and superintendents, will probably have little direct contact with the students and virtually no direct contact with the application of behavioral modification procedures, they are most definitely responsible for every service provided and every professional action taken within their given school system. It is therefore imperative that each administrator receive special attention when any educator wishes to implement behavioral modification procedures. This does not mean, for example, that the school psychologist should fully train the school principal to use all the techniques that he, the school psychologist, will use; the principal is not academically prepared for this role, just as the school psychologist is not academically prepared for the multiplicity of administrative duties inherent in the principalship. But the principal should be helped to understand what it is and why the educator, such as the school psychologist, chooses to modify behavior in the way that he does. And if the educator who wishes to use behavioral modification procedures is incapable of communicating the scientific rationale and other justifying principles to relevant persons, such as school administrators, then perhaps he is not prepared or competent to use the behavioral modification procedures.

In addition to the "coffee-cup seminars" that should occur daily and that allow communication between educators, another means of promoting better understanding and communication is to develop in-service training. In view of the diverse, probing, and potentially caustic critical questions that could and should arise from those who are unfamiliar with behavioral modification, it would be wise to begin any planned in-service training with a guest speaker who is capable of objectively answering and responding to queries and whose professional reputation will add an extra bit of stature to the proceedings. It is only through such an academically based approach as this that unnecessary fears and concerns can be allayed. Knowledgeable speakers should be available from the faculties of most universities or from the staffs of nearby mental hospitals or child guidance clinics. Audio-visual aids may be used for orientation; the use of films that reflect behavior is known to have a strong impact upon the viewers, even to the point of modifying their behavior. Likewise, there is nothing quite as effective as a demonstration, such as role-playing, to reveal to the group members the underlying processes of behavioral modification.

It should be noted that these formal in-service training activities are designed to orient the entire school faculty. Such a sophisticated approach is not, of course, necessary for the typical classroom teacher or school counselor who wishes merely to incorporate some of the more basic behavioral modification techniques into his regular functions. But if an intense, encompassing behavioral modification program is to be implemented, well-planned orientation and training activities should definitely be provided.

The involvement of persons in other professions, both affiliated with and outside of the school, necessitates consideration much in the same manner as the involvement of educational colleagues. Professionals in medicine, psychology, and social work merit special attention. With their understanding and cooperation, the implementation of behavioral modification procedures can be greatly facilitated, and there will be fostered an improved degree of consistency and coordination within the community. For example, interagency referrals will be facilitated, duplication of effort will be lessened, and better use of professional services will be achieved.

It is only fair to admit that there are professions—or, to be more exact, subsections of professions—whose specializations may condemn the use of behavioral modification procedures, particularly those techniques based almost entirely on conditioning principles. For example, evidence was previously cited that denied the efficacy of conventional psychotherapy and especially psychoanalysis (Eysenck, 1965; Wolpe, 1964). Thus it would not be a bit surprising if a member of a professional specialty that was based primarily on an insight or psychoanalytic theory (such as some in psychiatry, clinical psychology, and social work) would perceive efforts based on learning theory as being illogical, unnecessary, and perhaps even dangerous to the well-being of the clients. Any professional who has used behavioral modification techniques and has communicated his impressions has encountered skeptics and condemners of his theoretical approach. This is a professionally healthy situation; if the person using behavioral modification procedures cannot successfully defend and justify his actions on objective, empirical, scientific grounds, then perhaps he is not prepared to use the procedures (and the same might be said for persons endorsing other theoretical approaches). The degree of enthusiasm reflected at professional conferences and in professional journals readily attests that persons in medicine, psychology, social work, and education are willing to consider the merits and drawbacks of behavioral modification procedures; and more cannot be asked. Perhaps the person endorsing behavioral modification techniques can also learn from the skepticism of others, and it would be a credit to him if he did choose to alter some of his beliefs after being presented with contradictory scientific evidence (subjective opinion does not alone, however, constitute scientific evidence). Facetiously, it might be added that those who steadfastly refuse to consider the research and applied evidence in support of behavioral modification procedures should be provided with a psychoanalytic interpretation of their resistances.

Before attempting to inaugurate a comprehensive behavioral modification program in the schools, the would-be user is obligated to orient each educator, whether teacher or administrator, help them achieve understanding of the approach, and involve them in the planning and, in some cases, the application of the techniques. And by approaching allied professionals outside of the school systems, he will gain some degree of assurance of professional acceptance within the community. This is an invaluable benefit to the endorser of behavioral modification because the allied professionals will then be in a good position to further the behavioral modification program; their acceptance will also give the school's behavioral modification program access to resource or consulting personnel.

ORIENTING THE LAY COMMUNITY

The significance of and reasons for orienting relevant persons to the services for behavioral problem children have been repeatedly cited, and it would undoubtedly be redundant to belabor these points much further. Suffice it to say that the reasons for and values of involving colleagues and other allied professionals are essentially applicable in total to the lay community.

The orientation of the lay community has as its primary purpose the development of acceptance for the professional role played by the educator. Since the use of behavioral modification procedures will be new, this acceptance is requisite for effective implementation. The orientation of the lay community does not involve teaching how, specifically, behavior will be modified; rather the emphasis is on familiarizing them with the reasons why behavior should be modified, what behaviors should be modified, why the school and its professional personnel hold this responsibility, and how they, the lay community, can facilitate this process. When the lay community accepts the premise that the school is responsible and that its faculty members are professionals who are academically able and personally qualified to help behavioral problem children, the efforts for behavioral modification will meet with much less resistance, friction, and misunderstanding than if no orientation had been given.

Intrinsic to this is the secondary goal: active involvement of the lay community, in a nonprofessional manner. The reader may recall that there is evidence that lay persons, especially parents, can be beneficially involved in behavioral modification. Thus the educator using behavioral modification should try to provide a relatively unlimited amount of time, at least initially, for speaking about behavioral problem children and means to improve their behavior to parent-teacher organizations, church groups, other civic organizations, and individual parents. Laying the groundwork for behavioral modification procedures through a carefully planned orientation program can result in invaluable direct aid, such as support for personnel and supplies, and indirect aid, such as parental cooperation. And these orientation procedures may well result in lay persons volunteering for further training in order that they may serve as teachers' aids or in some other role in which they will be able to participate actively in the services provided to behavioral problem children.

Providing an orientation for the lay community does not always give immediate rewards; but in the long run, this is an invaluable part of the implementation stage. Although most of the emphasis on orientation will be at the beginning of the implementation stage, it must be recognized that orientation efforts never end.

PROFESSIONAL TRAINING

Professional training is the prerequisite for effective and comprehensive use of behavioral modification procedures. Even the materials in this book require the reader to have at least some familiarity with educational psychology. In all probability this means being at least on an advanced level in an undergraduate teacher training program; and it is apparent that many of the techniques described here are suited only to graduate-level students in educational psychology, guidance and counseling, and school, counseling, and clinical psychology.

It has been emphasized that the process of selecting and using a behavioral modification technique involves both personal and professional capabilities. Personal capabilities are cultivated during the professional training program. Comments regarding personal capabilities must always remain general, because the behavioral sciences have been unable to determine specifically what personal characteristics are absolutely necessary for the helping professions (Cottle, 1953; Polmantier, 1966).

Professional capabilities necessary for behavioral modification depend upon what procedures are to be used. For example, Kanfer and Phillips (1966), in distinguishing types of behavior therapy, seem to use the functions of the therapist as one of the most common differentiating factors; that is, the clinical functions that the therapist must be capable of performing vary with the type of behavior therapy that is being used. This would be especially applicable to the use of behavioral modification procedures in the schools. As has been discussed extensively in Chapters 7 and 8, there are techniques that the typical classroom teacher can use, and there are others that require that the user have more specialized training, particularly in psychological principles.

In general, the techniques set forth in Chapter 7 are appropriate to classroom teachers; other psychoeducational specialists, such as school counselors and school psychologists, can use the same techniques at different levels—for example, with more severe behavioral problems. Regardless of job title or position, it is important that there be intrastaff consultation on the use of behavioral modification procedures, and with more severe behavioral problems it would be advisable to have available consulting services from a clinical psychologist and medical physicians, especially a psychiatrist. Professional discretion, which must include moral and ethical codes, about when consultation services are needed should result from the intrastaff consultation. It is recommended that whenever behavioral modification techniques are to be used with relatively severe problem behaviors (and often with behaviors that do not seem very severe) a "screening meeting," involving all relevant psycho-educational personnel, be held. Any disposition of a case—that is, the proposed behavioral modification program for a given child—would then result from a professional consensus. This format would allow for an amalgamation of differences in professional training and experience.

The use of behavioral counseling techniques obviously requires that the user be a trained counselor. This usually means holding at least a Master of Arts degree in guidance and counseling or its equivalent. And according to McGowan and Schmidt (1962) this would mean having graduate training in personality organization and development; knowledge of social environmental factors, appraisal of the individual, and counseling theories and techniques; a well-developed professional orientation; a supervised practicum experience; and research skills. In view of the nature of behavioral counseling, it seems that a specific knowledge of learning theories and principles is essential.

There is virtually no reference in the professional literature to concrete guidelines for distinguishing what level of professional training is necessary for a given behavioral modification technique. As has been noted, it is quite possible that a lay person, such as a parent, can in fact perform the technical aspects of behavioral modification; but in these cases it is advisable that their efforts receive professional supervision. There are, however, a few references to the training of behavior therapists; but the term "behavior therapist" is so broadly defined that it encompasses the possibility of the therapist's treating any behavior problem and using essentially any behavioral modification procedure. Obviously this all-encompassing definition is not appropriate to educators in general, but it may be applicable to certain school counselors and school psychologists who would like to use the more specialized behavioral modification techniques with rather severe problem behaviors. Let us, then, examine the guidelines for the training of behavior therapists, since this will allow the would-be therapist to compare his own qualifications and to develop some criteria for what procedures he is ethically correct in using and what further training he should obtain.

It is generally held that the behavior therapist must be a professionally trained psychologist. Presumably this means holding at least a

Master of Arts degree in clinical psychology or its equivalent, and in view of current certification practices it is more probable that it means having training at the doctoral level in either clinical, counseling, or school psychology. The main academic requirements seem to be a knowledge of scientific methodology, knowledge of modern learning theory, and familiarity with relevant research (Wolpe and Lazarus, 1966). It has also been noted that psychoanalytically oriented psychology, which plays a prominent part in most clinical psychology training programs, is "largely irrelevant to the practice of behavior therapy and often proves to be a positive hindrance" (Wolpe and Lazarus, 1966, p. viii). Great importance is placed on the behavior therapist's receiving supervised clinical experience (Lazarus, 1966). As for personal characteristics, little attention is given to this matter because the personal relationship is not considered to be crucial to the outcome of behavior therapy; at least, this is the belief of some behaviorists (Eysenck, 1960). It has, however, been deemed important that the behavior therapy trainee strive for flexibility and versatility in selecting behavioral modification techniques and try to develop the ability to direct techniques at specific problem areas; in fact, it seems that these characteristics supersede the importance of the trainee's knowledge of learning theory and skill as a clinician in general (Lazarus, 1966).

Poser (1967) suggests that behavior therapists be trained on two levels: Level 1 trainees would serve as technicians or cotherapists with a professional therapist, and Level 2 trainees would be independent professional personnel. He also points out that behavior therapists should be trained in a setting that actually provides clinical behavior therapy, they should be exposed to diverse theories, not just the behavioral ones, they should have experience in presenting their work to nonbehaviorist professionals, and they should cultivate an appreciation of experimental research, particularly as it relates to learning principles.

Even though most educators will not need to receive training comparable to that required of behavior therapists, it is likely that the use of behavioral modification procedures in the schools will necessitate changes in the training of classroom teachers (in both regular and special education), school counselors, school psychologists, school administrators, and other specialized educators (such as school social workers, speech and hearing therapists, and teacher-consultants).

Three types of academic knowledge seem to be necessary. In view of the rationale, optimum use of behavioral modification procedures will require academic training in *general and/or experimental psychology,* with special emphasis on learning theory; this could quite easily be included in the regular block of educational psychology courses required in most teacher education programs. Second, since the types of problems differ in severity and the techniques vary in requirements for use, academic training in *psychopathology,* with emphasis on the psychology of behavioral problem children, and *personality theory* would be advisable; the extent or level necessary will depend upon the educational specialty and consequently the types of behavior that are to be serviced by the particular educator. Also advisable is a basic knowledge of *guidance and counseling theories and techniques;* as has been pointed out previously, behavioral modification is not an impersonal process, and there is reason to believe that factors typically associated with the counseling and psychotherapy continuum can contribute beneficially to the learning theory-oriented techniques of behavioral modification.

These three areas of academic knowledge seem to provide the basis for the didactic segment of professional training for educators who wish to use behavioral modification procedures. On this academic foundation behavioral modification techniques can be taught, either within existing courses, in new specialized courses, or in special institutes or workshops.

But there are also two other areas that are more personally developed than didactically attained: *self-understanding* and *supervised clinical experience.*

The reasons why counselors and psychotherapists need to develop self-understanding have already been discussed in detail. The basic premise is that the therapist's personal characteristics must be recognized and held in awareness in order that they may not adversely influence the therapeutic services. This seems equally important for counseling, psychotherapy, and behavior therapy. As was suggested, the most logical way to strive for this personal understanding is by means of a planned, systematic approach, such as actually receiving individual or group insight-oriented counseling. This may not be possible, nor is it absolutely necessary, for all who use behavioral modification procedures; that is, the techniques used and the problems serviced by classroom teachers probably do not necessitate extensive self-understanding. On the other hand, the techniques used and the problems serviced by school counselors and school psychologists, professionals dealing with more deeply rooted, personal-social difficulties, would require extensive self-knowledge. It seems imperative that the therapist, when working on the more advanced level, have an awareness of his own needs and characteristics, be able to recognize how they might affect the behavioral modification services, and be able to control them. Comprehensive professional training must accommodate this personal requirement.

Supervised clinical experience is necessary for essentially all helping-relationships. Just as teachers receive supervision during practice teaching placements, school counselors receive supervision in practicum settings and school psychologists receive supervision in internship settings. Likewise, the well-trained behavioral modification therapist must also receive supervised clinical experience. This personal apprenticeship should, of course, be under the guidance and supervision of a more highly trained professional who has had training and experience with behavioral modification procedures.

These two requirements—personal understanding and supervised clinical experience—are requisite for the optimum use of behavioral modification techniques. It is possible, however, for persons in each educational specialty to use some of the behavioral modification techniques, perhaps even on the basis of the information given in this book; but continued recognition must be given to the fact that certain types of behavior problems and certain techniques necessitate higher levels of professional competency. Thus, unlimited use of behavioral modification procedures is unwise, unjustified, and unethical unless one has received training comparable to the demands of the particular situation; and even then the services of consultants in other professions are advisable.

The necessity of training educators wishing to use behavioral modification procedures may create a number of curriculum and personnel problems for some college and university training programs. If it is accepted that these procedures can be used for certain problem behaviors by classroom teachers, as indeed they seem to be, it will be necessary to offer some degree of academic exposure to learning theories and general-experimental psychology to every student in a teacher training program on the undergraduate level; and materials relevant to psychopathology, personality theory, and guidance and counseling would also make a beneficial contribution to the preparation of teachers. Moreover, for those who wish advanced training in order to deal with more severe and complex behavior problems, graduate-level training programs, particularly in the areas of school counseling and school psychology, must add to their curriculums specialized courses, seminars, or workshops on behavioral modification procedures. Furthermore, these programs must provide faculty members or agency-clinical representatives who can give adequate supervision in the use of behavioral modification procedures during the trainee's practicum or internship experiences. Guidelines for counselor educators have been set forth elsewhere (Woody, 1968).

Diagnosis, as was pointed out in Chapter 4, varies according to the requirements of the particular educator. The level of diagnosis necessary for use by the classroom teacher need not be as sophisticated or complicated as that used by the school psychologist. It is therefore unrealistic to expect that each educator needs to be a comprehensive diagnostician, with the exception of the school psychologist—and he is, presumably, already only too familiar with the difficulties in diagnostic reliability and validity. Thus, training in diagnosis should be integrated into regular training programs, probably within existing courses.

If each type of educator can become familiar with what his role is in dealing with behavioral problem children and what behavioral modification procedures are within his professional and personal grasp, then it seems that, with the exception of the courses discussed in the last few paragraphs, currently required certification standards in most states will be adequate to allow the implementation of behavioral modification services.

It is recognized that these requirements for professional training are restricting. But they are not intended to dampen the enthusiasm of potential users of behavioral modification procedures. Optimum or comprehensive use of the procedures does, of course, require that the rigorous demands of a formal training program be fulfilled, but there are many behavioral principles that can be implemented without such an intensive and possibly exhausting undertaking. Nevertheless, the needs of the behavioral problem child are undeniable. His problem behaviors cause him and his family much personal suffering and anguish, and his classmates and his teachers share the ill effects of his inability to benefit fully from the educational program. Since there is such strong evidence for the efficacy of behavioral modification procedures for modifying problem behaviors in childhood, the needs of the child and professional commitment demand that each educator obtain training and that he implement behavioral modification approaches in his own educational role.

REFERENCES

Cottle, W. C. Personal characteristics of counselors: a review of the literature. *Personnel and Guidance Journal,* 1953, 31:445-450.

Eaton, M. T., Weathers, G., and Phillips, B. N. Some reactions of classroom teachers to problem behavior in school. *Educational Administration and Supervision,* 1957, 43:129-139.

Eysenck, H. J. (Ed.). *Behaviour therapy and the neuroses.* New York: Pergamon Press, 1960.

Eysenck, H. J. The effects of psychotherapy. *International Journal of Psychiatry,* 1965, 1:99-142.

Kanfer, F. H., and Phillips, Jeanne S. Behavior therapy: a panacea for all ills or a passing fancy? *Archives of General Psychiatry,* 1966, 15:114-128.

Kaplan, L. *Mental health and human relations in education.* New York: Harper and Brothers, 1959.

Lazarus, A. A. Broad-spectrum behaviour therapy and the treatment of agoraphobia. *Behaviour Research and Therapy*, 1966, 4:95-97.

McGowan, J. F., and Schmidt, L. D. *Counseling: readings in theory and practice.* New York: Holt, Rinehart and Winston, 1962.

Polmantier, P. C. The personality of the counselor. *Vocational Guidance Quarterly*, 1966, 15:95-100.

Poser, E. G. Training behavior therapists. *Behaviour Research and Therapy*, 1967, 5:37-41.

Wolpe, J. The comparative clinical status of conditioning therapies and psychoanalysis. In J. Wolpe, A. Salter, and L. J. Reyna (Eds.), *The conditioning therapies.* New York: Holt, Rinehart and Winston, 1964, 5-20.

Wolpe, J., and Lazarus, A. A. *Behavior therapy techniques.* Oxford, Eng.: Pergamon Press, 1966.

Woody, R. H. Preparation in behavioral counseling. *Counselor Education and Supervision*, 1968, 7:357-362.

Index of Authors

Index of Subjects